third edition

THE MELODY BOOK

300 Selections from the World of Music for Piano, Guitar, Autoharp, Recorder, and Voice

PATRICIA HACKETT
San Francisco State University

Cover and interior
illustrations by **Florence Holub**

PRENTICE HALL, *Upper Saddle River, New Jersey 07458*

Editorial director: *Charlyce Jones Owen*
Publisher: *Norwell F. Therien*
Editor: *Marion Gottlieb*
Project manager: *Carole R. Crouse*
Prepress and manufacturing buyer: *Bob Anderson*
Copy editor: *Carole R. Crouse*
Marketing manager: *Sheryl Adams*

This book was set in 9.5/12 Times Roman by Stratford Publishing Services, Inc., and was printed and bound by Courier Companies, Inc. The cover was printed by Courier Companies, Inc.

Acknowledgments appear on pages v and vi, which constitute a continuation of the copyright page.

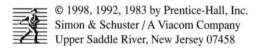
PRENTICE-HALL INTERNATIONAL (UK) LIMITED, *London*
PRENTICE-HALL OF AUSTRALIA PTY. LIMITED, *Sydney*
PRENTICE-HALL CANADA INC., *Toronto*
PRENTICE-HALL HISPANOAMERICANA, S.A., *Mexico*
PRENTICE-HALL OF INDIA PRIVATE LIMITED, *New Delhi*
PRENTICE-HALL OF JAPAN, INC., *Tokyo*
SIMON & SCHUSTER ASIA PTE. LTD., *Singapore*
EDITORA PRENTICE-HALL DO BRASIL, LTDA., *Rio de Janeiro*

CONTENTS

PREFACE

The 300 selections in *The Melody Book,* third edition, have been chosen for your musical enjoyment and satisfaction—whether you are a music teacher, a vocalist, a guitarist, a keyboardist, a music therapist, or a recreation leader. It is a comprehensive anthology that provides music for many different needs and situations, and one that reflects the goals of the "SingAmerica!" campaign initiated by Music Educators National Conference.

The Melody Book is a rich source of music for teachers in the elementary classroom and in special education, and for music therapy and recreational music. Vocalists will find it a songbook of exceptional variety and quality, with music of interest to both young and old, professional and amateur musician.

This major revision of *The Melody Book* includes 90 new pieces but retains many favorite songs and features of the second edition. As before, there are children's chants, traditional school songs, games and dances, rounds, songs in harmony, pop "standards," and foreign-language songs from around the world. (All have phonetic pronunciation, and English verses, as well.) To put the songs in context, you will find many cultural, historical, stylistic, and biographical descriptions. Teachers will recognize many songs from the elementary school music series and a number of selections from the "SingAmerica!" campaign.

In general, *The Melody Book* songs are notated in voice ranges that correspond to the maturity level of the song's text. Songs appropriate for youngsters are notated within limited ranges. For example, 80 percent of the book's songs lie within the range of an octave, and many are within the interval of a fifth or a sixth. Songs that will appeal mainly to adults may have wider ranges and are in lower keys. New in this edition are 19 songs with on-page xylophone parts, and four themes from classical music that can be used in elementary music lessons. Kodály Method teachers and Orff-*Schulwerk* specialists will find many songs for their respective programs.

Songs in *The Melody Book* are notated in keys suitable for particular instruments, and players will find a "Musical Instruments" section that contains basic information about piano, guitar and baritone ukulele, Autoharp, and soprano recorder. Included there are charts of chords and strums—all with fingerings. To help you choose an accompaniment, most songs have on-page ideas for strumming and chording patterns. The recorder section contains several children's chants for playing and singing that are grouped together for convenience.

The Appendixes provide reference material for musical terms, signs, and symbols, and conductor's patterns.

An extensive Classified Index lists music according to suitable instrument (and number of chords used); harmony (modal, part songs, rounds); appropriate movement (actions, dances, games); rhythm durations; sol-fa syllables; and songs with limited ranges. Additional groupings list holidays and special-occasion music and identify the biographies, cultural and musical style information, and song histories found throughout the anthology.

The national origin of the 300 musical selections and their keys are indicated in the Alphabetical Index of Songs and Melodies that concludes the book.

May the songs within these covers be your companions for many pleasant hours.

PATRICIA HACKETT

ACKNOWLEDGMENTS

Developing *The Melody Book* required the help and support of many people, and the author wishes to thank all of them: singers of songs in this country and overseas; colleagues whose experience, judgment, and good sense provided ideas for the preparation of this third edition; and friends who reviewed for accuracy songs from their respective backgrounds. Production editor Carole Crouse performed her usual miracles with pleasant, patient expertise. And, finally, I must thank my husband, Jim, whose vitality and musicality are always a source of inspiration.

Every effort has been made to locate owners of music included in this book. Omission of any copyright acknowledgment will be corrected if brought to our attention. Credit and appreciation are due to many contributors and to many copyright owners for their permission to use the following:

"A Zing-a Za," Brazilian rural samba arranged by Mary Goetze. © Copyright by Boosey & Hawkes, Inc. Used by permission.

"Ball-Bouncing Song" and lyrics of all Japanese songs reviewed for accuracy by Professor Ikuyo Yoshimura, Gifu Women's College, Gifu, Japan.

"The Bridge of Avignon" and lyrics of all French songs reviewed for accuracy by Patrick Blanche, Nyons, France.

"Bye, Bye, Blackbird," by Mort Dixon and Ray Henderson. © 1926 (Renewed) Warner Bros. Inc. Rights for Extended Renewal Term in U.S. controlled by Olde Clover Leaf Music and Ray Henderson Music Company. Canadian Rights controlled by Warner Bros. Inc. All Rights Reserved. Used by Permission Warner Bros. Publications U.S. Inc., Miami, FL. 33014.

"The Carolers" and "Celebration Song," music and Romanian lyrics provided by Michaela Codrescu

and Ion Codrescu, Constanţa, Romania. Copyright © 1996 by Michaela and Ion Codrescu. All Rights Reserved. Used by permission. Additional assistance by Mrs Simona Ionescu, Irvine, California

"Christmas Is a Time for Sharing" by David Eddleman. Copyright © 1982 by Shawnee Press, Inc. (ASCAP). International Copyright Secured. All Rights Reserved. Reprinted by Permission.

"Christmas Is Here!" Swedish text and pronunciation guide by Jeanni Nolting, San Francisco.

"Cielito Lindo" and lyrics of all Spanish songs reviewed for accuracy by Maria Flores-Schweinsberg, Pompano Beach, Florida.

"Circle 'round the Zero" used by permission of Maureen Kenney. Copyright © 1975, Magnamusic Baton, Inc., St. Louis.

"Clapping Land" from *Exploring Music,"* book one, by Eunice Boardman and Beth Landis. Copyright © 1966 by Holt, Rinehart and Winston, Publishers.

"The Condor" ("El Condor Pasa") from *The Music Connection.* English words by Aura Kontra for Silver Burdett Ginn, Simon & Schuster Elementary. Used by permission. Spanish text by Dolores Villagomez, San Francisco.

"Counting Song," by Lucille Wood and Roberta McLaughlin. © 1961 Bowmar ®. All Rights assigned to and controlled by Beam Me Up Music. All Rights Reserved. Used by permission Warner Bros. Publications U.S. Inc., Miami, FL. 33014.

"The Crocodile Song" used by permission of Dover Publications, Inc.

"De Colores," "Don Gato," "Hawaiian Rainbows," "La Raspa," "Laredo," "Morning Song," "Mister Sun," "Peace Like a River," "Ritsch Ratsch," and "Thanks for the Food" used by permission of Silver Burdett Ginn from *World of Music,* Copyright © 1988.

"Dry Bones" from *Growing with Music,* book six, by Harry Wilson et al. Copyright © 1966 by Prentice-Hall, Inc.

"The Eagle," music by Hap Palmer, words by Martha Cheney. © Hap Pal Music. From recording *Witch's Brew,* © Educational Activities.

"Ebeneezer Sneezer," by Georgia E. Garlid and Lynn Freeman Olson. © 1967 (Renewed) Belwin-Mills Publishing Corp. All Rights Reserved. Used by Permission Warner Bros. Publications U.S. Inc., Miami, FL. 33014.

"Feliz Navidad" by Jose Feliciano. Copyright by J & H Publishing. All rights reserved. Used by permission.

"Flower Drum Song" and "Song of Ali Mountains," Chinese lyrics and pronunciation by Lynn Tsai, San Francisco.

"Goodbye Round" / "A Round of Goodbyes" by Frederick Silver. Used by permission of Plymouth Music Co., Inc., Ft. Lauderdale, Florida.

"Grandpa Grigg" and orchestration for Orff ensemble by Doug Goodkin, San Francisco. Copyright © 1996. All rights reserved. Used by permission.

"Guantanamo Lady" ("Guantanamera") from *The Music Connec-*

tion. English words by Aura Kontra for Silver Burdett Ginn, Simon & Schuster Elementary. Used by permission.

"Haliwa-Saponi Canoe Song" from *Moving within the Circle: Contemporary Native American Music and Dance* by Dr. J. Bryan Burton. Danbury, Conn.: World Music Press. © 1993 World Music Press. Used by permission. Available as book with tape or CD; optional slide set.

"Harmony" by Artie Kaplan and Norman J. Simon. © 1972. Reprinted courtesy of Thrice Music, Inc., and Norman Simon Music Co., a division of Ennanden Prod. Inc. All rights reserved.

"Hello, Ev'rybody" by Charity Bailey and Eunice Holsaert. Used by permission of Plymouth Music Co., Inc.

"I'd Like to Teach the World to Sing." Words And Music By: Bill Backer, Billy Davis, Roger Cook, Roger Greenaway. © 1971 Shada Music Co., Inc. Original Record And Commercial Produced By Billy Davis.

"It's a Small World." Words and Music by Richard M. Sherman and Robert B. Sherman. © 1963 Wonderland Music Company, Inc., Copyright Renewed. All Rights Reserved. Used By Permission.

"It's Raining" ("¡Qué llueva!"), from *Hispanic Music for Arizona Children* (1993). Barbara Andress (Ed.). The Arizona Early Childhood Music Collaborative Project. Used with permission.

"Ka Mate" ("Te Rauparaha"), arr. Freedman. Copyright Sevenseas Publishing, Pty. Ltd; Box 152, Paraparaumu, New Zealand.

"Kang Ding City." Chinese lyrics by Muriel Chan, San Francisco.

"Kiowa Buffalo Dance," "Kiowa Handgame Song," "Kiowa Round Dance," "Sauk-Fox Pipe Dance Song," and "War Dance" learned from Don Patterson, Sauk-Fox/Tonkawa tribal singer, Tonkawa, Oklahoma.

"Korobushka," Russian lyrics reviewed for accuracy by David Lindeman, Washington, D.C.

"Let Music Surround You" used by permission of Fran Smartt Addicott. Copyright © 1966.

"Let's Go to the Sea" used with permission of the General Secretariat, Organization of American States.

"Little Bird," translation and pronunciation by Col. David P. Smith, Santa Rosa, California, with additional help from David Lindeman, Washington, D.C., and Professor Ron Levaco, San Francisco.

"Little Donkey" and "Spring Home," transcriptions and Chinese lyrics by D. J. Sun, San Francisco.

"Lost My Gold Ring" and "Thank You for the Chris'mus" collected and transcribed by Olive Lewin. Used by permission of the Organization of American States, Washington, D.C.

"Lovely Evening" and other songs in German reviewed for accuracy by Irmgard Albertson, Cotati, California.

"The Mango" used by permission of Miriam B. Factora.

"Mayo Nafwa" used by permission of Barbara Reeder-Lundquist of Seattle, Washington, and Grace Chiwama.

"Misty" by Erroll Garner and Johnny Burke. © 1954 & 1955 by Vernon Music Corp. (By arrangement with Octave Music Publishing Corp.) All Rights Reserved. Used by Permission.

"Moon, Moon" ("Lovely Moon"). © 1988 MMB Music, Inc., Saint Louis. Used by Permission. All Rights Reserved.

"My Body" provided by Sarah Pirtle, The Discovery Center, Shelburne Falls, Massachusetts.

"Over the Rainbow." E. Y. Harburg & Harold Arlen. Copyright © 1938, 1939 Metro-Goldwyn-Mayer, Inc. Copyright Renewed 1966, 1967 Metro-Goldwyn-Mayer, Inc. All Rights Assigned to Leo Feist, Inc. Rights of Leo Feist, Inc. Assigned to EMI Catalogue Partnership. All Rights Controlled and Administered by EMI Feist Catalog, Inc. International Copyright Secured. Made in USA. All Rights Reserved. Used by Permission.

"Royal Garden Blues" by Clarence Williams and Spencer Williams. Copyright © 1919, renewed by Shapiro, Bernstein & Co., Inc. Used by permission.

"Shabat, Shalom" courtesy of Ann Brostoff, San Diego, California.

"Shoes for Baby Jesus," music and Spanish lyrics courtesy of Gabriel Daneri, San Francisco.

"Singin' in the Rain," by Arthur Freed and Nacio Herb Brown. © 1929 (Renewed) Belwin-Mills Publishing Corp. All Rights Reserved. Used by Permission Warner Bros. Publications U.S. Inc., Miami, FL. 33014.

"Song of Peace," words by Lloyd Stone, adapted by Judy Bond. Copyright © by Westminster John Knox Press, Louisville, Kentucky. Used by permission.

"Sorida," from *Let Your Voice Be Heard! Songs from Ghana and Zimbabwe.* Copyright © 1986, 1997 (revised), World Music Press,

Danbury, Conn. Used by permission.

"The Sound of Silence," by Paul Simon. © 1964, 1965 Paul Simon. Used by permission.

"Take the 'A' Train." Copyright 1941 by Tempo Music, Inc. Used by permission of Ruth Ellington, New York, New York.

"This Beautiful World" used by permission of Patience Bacon, Honolulu, Hawaii.

"Tie a Yellow Ribbon 'round the Ole Oak Tree," by Irwin Levine and L. Russell Brown. © 1972, assigned 1973 Levine and Brown Music, Inc. All Rights Reserved. Used by Permission Warner Bros. Publications U.S. Inc., Miami, FL. 33014.

"Top of the World," by Richard Carpenter and John Bettis. © 1972 Almo Music Corp. & Hammer and Nails Music. All Rights Reserved. Used by Permission Warner Bros. Publications U.S. Inc., Miami, FL. 33014.

"Tzena, Tzena," by Julius Grossman, Issachor Miron, Mitchell Parish. © 1950 (Renewed) EMI Mills Music, Inc. All Rights Reserved. Used by Permission Warner Bros. Publications U.S. Inc., Miami, FL. 33014.

"Waddaly Atcha." Art Kassel, Ted Morse, and Mel Stitzel. Copyright © 1924 (Renewed 1952) Leo Feist, Inc. All Rights Assigned to EMI Catalogue Partnership. All Rights Controlled & Administered by EMI Feist Catalog, Inc. International Copyright Secured. Made in USA. All Rights Reserved. Used by Permission.

"We'll Meet Again" by Ross Parker and Hughie Charles. Copyright © 1939 (Renewed) by Irwin Dash Music Co., Ltd. All rights for the Western Hemisphere controlled by Music Sales Corporation. International Copyright Secured. All Rights Reserved. Reprinted by Permission.

"Winds of Morning," words and music by Tommy Makem. © 1966 Tin Whistle Music, BMI, 2 Longmeadow Road, Dover, N.H. 03820.

"Yesterday," by Paul McCartney and John Lennon. Copyright © 1965 Northern Songs Limited, 24 Bruxton Street, Mayfair, London WIX 7DA, England. All rights for the United States, Canada, Mexico and the Philippines controlled by Maclen Music, Inc., c/o ATV Music Corp., 6255 Sunset Blvd., Los Angeles, California 90028. International copyright secured. Made in U.S.A. All rights reserved.

"Yokuts Grinding Song" used by permission of the Lowie Museum of Anthropology, University of California, Berkeley, Tapes 115, 116.

ANTHOLOGY OF SONGS AND MELODIES

HOW TO USE ON-PAGE SYMBOLS AND SUGGESTIONS

- A letter or a number that follows a song identifies a particular accompaniment pattern for piano, guitar, or Autoharp. These letters and numbers are found on charts in the "Musical Instruments" section, on the following pages:

    Piano accompaniments, pp. 364–366
    Guitar strums, pp. 373, 374
    Autoharp strums, p. 379

- When soprano recorder is suitable for playing a melody, this is indicated following the music.

- Small numbers above or beside the notes indicate fingering for keyboard.

- The symbol ' identifies a breathing place for the recorder player and the singer.

- A curved line under a word means to sing more than one syllable on a single pitch.

- Percussion music (rhythms without pitch) has stems going in different directions. A downward stem means to play with the left hand; an upward stem means to play with the right hand.

- Large note heads and small note heads occur in some songs. The large note heads are usually melody, and the small note heads are the harmony.

- Two stems on a single note head indicate different rhythms for different verses or languages. An upward stem usually shows the rhythm for verse 1, and a downward stem shows the rhythm for subsequent verses (or for languages different from that in verse 1).

- Parentheses around a chord symbol mean that the chord is optional.

- Italic words under a foreign language are a pronunciation guide.

AIN'T GONNA STUDY WAR
(Down by the Riverside)

African American Spiritual

I ain't gon-na stud-y war no more, I ain't gon-na stud-y war no

more, I ain't gon-na stud-y _____ war no more. _____

Guitar, strum 6
Piano accompaniment pattern III

3

ALL AROUND THE KITCHEN

African American Play Song

♩ = 92

Call ... *Response*

All a-round the kitch-en, *Cock-a-doo-dle, doo-dle, doo.* All a-

round the kitch-en, *Cock-a-doo-dle, doo-dle, doo.* Now ___

stop right still, *Cock-a-doo-dle, doo-dle, doo.* Put your hand on your hip. *Cock-a-*

doo-dle, doo-dle, doo. Let your right foot slip, *Cock-a-doo-dle, doo-dle, doo,* Then, ___

do it like this. *Cock-a-doo-dle, doo-dle, doo.* All a-round the kitch-en, *Cock-a-*

rit.

doo-dle, doo-dle, doo. All a-round the kitch-en, *Cock-a-doo-dle, doo-dle, doo.*

Designate one person to sing the calls and all others to sing the response. The caller should perform different motions as suggested by each call. Responders can create one movement for *"Cock-a-doodle, doodle, doo"* and repeat it for every response.

ALLELUIA

Traditional Round

Al - le - lu - ia, Al - le - lu - ia,

A - - - - men, A - - - - men.

ALLELUIA

Wolfgang Amadeus Mozart
(Austria, 1756–1791)

♩ = 104

Al - le - lu - ia, Al - le - lu - ia, _____ Al - le -

lu - ia, Al - le - lu - ia. Al - le - lu - ia, Al -

le - lu - ia, _____ Al - le - lu - ia, Al - le - lu -

ia. Al - le - lu - ia, Al - le - lu - ia.

5

ALOHA OE
(Farewell to Thee)

Queen Liliuokalane
(Hawaii, 1838–1917)

Composer Unknown

With feeling ♩ = 66

Verse in English

E | A | E | B7

Dear the thoughts I take a-way with me, Sweet mem - 'ries of our hap - py

E | A | E

hours, It is sad that we must say good - bye, In our

A | B7 | E | 𝄋 *Refrain* | A

dreams we will meet a - gain some day.

{ *English:* Fare - well to thee, fare -
{ *Hawaiian:* A - lo - ha - 'oe, a -
Pronunciation: ah - low - ha oheh ah -

First time sing English, 𝄋 second time sing Hawaiian.

E | B7 | E

well to thee, To the friend of mine who lives a-mong the flow - ers, }
lo - ha - 'oe, E ke o - na-o-na no-ho i ka li - po, }
low - hah oheh eh keh oh - nah-oh - nah noe - hoe ih kah lih - poe

One

A | E | B7

fond em - brace

{ be - fore I de - part, }
{ hoi a - 'e a - u, }
hoy ah - eh ah - oo

Un - til we meet __ a -

Verse in Hawaiian

E | *Second time Fine* E | A | E

gain.

O ka ha - lia a - lo - ha i hi - ki mai Ke
oh kah hah - leeah ah - loe - hah ih hih-kih my keh

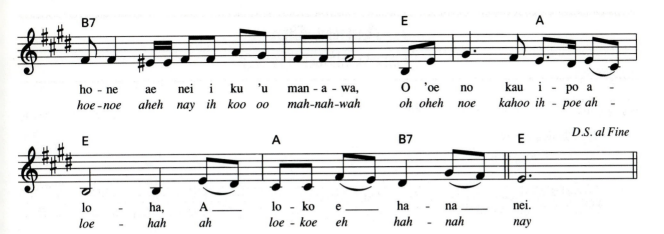

ho - ne   ae   nei   i   ku   'u   man - a - wa,   O   'oe   no   kau   i - po a -
hoe-noe   aheh   nay   ih   koo   oo   mah-nah-wah   oh oheh noe kahoo ih - poe ah -

D.S. al Fine

lo   -   ha,   A ____   lo - ko   e ____   ha - na ____   nei.
loe   -   hah   ah   loe - koe   eh   hah - nah   nay

Guitar, strum 23 (verse), strum 24 (refrain)

The symbol ' represents a glottal stop. The vowel following this mark should be separated from the preceding vowel with a separate articulation by the glottis, as in "oh-oh" pronounced quickly.

When missionaries from New England arrived in Hawaii in 1820, they introduced hymns (known as himeni) and established singing schools. In the late 1800s, the Hawaiian royal family and other, lesser-known musicians composed songs that combined Hawaiian and English languages with Western-style hymn tunes and instruments. "Aloha Oe," a song of farewell, is a himeni with lyrics composed by the last Hawaiian monarch, Queen Liliuokalani. (The composer of the melody is unknown.)

AMAZING GRACE

John Newell
(1779)

Early American Melody

Deliberately, but with a flow

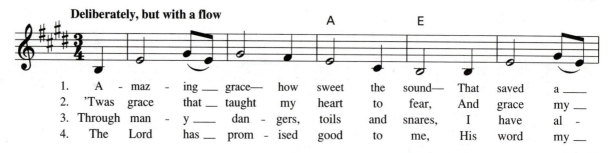

1. A - maz - ing __ grace— how sweet the sound— That saved a __
2. 'Twas grace that __ taught my heart to fear, And grace my __
3. Through man - y __ dan - gers, toils and snares, I have al -
4. The Lord has __ prom - ised good to me, His word my __

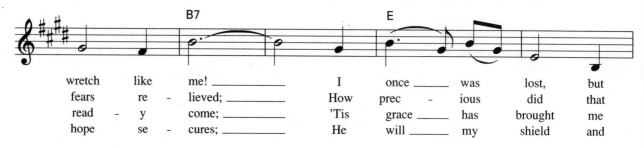

wretch like me! _____ I once ____ was lost, but
fears re - lieved; _____ How prec - ious did that
read - y come; _____ 'Tis grace ____ has brought me
hope se - cures; _____ He will ____ my shield and

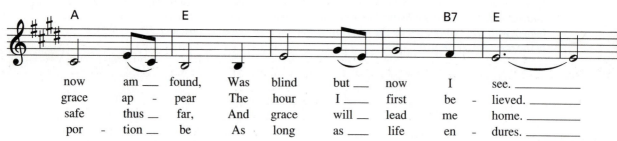

now am __ found, Was blind but __ now I see. _____
grace ap - pear The hour I ____ first be - lieved. _____
safe thus __ far, And grace will __ lead me home. _____
por - tion __ be As long as __ life en - dures. _____

**Guitar, strum 10 or 11. (To sing *Amazing Grace* in G major with guitar, place the capo
in fret 3 and play the chords shown above.)**
Piano, accompaniment pattern X

AMERICA

Samuel F. Smith
(United States, 1808–1895)

Composer Unknown

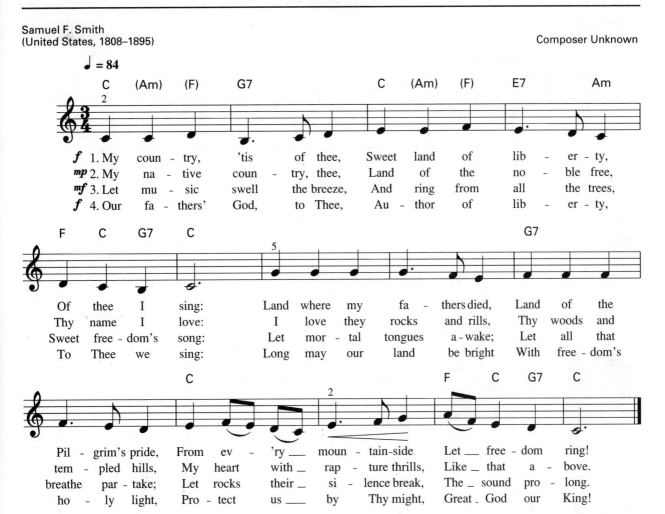

♩ = 84

f 1. My coun - try, 'tis of thee, Sweet land of lib - er - ty,
mp 2. My na - tive coun - try, thee, Land of the no - ble free,
mf 3. Let mu - sic swell the breeze, And ring from all the trees,
f 4. Our fa - thers' God, to Thee, Au - thor of lib - er - ty,

Of thee I sing: Land where my fa - thers died, Land of the
Thy name I love: I love they rocks and rills, Thy woods and
Sweet free - dom's song: Let mor - tal tongues a - wake; Let all that
To Thee we sing: Long may our land be bright With free - dom's

Pil - grim's pride, From ev - 'ry __ moun - tain-side Let __ free - dom ring!
tem - pled hills, My heart with __ rap - ture thrills, Like __ that a - bove.
breathe par - take; Let rocks their __ si - lence break, The __ sound pro - long.
ho - ly light, Pro - tect us __ by Thy might, Great _ God our King!

Autoharp, play melody rhythm
Piano, accompaniment pattern VI

On July 4, 1832, a choir trained by Lowell Mason gave the first public performance of what was then called "My Country, 'Tis of Thee." (Mason had successfully introduced music into public school education.) Samuel Francis Smith, a young divinity student, wrote these new patriotic words for a well-known tune from England that can be traced back to 1603. "God Save the Queen," the British national anthem, has at one time or another been borrowed by almost twenty countries as their national song. The tune was sung in the American colonies at many different times, to different words, including "God Save America," "God Save George Washington," and "God Save the Thirteen States." (Based on information in The Oxford Dictionary of Music, 1994.)

AMERICA, THE BEAUTIFUL

Katherine Lee Bates
(United States, 1859–1929)

Samuel A. Ward
(United States, 1847–1903)

1. O beau-ti-ful for spa-cious skies. For am-ber waves of grain, For
2. O beau-ti-ful for pil-grim feet, Whose stern im-pas-sion'd stress A
3. O beau-ti-ful for he-roes prov'd In lib-er-at-ing strife, Who
4. O beau-ti-ful for pa-triot dream That sees be-yond the years Thine

pur-ple moun-tain maj-es-ties A-bove the fruit-ed plain!
thor-ough-fare for free-dom beat A-cross the wil-der-ness!
more than self their coun-try lov'd And mer-cy more than life!
al-a-bas-ter cit-ies gleam, Un-dimmed by hu-man tears!

A-mer-i-ca! A-mer-i-ca!

God shed his grace on thee, And
God mend thine ev-'ry flaw, Con-
May God thy gold re-fine, Till
God shed His grace on thee, And

crown thy good with broth-er-hood From sea to shin-ing sea!
firm they soul in self-con-trol, Thy lib-er-ty in law!
all suc-cess be no-ble-ness, And ev-'ry gain di-vine!
crown thy good with broth-er-hood From sea to shin-ing sea!

Guitar, strum 24 (lines 1 and 2) and strum 18 (lines 3 and 4) (To sing in C major with the guitar, place the capo in fret 3 and play the chords shown above.)

Piano, accompaniment pattern XI

Inspired after a visit to the big sky country of the American West, a Wellesley professor of English wrote the poem she later joined with the tune of Ward's hymn "Materna." "America, the Beautiful" invites us to share the awe of Katherine Lee Bates, one hundred years after her journey to the summit of Pike's Peak.

ANGELS WE HAVE HEARD ON HIGH

French Carol

1. An - gels we have heard on high, Sweet - ly sing - ing o'er the plains,
2. Shep - herds, why this ju - bi - lee? Why your joy - ous strains pro - long?
3. Come to Beth - le - hem and see Him whose birth the an - gels sing;
4. See Him in a man - ger laid, Whom the choirs of an - gels praise;

And the moun - tains in re - ply Ech - o - ing their joy - ous strains.
What the glad - some tid - ings be, Which in - spire your heav'n - ly song?
Come, a - dore on bend - ed knee Christ, the Lord, the new - born King.
Mar - y, Jo - seph, lend your aid, While our hearts in love we raise.

Refrain

Glo - - - - - - - - - ri - a in ex - cel - sis De - o, De - o.
ihn ehx - chehl - sihs day - oh day - oh

Autoharp, strum A (verse) and strum L (refrain)
Guitar, strum 23 (verse) and strum 18 (refrain)

ARE YOU SLEEPING?
(Frère Jacques!)

French Round

	English:	Are	you	sleep-ing?	Are	you	sleep-ing?	Broth-er	John,	Broth-er	John?
	French:	Frè	re	Jacq-ues!	Frè	re	Jacq-ues!	Dorm-ez	vous?	Dorm-ez	vous?
	Pronunciation:	*freh*	*reh*	*jhah-keh*	*freh*	*reh*	*jhah-keh*	*dor-meh*	*voo*	*dor-meh*	*voo*

Morn-ing bells are ring-ing,	morn-ing bells are ring-ing,	Ding. ding, dong!	Ding, ding, dong!
Son-nez les ma-tin-es,	son-nez les ma-tin-es,	Din, din, don!	Din, din, don!
soe-neh lay mah-teen-eh	*soe-neh lay mah-teen-eh*	*dihn dihn dawn*	*dihn dihn dawn*

Autoharp (15-bar), strum C
Guitar, strum 8
Piano, accompaniment pattern II

Christmas version

1. Like a choir of angels singing
   O'er the dells, o'er the dells,
   Comes the sound of ringing, comes the sound of ringing,
   Christmas bells, Christmas bells.

2. "Christ is born!" their message bringing,
   Sound the bells, sound the bells!
   Hear them gaily ringing, hear them gaily ringing,
   Christmas bells, Christmas bells.

Play one or all of these patterns on a xylophone with "Are You Sleeping?"

ARTZA ALINU
(Our Land)

Israeli Dance Song

♩ = 100

Dm   Gm   Dm

Ar-tza a-li-nu, ar-tza a-li-nu, ar-tza a-li - nu.

Dm   Gm   Dm   *Fine*

Ar-tza a-li-nu, ar-tza a-li-nu, ar-tza a-li - nu.

Am   Dm   Am

La la la la la la la la la la la, La la la la la

Dm   Gm   Dm   Gm

la la la la la la, La la la la la la la; La la la la la

Dm   Gm   A7   Dm   Gm   A7   Dm   *D.C. al Fine*

la la. La la la la la la la. La la la la la la la.

Autoharp, strum A or P

Translation

We have come to our land.

Dance the hora along with "Our Land." See directions accompanying "Hava Nagila."

13

THE ASH GROVE

John Oxenford
(England, 1812–1877)

Welsh Folk Song

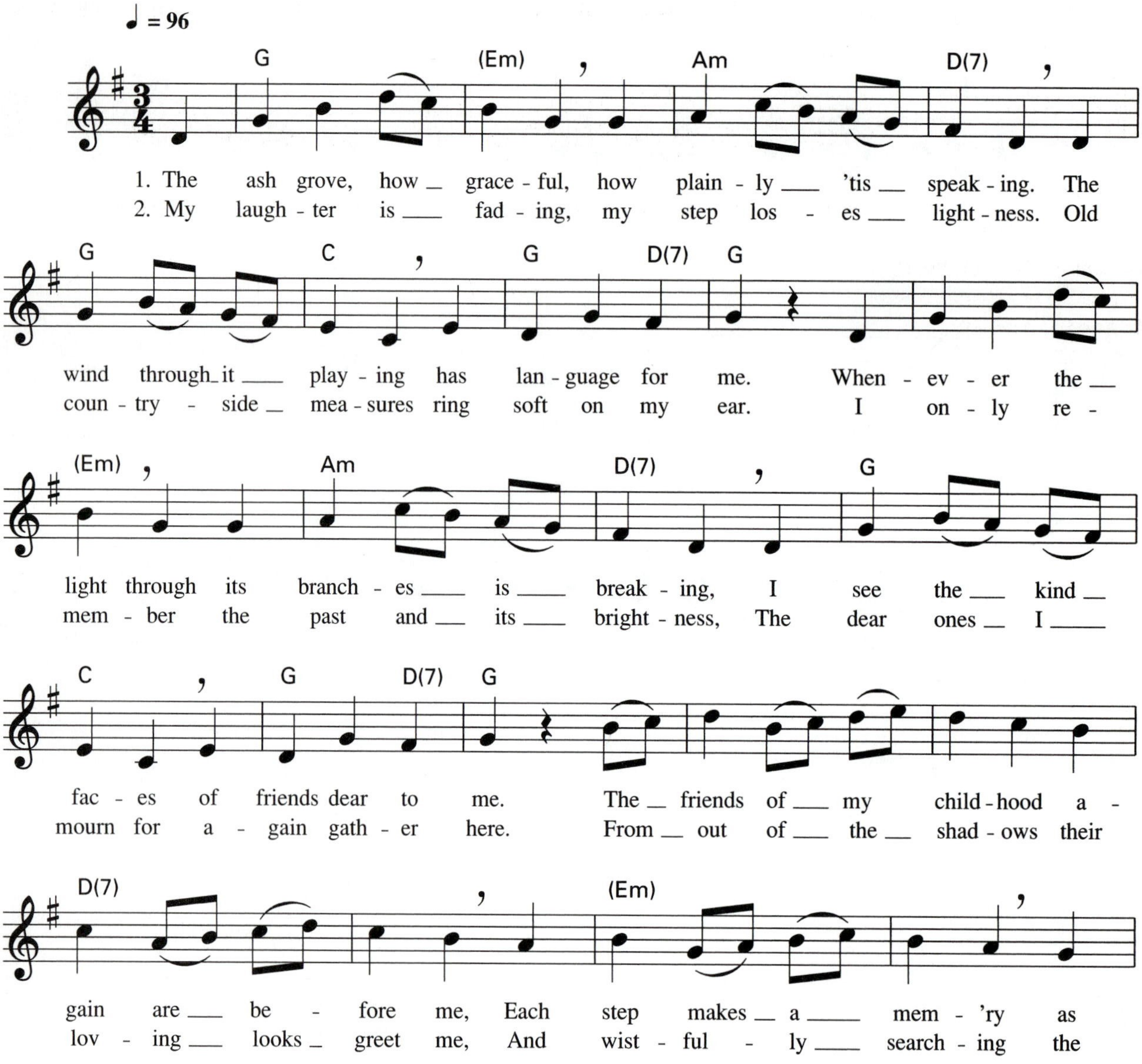

♩ = 96
G (Em) Am D(7)
1. The ash grove, how grace - ful, how plain - ly 'tis speak - ing. The
2. My laugh - ter is fad - ing, my step los - es light - ness. Old
G C G D(7) G
wind through it play - ing has lan - guage for me. When - ev - er the
coun - try - side mea - sures ring soft on my ear. I on - ly re -
(Em) Am D(7) G
light through its branch - es is break - ing, I see the kind
mem - ber the past and its bright - ness, The dear ones I
C G D(7) G
fac - es of friends dear to me. The friends of my child - hood a -
mourn for a - gain gath - er here. From out of the shad - ows their
D(7) (Em)
gain are be - fore me, Each step makes a mem - 'ry as
lov - ing looks greet me, And wist - ful - ly search - ing the

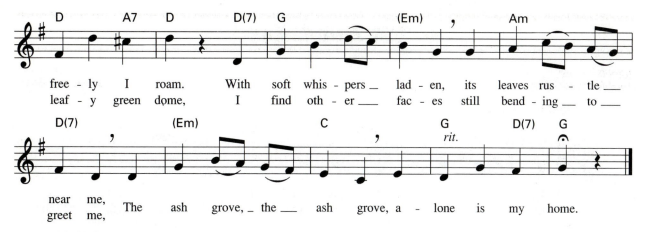

free - ly   I   roam.   With   soft   whis - pers __   lad - en,   its   leaves   rus - tle __
leaf - y   green   dome,   I   find   oth - er __   fac - es   still   bend - ing __   to __

near   me,   The   ash   grove, _ the __   ash   grove, a - lone   is   my   home.
greet   me,

Autoharp (15-bar), strum J
Guitar, play melody notes
Soprano recorder

A Zing-a Za

Brazilian Rural Samba
Arr. by Mary Goetze

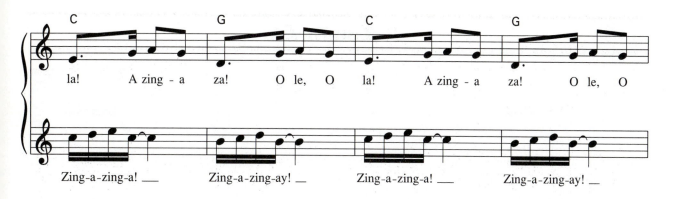

la! A zing - a za! O le, O la! A zing - a za! O le, O

Zing-a-zing-a! __ Zing-a-zing-ay! __ Zing-a-zing-a! __ Zing-a-zing-ay! __

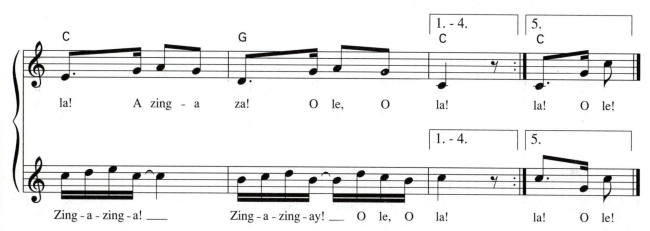

| 1. - 4. | 5. |

la! A zing - a za! O le, O la! la! O le!

Zing - a - zing - a! __ Zing - a - zing - ay! __ O le, O la! la! O le!

Autoharp, strum E
Piano, accompaniment pattern XVI

Play one or all of these patterns on percussion instruments with "A Zing-a Za!"

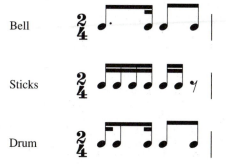

Bell

Sticks

Drum

B-A-BAY

American Folk Song

1. B - A - bay,   B - E - bee,   B - I - bid - dee - by,

B - O - bo, Bid-dee - by - bo   B - U - bu, Bid-dee by - bo - bu - bu! _____

Refrain

This   is   just   a   sil - ly   song!   The   words   don't   mean   a   thing.

Nev - er   mind   the   sil - ly   words,   Just   o - pen   up   and   sing.   Oh!

Autoharp, strum C
Piano, accompaniment pattern III

This song uses the vowels A, E, I, O, U preceded by a consonant. Select different consonants and create new verses, such as:

F
2. D-A-day, D-A-day,

C7
D-I-did-dee-dy, D-O-do,

Did-dee-dy-do D-U-du,

F
Did-dee-dy-do-du-du. (*Refrain*)

18

BALL-BOUNCING SONG
(*Maritsuki-uta*)

Japanese Children's Song

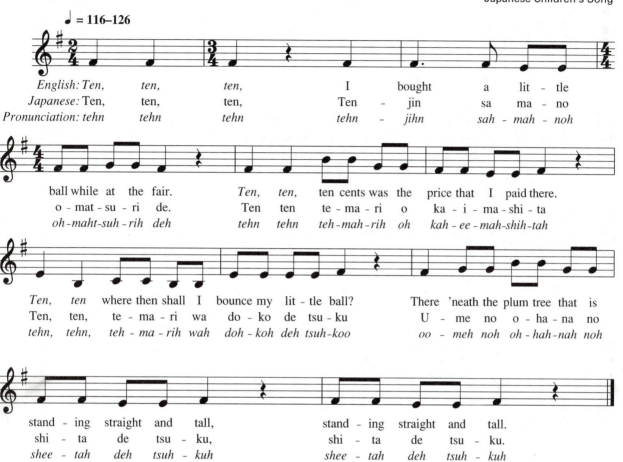

♩ = 116–126

English: Ten, ten, ten, I bought a lit - tle
Japanese: Ten, ten, ten, Ten - jin sa ma no
Pronunciation: *tehn tehn tehn tehn - jihn sah - mah - noh*

ball while at the fair. Ten, ten, ten cents was the price that I paid there.
o - mat - su - ri de. Ten ten te - ma - ri o ka - i - ma - shi - ta
oh - maht - suh - rih deh tehn tehn teh - mah - rih oh kah - ee - mah - shih - tah

Ten, ten where then shall I bounce my lit - tle ball? There 'neath the plum tree that is
Ten, ten, te - ma - ri wa do - ko de tsu - ku U - me no o - ha - na no
tehn, tehn, teh - ma - rih wah doh - koh deh tsuh - koo oo - meh noh oh - hah - nah noh

stand - ing straight and tall, stand - ing straight and tall.
shi - ta de tsu - ku, shi - ta de tsu - ku.
shee - tah deh tsuh - kuh shee - tah deh tsuh - kuh

Banuwa

Folk Song from Liberia

♩ = 168

① Ba - nu - wa, ba - nu - wa, ba - nu - wa yo. _____

② Ba - nu - wa, ba - nu - wa, ba - nu - wa yo. _____ **③**

③ A - la - no, neh - ni a - la - no; a - la - no, neh - ni a -

la - no. **④** Neh - ni a - la - no; Neh - ni a - la - no.

⑤ Neh - ni a - la - no; Neh - ni - a - la - no.

⑥ Ba - nu - wa, ba - nu - wa, ba - nu - wa yo. _____

Pronunciation guide

a as in F*a*ther

e as in *e*nd

i as in b*ee*

o as in *o*bey

u as in *u*nit

The words of this song mean "Don't cry, pretty little girl, don't cry."

Perform "Banuwa" in unison, and then as a cumulative song. Divide singers into six groups. Have group 1 begin, and then have groups 2–6 enter as in a round. Instead of ending simultaneously, have groups drop out in reverse order, beginning with group 6.

The dynamics can gradually increase from *piano,* as group 1 begins, to *forte,* as groups 5 and 6 enter, and then diminish as the groups drop out, ending *piano.*

Play instrumental parts with "Banuwa," using either patterns from the song's words or the patterns that follow. Have the players enter as described for the groups of singers. Player 1 can sit near group 1 singers, and so forth.

* Player 1 can play a soft introduction before singers begin and after singers drop out.

BARB'RA ALLEN

Anglo-American Ballad

1. In Scar-let town where I was born, There was a fair maid dwell-in', Made
2. 'Twas in the mer - ry month of May, When flow - er buds were swell-in', Sweet
3. He sent his ser - vant to the town, To the place where she was dwell-in', Said
4. Then slow-ly, slow - ly, she came up, And slow - ly she drew near him, But

man-y a youth cry _ "Well a day," Her name was Bar - b'ra Al - len.
Wil-liam on his _ death-bed lay, For love of Bar - b'ra Al - len.
"Mas-ter bids you to come with me, If your name be Bar - b'ra Al - len."
all she said when _ she got there: "Young man, I think you're dy - in'."

Guitar, strum 13, strum 17 on verses 4–7

5. *A*
He turned his face unto the wall,

E
For death was in him wellin';

D   *A*
"Goodbye," he said, "to all my friends;

E   *A*
Be good to Barb'ra Allen."

6. *A*
"Oh mother, oh Mother, go dig my grave,

E
And make it long and narrow;

D   *A*
Sweet William died for love of me,

E   *A*
And I will die of sorrow."

7. *A*
They buried her in the old church yard;

E
Sweet William was laid beside her.

D   *A*
And from his heart grew a red, red rose;

E   *A*
From Barb'ra Allen's: a briar.

8. *A*
They grew and grew in the old church yard

E
Till they could grow no higher;

D   *A*
At last they formed a true lover's knot,

E   *A*
And the rose grew 'round the briar.

"Barb'ra Allen" is an old ballad. Englishman Samuel Pepys wrote about hearing it sung in London on January 2, 1666. Ballads were performed by common people, and by professional minstrels of the Middle Ages who roamed the countryside or attached themselves to courts or great houses. Minstrels were succeeded by tavern poets during the reign of Queen Elizabeth I, and these poets composed new, topical texts for already familiar ballad melodies. These texts (not tunes) were printed on large sheets of paper called "broadsides," and through them, news and rumor were spread far and wide. When Samuel Pepys died in 1703, he had collected some 1,800 of these broadsides. They still exist at the Cambridge University Library, and through them, we can trace many song texts. In addition, many of these old narrative ballads crossed the Atlantic with British colonizers and have survived into the twentieth century. Folklorists discovered a living ballad tradition in the backwoods of the rural south—a tradition that had almost disappeared in the British Isles. Thanks to collectors, performers, and sound recordings, this rich Anglo-American ballad tradition has survived into modern times.

THE BATTLE HYMN OF THE REPUBLIC

Julia Ward Howe
(United States, 1819–1910)

William Steffe
(United States, 1830–ca. 1890)

Autoharp, strum M on the verse, strum O on the refrain
Piano, accompaniment pattern XVII, rolled chords (verse) and solid chords (refrain)

G
4. I have read a fiery gospel, writ in burnished rows of steel:

      C   G   D7
"As ye deal with my condemners, so with you my grace shall deal:

     G
Let the Hero, born of woman, crush the serpent with His heel,

     C   G   D7 G
Since God is marching on." *(Refrain)*

     G
5. In the beauty of the lilies Christ was born across the sea,

      C   G   D7
With a glory in His bosom that transfigures you and me;

     G
As He died to make men holy, let us die to make men free,

     C   G   D7 G
While God is marching on. *(Refrain)*

     G
6. He is coming like the glory of the morning on the wave,

     C   G   D7
He is wisdom to the mighty, He is honor to the brave,

     G
So the world shall be His footstool, and the soul of wrong His slave,

     C   G   D7 G
Our God is marching on! *(Refrain)*

The ordeal of battle was all too familiar to Civil War soldiers who sang "John Brown's Body" as a marching song. But to Julia Ward Howe, wartime Washington, D.C., was a frenzied and frightening place to visit. After inadvertently witnessing a battle at a nearby army camp, Howe returned to her hotel. There she penned—in just a few hours—the now famous verses set to a hymn tune of William Steffe. Published in 1862, "The Battle Hymn of the Republic" quickly became a favorite with the Union army, and these new words replaced the "John Brown's Body" text.

BICYCLE BUILT FOR TWO

Harry Dacre

♩. = 69

G   C

Dai - sy,   Dai - sy,   give me your an - swer

G   D7   G   A7

true, _____ I'm half cra - zy all for the

D7   G

love of you. _____ It won't be a styl - ish mar - riage; _____ I

C   G   D7   G   D7

can't af - ford a car - riage, _____ But you'll look sweet up -

G   D7   G   D7   G

on the seat Of a bi - cy - cle built for two. _____

Autoharp, strum each downbeat
Guitar, strum 15
Soprano recorder

BIG BUNCH, A LITTLE BUNCH

African American Game Song

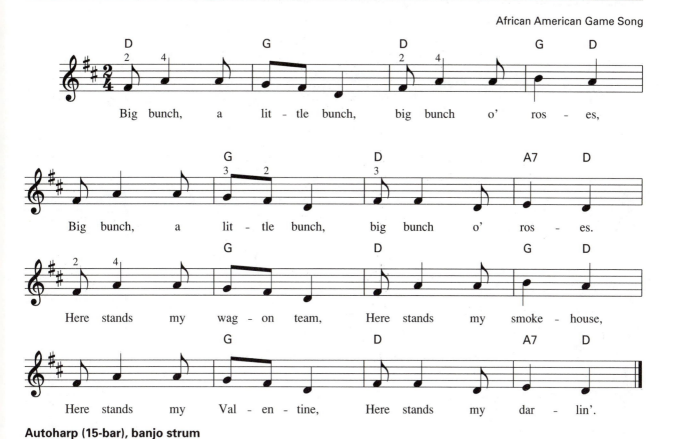

Big bunch, a lit – tle bunch, big bunch o' ros – es,

Big bunch, a lit – tle bunch, big bunch o' ros – es.

Here stands my wag – on team, Here stands my smoke – house,

Here stands my Val – en – tine, Here stands my dar – lin'.

Autoharp (15-bar), banjo strum

Insert child's name in place of "darlin' " at the end of the song.

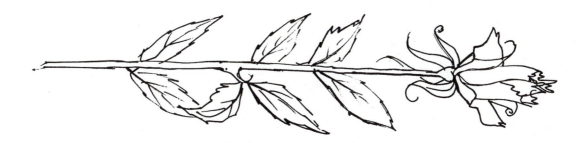

THE BIG CORRAL

American Cowboy Song

The big hus - ky brute from the cat - tle chute, Press a - long to the big cor -

ral! He should be brand - ed on the snoot, Press a - long to the big cor -

Refrain

ral! Press a - long, cow - boy, Press a - long with a cow - boy

yell, Ya - hoo! Press a - long, cow - boy, Press a - long to the big cor - ral!

Autoharp, strum L

Play this pattern on a xylophone during the first section.

Play 7 times

Play this pattern on a wood block during the refrain.

Play 4 times

28

BINGO

American Song

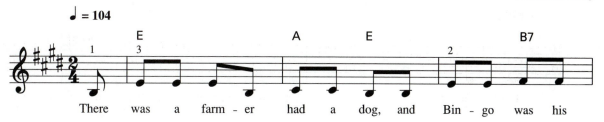

There was a farm – er had a dog, and Bin – go was his

name, O, B – i – n – g – o, B – i – n – g – o,

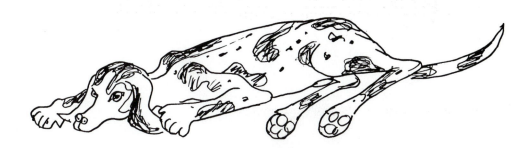

B – i – n – g – o, and Bin – go was his name, O.

Guitar, strum 3
Piano, accompany using chord roots

Sing and play the traditional game for "Bingo." Omit a letter each time the song is repeated, inserting a clap where a letter should occur. Begin by omitting B, then both the B and the I, until all five letters are omitted and are replaced by five claps.

29

BLACK IS THE COLOR

Appalachian Ballad

Freely

1. Black, black, black is the col - or of my true love's hair. Those
2. How I love my __ love and well s/he knows, _____ I

lips are like some ros - y fair; The pur - est __ eyes and the
love the grass where - on s/he goes; When s/he on __ earth no __

neat - est __ hands, I love the grass where - on s/he stands.
more __ I ____ see, My life will quick - ly o - ver be.

Guitar, free brush
Piano, accompaniment pattern XI

The ballad is a sung story. Every narrative focuses on a single incident of universal appeal—romantic, gruesome, fabulous, or even miraculous. Tales are about faithful lovers, abandoned sweethearts, or brave soldiers or sailors. Real people are also subjects: pirates, coal miners, or highwaymen. And disasters such as shipwrecks are popular ballad topics. Each tale has several stanzas, each stanza four (or five) phrases long. In old-style balladry, the singer performs with great precision and economy. Eccentricities are shunned in favor of an impersonal, yet intense, rendition.

"Black Is the Color" inspired the music for Mel Gibson's film Braveheart.

BLOW THE MAN DOWN

American Halyard Shanty

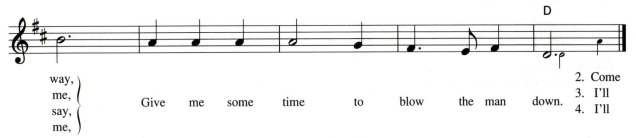

Heavily, in one ($\dot{\jmath}$ = 60)

1. Blow the man down, bul-lies, blow the man down!
(2.) all you young fel-lows who fol-low the sea,
(3.) give you fair warn-ing be-fore we be-lay,
(4.) sing you a song, a good song of the sea,

To me way,

hey, blow the man down!

Blow the man down, bul-lies, blow him a-
Please pay at-ten-tion and lis-ten to
Don't ev-er take heed of what pret-ty girls
And trust that you'll join in the cho-rus with

way,
me,
say,
me,

Give me some time to blow the man down.

2. Come
3. I'll
4. I'll

Autoharp (15-bar), strum each downbeat
Guitar, strum 15
Piano, accompaniment pattern VI

The heavy, straining work on the great square-rigged merchant vessels was done to the strong rhythm of a sea shanty. These lusty work songs could time the group pull and also the interval of relaxation as the crew handled the halyards—the ropes used to hoist or lower a sail. In this halyard shanty, "blow the man down" probably means to "knock the man out" so he could be "shanghaied" to fill out a ship's crew.

BLUEBIRD

Blue-bird, blue-bird, through my win-dow, Blue-bird, blue-bird, through my win-dow,

Blue-bird, blue-bird, through my win-dow, To find an-oth-er bird.

Autoharp (15-bar), strum C
Guitar, strum 5
Piano, accompaniment pattern III

Game

Children stand in a circle with hands joined and arms raised to form windows. One child is "it" (the bird), and he or she weaves inside then outside through the windows. On the last phrase, he or she stands in place, facing one of the children in the circle. The singing stops, and the child who is it asks, "What bird do you want to be?" The child in the circle answers, then becomes it for the next repetition of the song.

BLUETAIL FLY

American Minstrel Song

Freely

Verse

Gm   B♭   F   C7

1. When I was young I used to wait on Mas - ter and hand him his plate, And
2. And when he'd ride in the af - ter - noon, I'd fol - low af - ter with a hick-o - ry broom; The
3. One day while rid - ing round the farm, The flies so numerous they _ did swarm; One
4. The po - ny run, he jump, he kick, He throw my Mas-ter in _ the ditch; He
5. They laid him under a 'sim-mon tree, His ep - i - taph is there _ to see: "Be -

Gm   B♭   *a tempo* C7   F

pass the bot - tle when he got dry, And brush a - way the blue - tail fly!
po - ny be - ing ver - y shy, When bit - ten by the blue - tail fly!
chanced to bite him on the thigh, The dev - il take the blue - tail fly!
died and the ju - ry won-dered why, The ver - dict was the blue - tail fly!
neath this stone I'm forced to lie, A vic - tim of the blue - tail fly!"

Refrain

C7   F

Jim - my crack corn, and I don't care, Jim - my crack corn, and I don't care,

F(7)   B♭   C7   F

Jim - my crack corn, and I don't care, My Mas - ter's gone a - way.

Autoharp, strum freely until *a tempo,* then strum C
Piano, accompaniment pattern V until *a tempo,* then III

THE BRIDGE OF AVIGNON
(*Sur le pont d'Avignon*)

French Folk Song

English:	On	the bridge,	A - vi - gnon,	there	is	danc - ing,	there	is	danc - ing,
French:	Sur	le pont	d'A - vi - gnon,	l'on	y	dan - se,	l'on	y	dan - se,
Pronunciation:	sir	luh puhn	dah - veen - yahn	luhn	ee	dahn - seh	luhn	ee	dahn - seh

Fine

On	the bridge,	A - vi - gnon,	there	is	danc - ing	all a - round.
Sur	le pont	d'A - vi - gnon,	l'on	y	dan - se	tout en rond.
sir	*luh puhn*	*dah - veen - yahn*	*luhn*	*ee*	*dahn - seh*	*too tehn rahn*

Verse

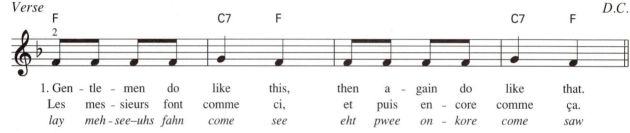

D.C.

1. Gen - tle - men	do	like	this,	then	a - gain	do like	that.
Les mes - sieurs	font	comme	ci,	et	puis	en - core	comme ça.
lay meh - see–uhs	*fahn*	*come*	*see*	*eht*	*pwee*	*on - kore*	*come saw*

Autoharp, strum C
Piano, accompaniment pattern II

              F   *C7 F*   *C7 F*

2. La-dies all do like this, then a-gain do like that.
   Les da-mes font comme ci, et puis en-core comme ça.

              F   *C7 F*   *C7 F*

3. Sold-iers all do like this, then a-gain do like that.
   Les sold-ats font comme ci, et puis en-core comme ça.

              F   *C7 F*   *C7 F*

4. Child-ren all do like this, then a-gain do like that.
   Les gam-ins font comme ci, et puis en-core comme ça.

Pronunciation guide

dames: *dah-meh*

soldats: *sole-dot*

gamins: *gah-meen*

    At "do like this" and "do like that," create a suitable body movement for each verse, such as bowing (*gentleman*) and skipping rope (*children*).

Avignon is a large and ancient city in southeastern France. It is dominated by a Romanesque palace of the popes and a cathedral, both built on a steep hill overlooking the Rhone River. The power and width of the Rhone at Avignon made it impossible for even the Romans to build a bridge there. However, in 1178–88 St Bénézet built one, which was broken down and repaired several times and finally abandoned in 1680. Only part of the bridge supported by four arches nearest to Avignon still stands.

An accurate version of this famous song, "Sur le pont d'Avignon," should read "Sous le pont . . ." ("under the bridge") because any dancing would probably have taken place in the shade of the bridge on the Île de la Barthelasse.

BYE, BYE, BLACKBIRD

Mort Dixon

Ray Henderson

Piano, accompaniment pattern XVI

Create a medley of Gay Nineties songs by linking "Bye, Bye, Blackbird," "Bicycle Built for Two," "Mister Sun," "Side by Side," and "The Sidewalks of New York."

CAMPTOWN RACES

Stephen C. Foster
(United States 1826–1864)

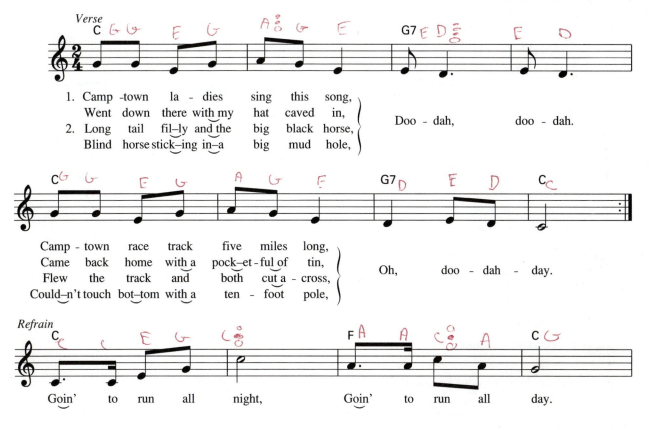

Verse

1. Camp-town la-dies sing this song, Doo - dah, doo - dah.
   Went down there with my hat caved in,
2. Long tail fil-ly and the big black horse,
   Blind horse stick-ing in-a big mud hole,

Camp-town race track five miles long, Oh, doo - dah - day.
Came back home with a pock-et-ful of tin,
Flew the track and both cut a-cross,
Could-n't touch bot-tom with a ten - foot pole,

Refrain

Goin' to run all night, Goin' to run all day.

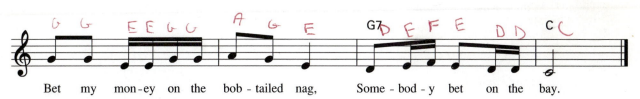

Bet my mon-ey on the bob - tailed nag, Some - bod - y bet on the bay.

Autoharp, strum C on verse, banjo strum on refrain
Piano, accompaniment pattern III

Self-taught composer Stephen Collins Foster was born in Lawrenceville, Pennsylvania. Some of his over two hundred songs are regarded almost as American folk songs. Even though he was a northerner, many of his songs depict southern plantation life in an eloquent and poignant manner. His best-known songs include "Oh! Susanna," "Beautiful Dreamer," and "Camptown Races."

THE CAROLERS
(*Íată Vin Colindători*)

English words by
Patricia Hackett

Traditional Romanian Carol
as sung by Ion Codrescu

Quickly (♩ = 208)

English: 1. Young and old will bring a song, Sing in the white __ dawn, __
Romanian: Ia - tă vin co - lin - dă - tori, Zo - ri - le-s dal - be, ___
Pronunciation: ih–ah - tuh veen koe - lihn - dah - toree zoe - rih - lehss dahl - bay

Hear them ca - rol Christ - mas joy, Sing in the white dawn.
Noap - tea* pe la cân - tă - tori, Zo - ri - le-s dal - be.
noh–ahp-ta peh lah kuhn - tuh - toree zoe - rih - less dahl - bay

* Pronounce *ea* as in h*a*t.

Guitar, brush each downbeat

Em
2. Now they bring the love of God,

Am   *Em*
Sing in the white dawn;

Hear them carol Christmas peace,

Em
Sing in the white dawn.

Em
3. Give the singers food and drink,

Am   *Em*
Sing in the white dawn;

Hear them carol Christmas love,

Em
Sing in the white dawn.

Literal translation

Children and young people
Go to sing carols early at dawn
When there is just a white light;
Their songs bring us the message of God.

"The Carolers" describes an hour when the light of dawn reveals a world of snowy one-ness. The carol is probably from the mountains of Romania, a beautiful country in southeastern Europe that has varied topography. Romania's rich body of folk music developed from regional isolation and from a devout peasant culture. The somber folklore of Transylvania is misleading, because most Romanian folk music, dance, costumes, and visual arts are bright and dynamic. Internationally known Romanian artists include classical violinist and composer Georges Enesco (1881–1955) and abstract sculptor Constantin Brancusi (1876–1957). Today's artists and intellectuals (who typically speak several languages) are enjoying their new freedom to travel and to communicate with colleagues throughout the world. (Romania is further described with "Celebration Song" and "The Lamb.")

CELEBRATION SONG
(*La Mulţi Ani Cu Sănătate*)

English words by
Patricia Hackett

Traditional Romanian Song
as sung by Ion Codrescu

English: Now, to-day I come to greet you, May you be blessed with health and good cheer,
Romanian: La mulţi ani eu să - nă -ta - te, Să vă dea* Dom - nul tot ce do - riţi,
Pronunciation: lah mooltz ahn koo suh - nuh-tah - tay suh vuh da dome - nool tote cheh doe - reets

Cel - e - brate here with fine friends to meet you, Hap - py and strong, a - noth - er year!
Zi - le se - ni - ne şi fe - ri - ci - te, La mulţi ani, să tră - iţi!
zee - leh seh - nee - nay shih feh - rih-chee - tay lah mooltz ahn suh truh-eets

* Pronounce *ea* as in h*a*t.

Autoharp (15-bar), strum B
Soprano recorder

Literal translation

Many healthy returns of the day,
May God grant your wishes;
Happy and serene days,
Many healthy returns.

"Celebration Song" is Romania's "Happy Birthday Song"; it is performed on other occasions, as well. Romania's history is long and fascinating. Archeological remains from the Stone Age have been discovered in the mountains, and Roman ruins from the beginning of the Christian era are found near the Black Sea port of Constanţa. (The Romanian language developed from Latin as a result of the Roman conquest of Romania and the Balkan peninsula.) Over the centuries, there has been much intermixing of Romanians with their Yugoslav and Hungarian neighbors, and borders have changed often since the Romanian state was created in 1859. Now the people are recovering from four decades of tyranny that ended with the execution of dictator Nicolae Ceauşescu in 1989. (Romania is further described with "The Carolers" and "The Lamb.")

Bran Castle

CHANSON RUSSE
(for recorder and guitar)

Anonymous French Melody

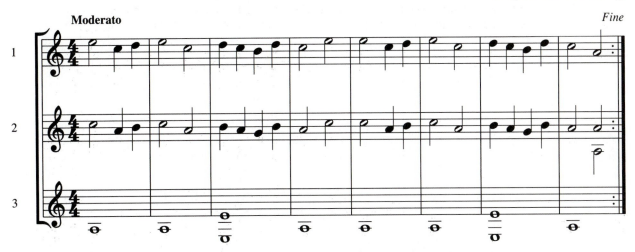

Perform this chanson with soprano recorders on parts 1 and 2, and guitar on part 3. Or, perform with a guitar on each part: 1, 2, and 3.

CHEH CHEH KOOLAY

West African Song (Ghana)

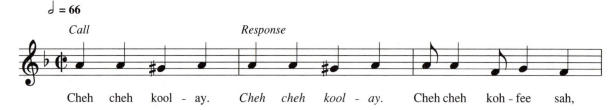

Cheh   cheh   kool - ay.   *Cheh   cheh   kool - ay.*   Cheh cheh   koh - fee   sah,

Cheh cheh   koh - fee   sah.   Kah - fee   sah lang - ah,   *Kah - fee   sah lahn - gah.*

Tah-tah   shee lahn - gah,   *Tah-tah   shee lahn - gah.*   Coom   ah - dye - day,   *Coom   ah - dye - day.*

Game

Children form a circle around a leader. The leader sings the calls and makes the motions described below. The players in the circle respond by singing and imitating the caller. Players move constantly during the singing, twisting their bodies or bouncing up and down.

Cheh cheh koo-lay: Hands on head; all twist their bodies along with the beat as they sing.

Cheh cheh koh-fee sah: Hands on shoulders; twisting continues.

Kah-fee sah lahn-gah: Hands on waist; twisting continues.

Tah-tah shee lahn-gah: Hands on knees. All change to an up-and-down movement, bending the knees along with the beat.

Coom ah-dye-day: Hands on ankles; up-and-down movement continues. At the end of the song, players jump as they shout, "Hey!"

CHILDREN, GO WHERE I SEND THEE

African American Song

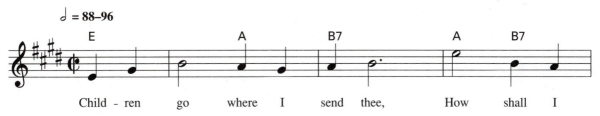

Child - ren go where I send thee, How shall I

send thee? I'm a - gon - na send thee one by one:

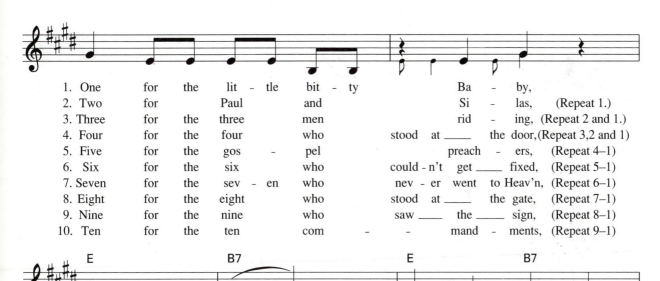

1. One for the lit - tle bit - ty Ba - by,
2. Two for Paul and Si - las, (Repeat 1.)
3. Three for the three men rid - ing, (Repeat 2 and 1.)
4. Four for the four who stood at ____ the door,(Repeat 3,2 and 1)
5. Five for the gos - pel preach - ers, (Repeat 4–1)
6. Six for the six who could-n't get ____ fixed, (Repeat 5–1)
7. Seven for the sev - en who nev - er went to Heav'n, (Repeat 6–1)
8. Eight for the eight who stood at ____ the gate, (Repeat 7–1)
9. Nine for the nine who saw ____ the ____ sign, (Repeat 8–1)
10. Ten for the ten com - - mand - ments, (Repeat 9–1)

Born, born, ____ born in Beth - le - -

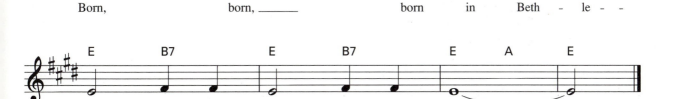

hem, Beth - le - hem, Beth - le - hem. ____

Guitar, strum 2

43

CHRISTMAS IS A TIME FOR SHARING

David Eddleman

time, set a can - dle blaz - ing, Sing a song with a voice a-rais - ing, Sing of

Christ - mas time is giv - ing time, a
Christ - mas time is can - dle time, a

peace on earth and hu - man worth in ev - 'ry - one we see. ___ Christ-mas

time for ev - 'ry - one to care. ___
time for you, a

1.

2.

ev - 'ry one we see. ___ Sing a Christ - mas song of

time for me. ___ Sing a Christ - mas song of

love for you and me. ___

love for you and me. ___

CHRISTMAS IS HERE!

Swedish Folk Song

♩ = 96

f F

English:	Christ - mas is here a - gain, Oh,	Christ - mas is here a - gain, Our
Swedish:	Nur är det jul i - gen, och	nu är det jul i - gen, och
Pronunciation:	*new air deh yule ee - yen, oh*	*new air deh yule ee - yen oh*

Dm

1. C

2. B♭ F *Fine*

Gm B♭

hap - py days will last till East - er.
ju - len va - ra skall til på - ska.
you - len vah - rah skahl teel poh - skah

East - er.
på - ska.
poh - skah

Then it is East - er - time, Oh,
Så är det påsk i - gen, och
soh air deh posk ee - yen oh

F Am Gm C7

D.C. al Fine

F

then it is East - er - time, And East - er joy will last till Christ - mas.
så är det påsk i - gen. Och på - sken va - ra skall til ju - la.
soh air deh posk ee - yen oh posk - ken vah - rah skahl teel you - lah

Autoharp, strum I
Piano, accompaniment pattern IX

46

CIELITO LINDO

English words by
Samuel Maqui

Quirino Mendoza y Cortez
(Mexico)

♩ = 152–160

A   **E7**   **A**   **E7**

English: 1. Night and day _____ 'neath your win - dow, *Cie - - li - to*
Spanish: 1. E - se lu - - nar que tie - nes. *Cie - - li - to*
Pronunciation: eh - seh loo - - nahr keh tyeh - nehs syeh - lee - toh

A   **E7**

Lin - do, play - - ing and sing - ing, _____
Lin - do. Jun - - to a la bo - ca, _____
leen - doh hoon - - toh a lah boh - kah

My gui - tar _____ strum - ming from a - far _____ Brings my
No se lo _____ des a na - die. *Cie - - li - to*
noh seh loh dehs ah nah - dyeh syeh - - lee - toh

A

song to you _____ soft - ly wing - ing. _____
Lin - do. Que a _____ mi me to - ca. _____
leen - doh keh ah mee meh toh - kah

Refrain

A   **(C#7)**   **D**

¡Ay, ay, ay, ay! _____

E7   **A**

Hush, now your weep - ing; _____ We'll sing and dance _
Can - - ta y no llo - res; _____ Por - que can - tan -
kahn - tah ee noh yoh - rehs pohr - keh kahn - tahn -

47

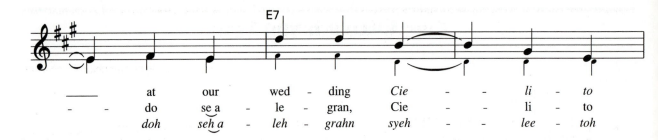

at our wed - ding Cie - - li - to
- - do se a - le - gran, Cie - - li - to
doh seh a - leh - grahn syeh - - lee - toh

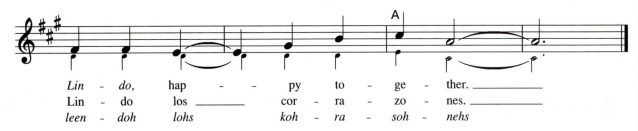

Lin - do, hap - - py to - ge - ther. _____
Lin - do los _____ cor - ra - zo - nes. _____
leen - doh lohs koh - ra - soh - nehs

Guitar, strum 11

A   E7   A
2. If your mother should tell you,

E7 A   E7
"Cielito Lindo, come from your window,"

I will wait by the garden gate,

                     A
You're my fate, my Cielito Lindo. (*Refrain*)

Spanish

A   E7   A
2. Si tu mama te dice,
see too mah-mah teh dee-seh

E7   A   E7
"Cielito Lindo, cierra la puerta,"
syeh-lee-toe leen-doh syeh-rah lah pwehr-tah

Hace ruido a la llave, Cie-
hah-seh rwee-doh ah lah yah-veh syeh-

                     A
lito Lindo, Y dejala abierta. (*Refrain*)
lee-toe leen-doh ee deh-hah-la ah-byehr-tah

Spaniards found sophisticated musical instruments and a complex melodic system in Mexico at the time of the conquest. Modern Mexican folk music strongly reflects Spanish music in its melodies, dances, and instruments. European violins, harps, guitars, and trumpets all became popular in folk music. From three to twelve of these instruments make up today's mariachi ensemble of violins, trumpets, arpón (harp), guitarron (a large bass guitar), and jarana (a smaller, 8-gut-stringed version of the guitar). Mariachi ensembles perform "Cielito Lindo," which is based on the jarabe, a popular dance in $\frac{6}{8}$ or a fast $\frac{3}{4}$ meter. The song is also popular with wandering street musicians of Mexico.

CIRCLE 'ROUND THE ZERO

African American Game Song

Cir - cle round the ze - ro,   Find your lov - in' ze - ro.   Back, back ze - ro,

Side,   side   ze - ro,   Front, front   ze - ro,   Tap your lov - in' ze - ro.

Autoharp, strum M

Formation

Players in a circle, doing a patschen-clap motion throughout the game.

Game

Measures 1–2: A leader moves around the outside of the group, stopping behind a player on "your loving zero."

Measure 3: Back-to-back, the two players bump twice.

Measure 4: They bump hips twice.

Measure 5: The two players face each other, and clap hands twice.

Measure 6: On "tap," the leader taps his zero's shoulder and takes his or her place.

Play one or both of these patterns, on a xylophone with "Circle 'round the Zero."

CLAPPING LAND

Danish Folk Song

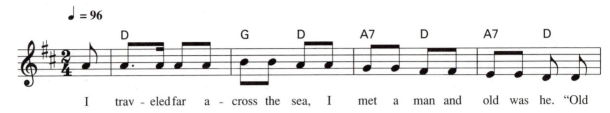

I trav - eled far a - cross the sea, I met a man and old was he. "Old

man," I said, "where do you live?" and this is what he told me:

Refrain

"Come with me to
clap - png land,	clap - ping land,	clap - ping land.
nod - ding land,	nod - ding land,	nod - ding land.
danc - ing land,	danc - ing land,	danc - ing land.
skip - ping land,	skip - ping land,	skip - ping land.

All who want to live with me, Fol - low me to
| clap - ping |
| nod - ding | land."
| danc - ing |
| skip - ping |

Autoharp (15-bar), strum C
Guitar, strum 7 or play melody notes
Piano, accompaniment pattern II (play chord on each beat)

On the refrain, do body rhythms along with the words "clapping land," "nodding land," and so forth. For example, clap the rhythm of the words "clapping land" each time they occur.

COFFEE GROWS ON WHITE OAK TREES

American Play-Party Song

Refrain

Cof-fee grows on white oak trees, The riv-er flows with hon-ey-O. Go

choose some-one to walk with you As sweet as choc-'late can-dy-O!

Verse

1. Two in the mid-dle and I can't dance, Bet-sy! Two in the mid-dle and I can't dance, Bet-sy!
2. Four   Four
3. Eight   Eight

Two in the mid-dle and I can't dance, Bet-sy! Hel-lo, Nan-cy Brown!
Four
Eight

Autoharp (15-bar), strum H (refrain) and strum D (verse)
Guitar, strum 10 (refrain) and strum 4 (verse)

Formation

Couples stand side by side with hands joined, forming two concentric circles; girls are on the inside. One boy stands in the center of the circle.

Dance

Measures 1–8: Couples walk clockwise in a circle. The boy in the center selects a girl from the circle to join him for measure 9 actions.

Measures 9–16: Couples skip around the circle. The boy in the center swings his partner, first by the right hand (measures 9–12) and then by the left hand (measures 13–16).

When the song is repeated, the two dancers in the center each select a partner from the circle as the couples walk clockwise. During measures 9–16, the four dancers in the center swing; those in the outside circle skip.

On the next repetition, 8 dancers will swing in the center, then 16, and finally 32. (The song's words change to "sixteen" or "thirty-two," as needed.) The dance is repeated until everyone is in the center.

THE CONDOR
(*El Condor*)

English words by
Aura Kontra

Daniel Almonica Robles

Moderately ($\quarternote$ = 80–84)

Am

English: Love is like a con - dor glid - ing toward the earth. It comes to
Spanish: El a - mor co - mo un con - dor ba - ja - ra, mi ko - ra
Pronunciation: *ehl ah - mohr koh-moh oon kohn-dohr bah - hah - rah mee coh - rah*

C

E7 **Am** **E7**

me, fil-ling me with hap-pi-ness. And then it's gone. Mm
zón. gol-pea - rá. des pues se i - rá. Mm
ssohn gohl-pay - rah dehs pwes seh ee - rah

Am **C**

As the moon-light leaves its glow on de - sert sands, You ap -
La lu - na en el des - ier to bril - la - rá. Tu ven -
lah loo-nah ehn ehl dah-sseair toh bree - yah - rah too ven -

E7 **Am** **E7**

pear, bring-ing back the love I lost. And then you, too, are gone. Mm
dras. So - la - men - te un be - so. me de - ja - rás. Mm
drahss so - lah - men-teh oon beh - so meh day - ha - rass

Am **(F)**

Who knows when my love will draw you back-a - gain. What to
Quién sa - be ma - ña - na vol - ve - rás. Qué ha -
kyehn sah - bay mah-nyah-nah vowl-vay - rahss kay ah -

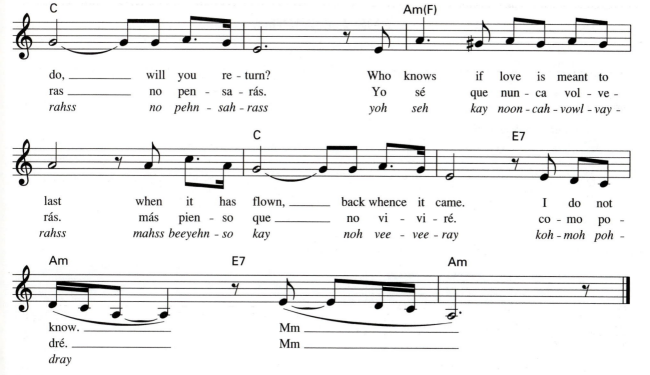

do, _____ will you re - turn? | Who knows if love is meant to
ras _____ no pen - sa - rás. | Yo sé que nun - ca vol - ve -
rahss | *no pehn - sah - rass* | *yoh seh kay noon - cah - vowl - vay -*

last when it has flown, _____ back whence it came. | I do not
rás. más pien - so que _____ no vi - vi - ré. | co - mo po -
rahss | *mahss beeyehn - so kay* | *noh vee - vee - ray* | *koh - moh poh -*

know. _____ | Mm _____
dré. _____ | Mm _____
dray

Autoharp, strum L
Guitar, strum 23

Literal translation
Like the condor, love descends to strike my heart, then takes flight again;
  like the bright moon, love comes, leaving but a kiss.
Who knows? Tomorrow love may return . . . or never. How can I go on,
  with such sadness and pain in my heart?

Most Latin American folk music shows the influence of Spain and Portugal. Although there are places where African influences dominate—and in remote regions of the Andes or the Upper Amazon the music is strongly Indian—nearly everywhere in Latin America there are hybrid styles: mestizo (Native American and Spanish), mulato (African and European), and zambo (African and Native American). Pre-Hispanic flutes and panpipes are still played in Bolivia, Chile, Ecuador, and Peru, and indigenous Indian dances have been woven into Christian celebrations. Afro-Hispanic music, with its intense, percussive rhythms, permeates life in parts of Brazil, Colombia, and Venezuela. But nearly everywhere in Latin America, Hispanic musical traits tend to dominate. Guitars, violins, and harps accompany melodies that are sometimes harmonized in the parallel thirds of Portugal.

COUNTING SONG

English words by
Lucille Wood

Mexican Children's Song

Verse

1. U - no, dos y tres,   Cua - tro, cin - co, seis;   Sie - te, o - cho,
   oo - noh dohs ee trehs   *kwah - troh seen - koh seh—ees*   *see—eh - teh oh - choh*
2. Ten - go un som - brero,   I have a lit - tle hat;   Ten - go un sa -
   tehn - goh oon sohm - breh—roh   *ten - goh oon sah -*

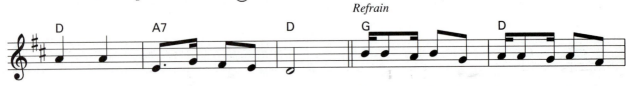

Refrain

nue - ve, I can count to diez.   La la la la la, La la la la la,
nweh - veh   *dee—ehs*

ra - pe, What do you think of that?
rah - peh

La la la la la la;   La la la la la, La la la la la, La la la la la.

Autoharp (15-bar), strum D (verse) and strum C (refrain)
Guitar, strum 5 (verse), scratch melody rhythm (refrain)

     D
3. Adios,   amigo,
   ah-dee-ohs ah-mee-goh

   A7   D
   Adios, my friend;

   G   D
   Hasta   la vista,
   ah-stah lah vee-stah

   A7   D
   Till we meet again. (*Refrain*)

THE CROCODILE SONG

Nova Scotia Folk Song

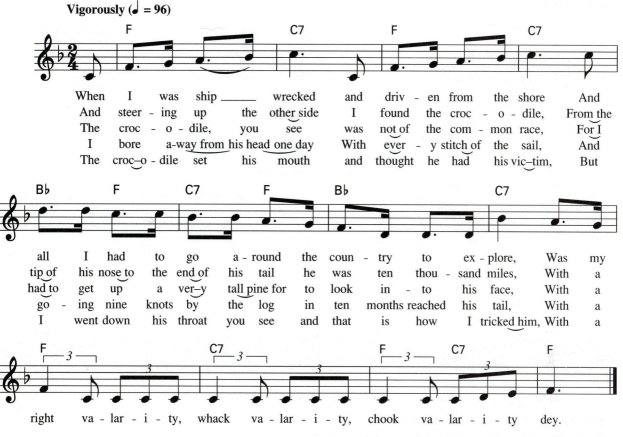

Vigorously (♩ = 96)

When I was ship——— wrecked and driv-en from the shore And
And steer-ing up the other side I found the croc-o-dile, From the
The croc-o-dile, you see was not of the com-mon race, For I
I bore a-way from his head one day With ever-y stitch of the sail, And
The croc-o-dile set his mouth and thought he had his vic-tim, But

all I had to go a-round the coun-try to ex-plore, Was my
tip of his nose to the end of his tail he was ten thou-sand miles, With a
had to get up a ver-y tall pine for to look in-to his face, With a
go-ing nine knots by the log in ten months reached his tail, With a
I went down his throat you see and that is how I tricked him, With a

right va-lar-i-ty, whack va-lar-i-ty, chook va-lar-i-ty dey.

"The Crocodile Song" was taken from *Songs and Ballads of Nova
Scotia* by Helen Creighton. Dover Publications, New York, 1966.

Autoharp, strum G (lines 1 and 2) and strum C (line 3)

Danny Boy
(A Londonderry Air)

Words by Frederic E. Weatherly
(England, 1848–1929)

Traditional Irish Melody

1. Oh, Dan - ny boy, the pipes, the pipes are call - ing, From glen to
2. But come ye back when all the flow'rs are dy - 'in, If I am

glen, and down the moun-tain side, The sum-mer's gone, and all the ros - es
dead, as dead I may well be, Ye'll come and find the place where I am

fal - ling; It's you, it's you must go and I must bide. But come ye
ly - in', And kneel and say an A - ve there for me. And I shall

back when sum - mer's in the mead - ow, Or when the
hear, tho' soft you tread a - bove _____ me, And all my

val - ley's hush'd and white with snow, 'Tis I'll be here in sun-shine and in
grave will warm - er, sweet - er be, For you will bend and tell me that you

shad - ow, Oh, Dan - ny Boy, Oh, Dan - ny Boy, I love you so. _____
love _____ me, And I shall sleep in peace un - til you come to me. _____

Autoharp, free strum
Piano, accompaniment pattern XI on each chord change

The "Danny Boy" melody was composed at the beginning of the seventeenth century as a lament for the ancient Irish O'Cahan Clan, probably by the clan's blind harpist Rory Dall O'Cahan. The tune itself was handed down by later Irish harpists. In 1851, Irish music teacher Jane Ross notated the melody as played by blind Jimmy McCurry, a street fiddler of Londonderry County. Ross then gave the tune to Irish folk-song collector Charles Petrie, who published it in 1855 with the title "A Londonderry Air." Various lyrics for the melody were later written by Irishmen A. P. Graves ("Would I were Erin's apple blossom" and "Elmer's Farewell") and Thomas Moore ("The harp that once in Tara's halls"). In 1912, English barrister and songwriter F. E. Weatherly fitted his "Danny Boy" lyrics (written in 1910) to the Londonderry Air melody, and from then on the haunting O'Cahan lament became a song that is internationally known and loved. (Based on information provided by Retired Ambassador Sean G. Ronan, Dublin, and by The Danny Boy Trading Co. Ltd., Bangor, Northern Ireland.)

DE COLORES

English words by Alice Firgau

Traditional Mexican Song

♩ = 132

English: When _____ the mead - ows, _____ When the mead - ows burst
Spanish: De _____ co - lo - res, _____ De co - lo - res se
Pronunciation: deh coh - loh - rehs deh coh - loh - rehs seh

forth in the cool, dew - y col - ors of spring - time; _____
vis - ten los cam - pos en la pri - ma - ve - ra; _____
vees - tehn lohs cahm - pohs ehn lah pree - mah - veh - rah

____ When the swal - lows, _____ When the swal - lows come
____ De _____ co - lo - res, _____ De co - lo - res son
deh coh - loh - rehs deh coh - loh - rehs sone

wing - ing in clouds of bright col - ors from far off, _____
los pa - ja - ri - tos que vie - nen de a - fue - ra, _____
lohs pah - ha - ree - tohs keh vee eh-nehn deh ah - fooeh - rah

____ When _____ the rain - bow, _____ When the rain - bow spreads
____ De _____ co - lo - res, _____ De co - lo - res es
deh coh - loh - res deh coh - loh - res ehs

rib - bons of col - or all o - ver the sky, _____ Then I
el ar - co i - res que ve - mos lu - cir. _____ Y por
ehl ahr - coh ee - rehs keh veh - mohs loo - seer ee pore

58

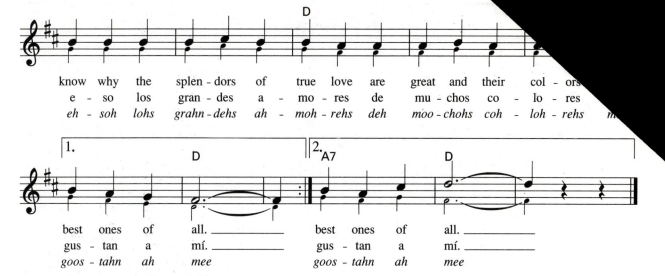

know   why   the   splen - dors   of   true   love   are   great   and   their   col - ors
e - so   los   gran - des   a - mo - res   de   mu - chos   co - lo - res
eh - soh   lohs   grahn - dehs   ah - moh - rehs   deh   moo - chohs   coh - loh - rehs

1.
D
2. A7
D

best   ones   of   all. _____   best   ones   of   all. _____
gus - tan   a   mí. _____   gus - tan   a   mí. _____
goos - tahn   ah   mee   goos - tahn   ah   mee

Autoharp (15-bar), strum each downbeat
Guitar, strum 12
Piano, accompaniment pattern VIII

In the nineteenth century, fashionable European dances such as the waltz, the polka, and the bolero provided the basis for popular Mexican and Latin American music. "De Colores" is a valse rancheras, associated with the states of Jalisco and Michoacan (northwest of Mexico City). Ranchera songs have a special Mexican flavor and became popular favorites through their use in Mexican films of the 1930s and 1940s. "De Colores" was used as a theme song in the labor struggle of California farmworkers in the 1960s and was popularized by Joan Baez, the American folk singer. Many other Mexican songs have become internationally known, such as "Granada," by Agustín Lara (1897–1970), and "La Bamba," Richie Valens's arrangement of a Mexican wedding song.

Do, Lord

African American Spiritual

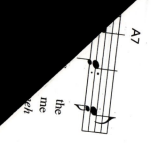

Do, Lord, oh do re-mem-ber me, Do, Lord, oh do, Lord oh

rit. last time

do re-mem-ber me. Do, Lord, oh do, Lord, oh do re-mem-ber me, Look a -

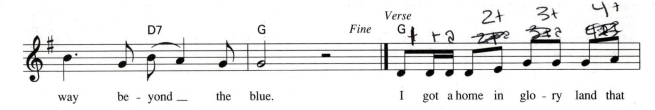

Fine *Verse*

way be - yond ___ the blue. I got a home in glo - ry land that

out-shines the sun, I got a home in glo - ry land that out-shines the sun.

D.C. al Fine

I got a home in glo - ry land that out-shines the sun, Look a - way be - yond ___ the blue.

Autoharp, strum L (refrain) and strum A (verse)
Piano, accompaniment pattern III

355

60

DON GATO
(Mister Cat)

English words by Margaret Marks

Mexican Folk Song

1. Oh, Se - ñor Don Ga - to was a cat, _____ On a
2. "I a - dore you!" wrote the la - dy cat, _____ Who was
3. Oh, Don Ga - to jumped so hap - pi - ly, _____ He fell
4. Then the doc - tors all came on the run, _____ Just to

high, red roof Don Ga - to sat. _____ He went there to read a
fluff - y, white, and nice and fat. _____ There was not a sweet - er
off the roof and broke his knee, _____ Broke his ribs and all his
see if some - thing could be done, _____ And they held a con - sul -

let - ter, ⎫
kit - ty, ⎪ meow, meow, meow,
whisk - ers, ⎬
ta - tion, ⎭

⎧ Where the read - ing ligth was bet - ter, ⎫
⎪ In the coun - try or the cit - y, ⎪ meow, meow,
⎨ And his lit - tle so - lar plex - us, ⎬
⎩ A - bout how to save their pat - ient, ⎭

meow.

⎧ 'Twas a love note for Don Ga - to! _____
⎪ And she said she'd wed Don Ga - to! _____
⎨ "¡Ay car - ram - ba!" cried Don Ga - to! _____
⎩ How to save Señ - or Don Ga - to! _____

Autoharp, strum F (verses 1–5), harp (verse 6)

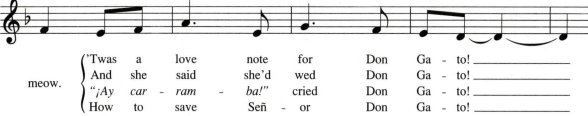

      Dm C Dm
5. But in spite of ev'rything they tried

          C Dm
Poor Séñor Don Gato up and died,

          D7   Gm
Oh, it wasn't very merry, meow, meow, meow,

         A7   Dm
Going to the cemetery, meow, meow, meow,

   A7   Dm
For the ending of Don Gato!

Sing verse 6 slowly.

      Dm C   Dm
6. When the funeral passed the market square

          C   Dm
Such a smell of fish was in the air.

          D7   Gm
Though his burial was slated, meow, meow, meow,

         A7   Dm
He became re-animated: Meow, meow, meow.

   A7   Dm
He came back to life. Don Gato!

Spanish words

1. El señor don Gato estaba,

   sentadito en el tejado,

   cuando le vinieron cartas, . . .

   cuando le vinieron cartas, . . .

   si quería ser casado.

2. Con una gatita blanca,

   sobrina de un gato pardo,

   que no la había más linda, . . .

   que no la había más linda, . . .

   en las casas de aquel barrio.

3. Don Gato con la alegría,

   se ha caído del tejado;

   ha roto siete costillas, . . .

   ha roto siete costillas, . . .

   las dos orejas y el rabo.

4. A visitar lo venían,

   médicos y cirujanos;

   todos dicen que se muere, . . .

   todos dicen que se muere, . . .

   que don Gato está muy malo.

5. El gatito ya se ha muerto,

   ya se ha muerto el buen don Gato;

   a enterrar ya se lo llevan, . . .

   a enterrar ya se lo llevan, . . .

   todos las gatos llorando.

6. Cuando pasaba el entierro,

   por la plaza del pescado,

   al olor de las sardinas, . . .

   al olor de las sardinas, . . .

   don Gato ha resucitado.

DOWN BY THE BAY

American Folk Song

Piano, accompaniment pattern XVI

Divide into two groups and sing "Down by the Bay" as an echo song. After group 1 sings "down by the bay," group 2 begins.

DOWN BY THE STATION

American Song

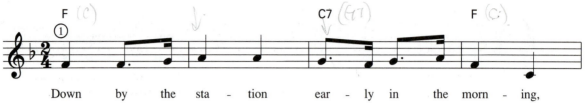

Down by the sta – tion ear – ly in the morn – ing,

See the lit – tle puf – fer-bil – lies all in a row. See the en – gine driv – er

pull the lit – tle han – dle. Choo! Choo! Toot! Toot! Off they go!

Autoharp, strum G
Piano, accompaniment pattern IV

Create a pantomime for the song's words.

DOWN IN THE VALLEY

American Folk Song

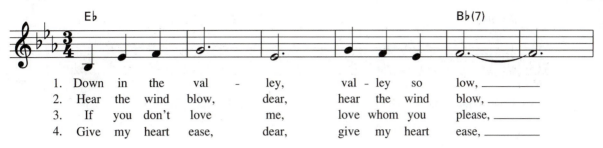

Eb   Bb(7)

1. Down in the val - ley,   val - ley so   low, _____
2. Hear the wind blow,   dear,   hear the wind   blow, _____
3. If you don't love   me,   love whom you   please, _____
4. Give my heart ease,   dear,   give my heart   ease, _____

                                                            Eb

1., 2. Hang your head   o - ver,   hear the wind   blow. _____
3., 4. Throw your arms 'round me,   give my heart   ease. _____

Autoharp (15-bar), strum H
Guitar, strum 10 (play one half step higher, using E and B7 chords.)

Eb   *Bb7*
5. Write me a letter, send it by mail,

           Eb
   Send it in care of Birmingham Jail.

Eb   *Bb7*
6. Birmingham Jail, love, Birmingham
   Jail,

           Eb
   Send it in care of Birmingham Jail.

Eb   *Bb7*
7. Build me a castle forty feet high,

           Eb
   So I can see her, as she rides by.

Eb   *Bb7*
8. As she rides by love, as she rides by,

           Eb
   So I can see her, as she rides by.

Eb   *Bb7*
9. Roses love sunshine, violets love dew,

           Eb
   Angels in heaven know I love you.

Eb   *Bb7*
10. Know I love you, dear, know I love you,

            Eb
    Angels in heaven know I love you.

DRAW ME A BUCKET OF WATER

African American Singing Game

1.–4 Draw me a buck-et of wa - ter For my on - ly daugh - ter. There's

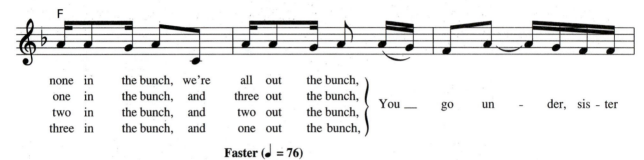

none	in	the bunch,	we're	all	out	the bunch,
one	in	the bunch,	and	three	out	the bunch,
two	in	the bunch,	and	two	out	the bunch,
three	in	the bunch,	and	one	out	the bunch,

You ___ go un - der, sis - ter

Faster (♩ = 76)

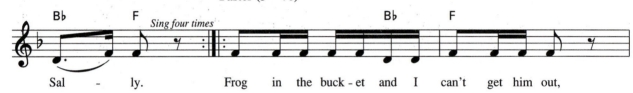

Sing four times

Sal - ly.   Frog   in the buck - et and I can't get him out,

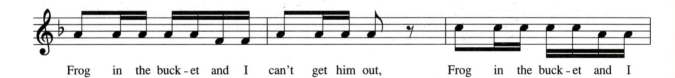

Frog   in the buck - et and I can't get him out,   Frog   in the buck - et and I

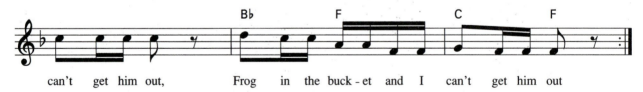

can't get him out,   Frog   in the buck - et and I can't get him out

"Draw Me a Bucket of Water." Written and adapted by Bessie Jones. Collected and Edited by Alan Lomax.
TRO–© Copyright 1972 by Ludlow Music, Inc., New York, New York. Used by Permission.

Autoharp, strum D

Formation

Players form groups of four in a tight circle, with partners standing opposite one another. Number each player from 1 to 4. Partners extend arms across the circle to hold hands in the "weave a basket" position: One pair's arms are under; the other pair's arms are on top.

Game (sing all four verses)

Phrases 1–3: Pairs do a rope-pulling motion by pulling/pushing alternately with right and then left arms.

Phrase 4: Player 1 ducks under the players' arms (players keep hands clasped). As a result, player 1 is encircled by arms around his or her back.

Repeat three times, until players 2, 3, and 4 have been let under. The basket is now "woven," and players' arms are around one another's back.

Ending: Remaining in "woven" formation, groups move clockwise with small, fast, running steps.

DRY BONES

African American Spiritual

Rhythmically (♩ = 152–168)

E - ze - kiel cried, "Them dry __ bones!" E - ze - kiel cried, "Them

dry __ bones!" Oh, hear the word of the Lord! The foot bone con-nect-ed to the

leg bone, the leg bone con-nect - ed to the knee bone, The

knee bone con-nect - ed to the thigh bone, The thigh bone con-nect - ed to the

back bone, The back bone con-nect - ed to the neck bone, The

neck bone con-nect - ed to the head bone, Oh, hear the word of the Lord!

Them bones, them bones gon-na walk a-roun',them bones, them bones gon-na walk a-roun',

Oh, hear the word of the Lord! The head bone con-nect - ed to the

neck bone, the neck bone con-nect - ed to the back bone, The

back bone con-nect-ed to the thigh bone, the thigh bone con-nect-ed to the knee bone, The

knee bone con-nect - ed to the leg bone, the leg bone con-nect - ed to the

foot bone, Oh, hear the word of the Lord! _____

Piano, accompaniment XVI, then use XI (solid chords)
measures 9–21 and measure 31 to the end

Play a different percussion instrument on the rest preceding each body part's name. Play all instruments simultaneously during measures 23 to 30.

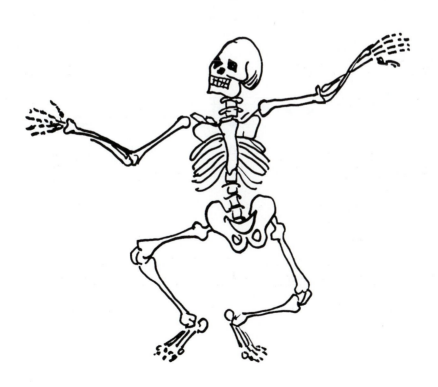

THE EAGLE

Martha Cheney

Hap Palmer

mf Born for a west-ern sky, _ sweep-ing a cir-cle as he flies._
mp Brave and a hunt-er's son, _ the land was his 'til he met a gun._
p There on a moun-tain high,_ wound-ed _ ea-gle wants to die._
mf Dream - ing of days gone by, _ when lit-tle chil-dren watched him fly. _

He was

free _____ when they let him be. _____

1., 3.

2., 4.

In a land with-out a friend, _ will there be an emp-ty sky_

Verse 2 — Go back to the beginning
Verse 4 — Go to Coda

_____ where the ea - gle used to fly _____ in the wind? _____

dim.

Coda

Born   for a   west-ern   sky, __   sweep-ing a cir - cle   as   he   flies. _   He was

free _____   when they let him   be. _____   He was

free _____   when they let him   be. _____

Guitar, strum 23 (verses and coda), strum 22 (endings 2 and 4)

Hap Palmer began writing children's songs as he developed a curriculum for teaching students with learning disabilities. A school administrator encouraged Palmer to record these enjoyable songs and even contacted the company that produced Palmer's first recordings.

EBENEEZER SNEEZER

Lynn Freeman Olson

E - be - nee - zer Snee - zer, ___ Top - sy - tur - vy man, Walks up - on his el - bows ___

Eve - ry - time he can, Dres - es up in pa - per ___ Eve - ry - time it pours,

Whis - tles "Yan-kee Doo-dle" _ Eve -ry-time he snores. Oh, E - be -nee-zer, what a man!

Autoharp, strum N
Piano, accompaniment pattern XIV

EENCY, WEENCY SPIDER

Traditional American Finger Play

Een - cy, ween - cy spi - der went up the wa - ter spout,
"Climb" up, touching one little finger to the thumb of the other hand. Then rotate wrists,
alternately touching thumbs to little fingers.

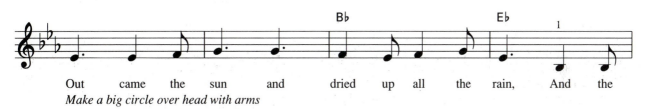

Down came the rain and washed the spi - der out.
Bring hands down and out to sides

Out came the sun and dried up all the rain, And the
Make a big circle over head with arms

een - cy, ween - cy spi - der went up the spout a - gain.
"Climb" up again

Autoharp (15-bar), strum S
Guitar, strum 1 (play one half step higher, using E and B7 chords)

El Coquí
(The Tree Frog)

Puerto Rican Folk Song

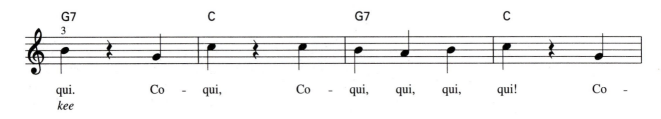

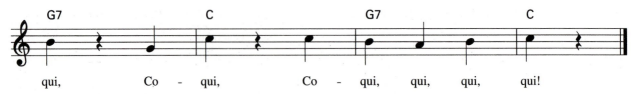

Autoharp, strum H
Piano, accompaniment pattern VIII

THE ENTERTAINER
Rag

Scott Joplin
(United States, 1868–1917)

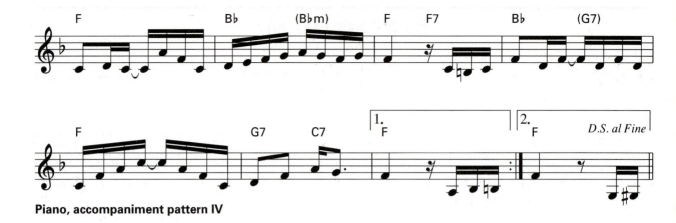

Piano, accompaniment pattern IV

Near the turn of the century, a fellowship of pianists—mostly Black—entertained from New Orleans to Chicago. These piano "professors" were to develop one of the most engaging styles of the twentieth century: the rag. They played dance music for the white underworld, "ragging the time" in the Black districts and the tenderloins of the Mississippi Valley. In 1899, the young Scott Joplin was in Sedalia, Missouri, at clubs like the Maple Leaf, creating his classic piano rags. Graceful and never too fast, these ragtime two-steps almost sound like "two different times at once." Over an unwavering, even "oom-pah" in the bass, syncopation throbs in the melody. These rags were an outgrowth of several styles that had gone before: the cakewalk, the minstrel show band, banjo music, and brass marching bands. After 1900, ragtime became the popular music of Broadway and of vaudeville for two decades, until blues and jazz swept the nation. Ragtime faded, but it was revived after World War II to charm and delight new generations.

EV'RYONE BUT ME

Verses 2 and 3 by
Patricia Hackett

New England Folk Song

♩ = 72–84

F

1. Oh, the fox and the hare, And the bad - ger and the bear, And the
2. Oh, the lark and the wren, And the cuck - oo in the glen, And the
3. Oh, the fish and the frog, And the tur - tle and the dog, And the

B♭   F   C7

squirrel in the wal - nut tree; And the fur - ry lit - tle rab - bits, So en -
owl in the hol - low tree; And the jay - bird and the hawk __ With a
worm in the old oak tree; And the fris - ky lit - tle rat ___ And the

F   C7   F

gag - ing in their hab - its, Have all got a friend but me.
cry ___ and a squawk, _ Have all got a nest but me.
big ___ fat ___ cat, ___ Have all got a home but me.

Autoharp (15-bar), strum A

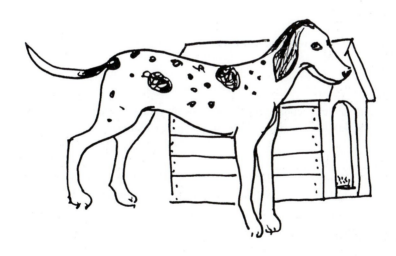

77

THE FARMER IN THE DELL

American Game Song

1. The farm - er in the dell, _____ The farm - er in the dell,
2. The farm - er takes a wife, _____ The farm - er takes a wife,
3. The wife ___ takes the child, _____ The wife ___ takes the child,
4. The child ___ takes the nurse, _____ The child ___ takes the nurse,

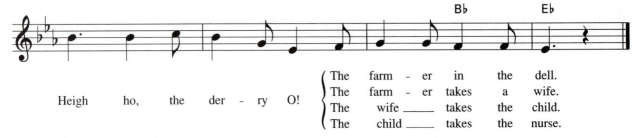

Heigh ho, the der - ry O!

{
The farm - er in the dell.
The farm - er takes a wife.
The wife _____ takes the child.
The child _____ takes the nurse.
}

Autoharp (15-bar), strum S
Guitar, strum 29 (play one half step higher, using E and B7 chords)

5. The nurse takes the dog, . . .

6. The dog takes the cat, . . .

7. The cat takes the rat, . . .

8. The rat takes the cheese, . . .

9. The cheese stands alone. . . .

Formation

Players form a circle. One player is selected as the farmer and stands alone in the middle of the circle.

Game

Players forming the circle either stand in place as they sing (clapping steady beats) or skip around the circle. In each case, they always stop singing and moving at the conclusion of each verse.

Verse 1: The farmer walks around inside the circle, and chooses a wife when the singing stops.

Verse 2: The wife and the farmer walk around inside the circle, and the wife selects a child.

Verse 3–8: The last player to join those inside the circle chooses a person to become the next character mentioned in the song (nurse, dog, cat, rat, and cheese).

Verse 9: Everyone in the middle rejoins the outer circle except the cheese. The cheese stands alone during the singing of verse 9.

The cheese can become the farmer when the game is played again.

FELIZ NAVIDAD

José Feliciano
(Puerto Rico, b. 1945)

Spanish: Fe - liz Na - vi - dad. _____ Fe - liz Na - vi - dad. _____
Pronunciation: *fe - lees nah-vee - dahd feh-lees nah-vee - dahd*

_____ Fe - liz Na - vi - dad, Pros-pe - ro a - ño y fe - li - ci - dad. __
feh-lees. nah-vee - dahd pros-peh - roh ah-nyoh ee feh-lih - see - dahd

I want to wish you a Mer - ry Christ-mas With lots of pres - ents to make you hap-py.

I want to wish you a Mer - ry Christ-mas from the bot-tom of my heart. _____

_____ I want to wish you a Mer - ry Christ-mas with mis-tle-toe and _ lots of cheer. __

With lots of laugh-ter through-out the years from the bot-tom of my heart. ____

Guitar, strum 23 (Spanish section), strum 18 (English section)

Sing the two sections of "Feliz Navidad" together as partner songs.

José Feliciano is a singer, songwriter, and guitarist. Born in Puerto Rico, he moved with his family to New York when he was five years old. Feliciano began his career by teaching himself to play guitar. The winner of several Grammy Awards, he continues to compose, record, and per-form throughout the United States and Europe.

FIVE LITTLE SKELETONS

Walter Bates

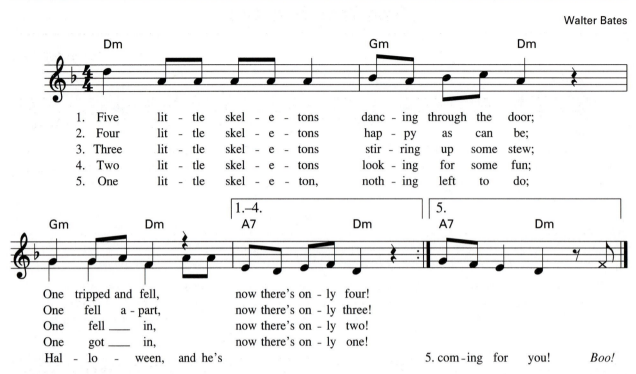

1. Five	lit – tle	skel – e – tons	danc – ing	through	the	door;
2. Four	lit – tle	skel – e – tons	hap – py	as	can	be;
3. Three	lit – tle	skel – e – tons	stir – ring	up	some	stew;
4. Two	lit – tle	skel – e – tons	look – ing	for	some	fun;
5. One	lit – tle	skel – e – ton,	noth – ing	left	to	do;

1.–4.   **5.**

One tripped and fell,   now there's on – ly four!
One fell a - part,   now there's on – ly three!
One fell ___ in,   now there's on – ly two!
One got ___ in,   now there's on – ly one!
Hal - lo - ween, and he's   5. com -ing for you!   *Boo!*

Autoharp, Middle Eastern strum

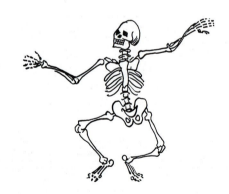

FLOWER DRUM SONG
(Feng Yang Hwa Gu)

Chinese Folk Song

♩ = 96

English: Sing-ing as we walk, sing-ing as we sell, Sing-ing our song, we will
Mandarin: Dzwo _ shou _ lwo, you _ shou _ gu, shou na je lwo gu _
Pronunciation: tzwoh show loowoh yoh show goo show nah juh loh goo

beat the drum and gong. Come to our stall, take a look at what we sell,
lai _ chang _ ge. Bye de _ ge er _ wo ye bu hwei chang,
lye chahng guh beeyeh duh guh ehr woh yeh boo hway chahng

Sing-ing our song, we will beat the drum and gong. Flow - er drums of Feng Yang, we will
jr hwei _ chang ge _ Feng _ Yang _ ge. Feng lai Feng Yang ge _ lai _
jer hway chahng guh fuhng yahng guh fuhng lye fuhng yahng guh lye

Refrain

play them all day long! Drrr!* Hit the drum and gong, Drrr! Hit the drum and gong,
Ai ya ai you ya! Drrr! Ling ding pyao yi pyao. Drrr! Ling ding pyao yi pyao.
aye yah aye yoh yah der ling ding pyaow ee pyaow der ling ding pyaow ee pyaow

Drrr! Pyao!* Drrr! Pyao! Drrr! Pyao! Drrr! Pyao! Pyao! Yo Drrr! Pyao! Pyao! Pyao yi pyao!
der pyaow der pyaow der pyaow der pyaow pyaow yoh der pyaow pyaow pyaow ee pyaow

*Drrr and Pyao are words imitating the drum and gong sounds.

Play these patterns on sticks, gong, and drum during "Flower Drum Song." Have each
instrument begin at a different time.

FUGUE
("The Little")
BWV 578 (ca. 1709)

Johann Sebastian Bach
(Germany, 1685–1750)

♩ = 69

A fugue is a musical procedure that uses imitation. Three or four parts enter at different times, as in a round. However, a fugue has many rather complex musical characteristics that make it a special challenge for composer, performer, and listener. Bach is acknowledged as having brought the fugue to perfection. The subject (theme) of Bach's organ fugue is in the key of G minor, so it is sometimes called the "Little Fugue in G Minor."[1]

The Baroque was an exuberant and dynamic period (from about 1600 to about 1750) during which artists expressed a wide range of human feeling and ideas. Baroque music made extensive use of ornamentation and improvisation, and this era saw the beginning of idiomatic composition for specific instruments. Not only was our major/minor system crystallized in that period, but also Baroque dance rhythms contributed to our modern predilection for the four-measure phrase. The towering genius of Johann Sebastian Bach brought the Baroque style to perfection with his creation of an immense quantity of sacred and secular music for varied instruments and voices. Although Bach's music was neglected after his death, it was revived in the nineteenth century, and his spirit speaks to us as profoundly today as in his own time—truly a music for the ages.

---

[1] *Found in* Bowmar Orchestral Library, Series 2, "Fashions in Music."

GERAKINA

Greek Folk Song

♩ = 200

English:	Ger - a - ki-na's at the	fair, ____	Ger - a - ki-na with her	gol - den ban-gles on,
Greek:	Ki - ni - - se ____		i Ye - ra -	ki - na, ____
Pronunciation:	kee - neh - - seh		ee yeh - rah -	kee - na

There's	mu - sic ev - 'ry - where. ____	Ring,	pret - ty gol - den	ban - gles, jin - gle, jin - gle,
ya	ne - - ro. ____	Kri -	o ____ na ____	fe - ri ____ droom - a
yah	neh - - roh	kree -	oh nah	feh - ree droom -ah

jan - gle. Sing	in the	air,	Ger - a - ki - na danc - ing at the	fair. All the vil - lage
droom - a drun	drun - a	drun,	Ta ____ vra - chio - lia tis vro - dun.	Ta ____ vra -
droom - ah droon	droon-ah	droon	tah vrah - choh - lyah tees vroh - doon	tah vrah -

boys will come	to the square	For the jin - gle	jan - gle dance at the	fair. ____
chio - lia tis	vro - dun,	Droom-a, droom - a	drun - a, drun, drun - a	drun. ____
choh - lyah tees	vroh - doon	droom-ah droom-ah	droon - ah droon droon-ah	droon

Autoharp, brush each accent (see dance that follows), or use a Middle Eastern strum

A group of singers can sing harmony throughout, a third below the melody.

The *kalamatianos* that follows is a Greek folk dance distinguished by its seven-beat meter.

Preliminary activities

Practice the dance rhythm by speaking these words and clapping the accents:

Speak: My - ko - nos, Del - phi, Ath - ens*

Clap: ♩ ♩ ♩ ♩ ♩ ♩ ♩
    >   >   >

Mykonos ("MIH-kuh-nohss") is a Greek island in the Aegean Sea, midway between Athens and the Turkish coast. Delphi ("DELL-fee") is an ancient religious site on the Greek mainland. Athens is the capital city of Greece, home to the famous Parthenon atop the Acropolis.

Transfer the clapping rhythm to the feet, and lightly stamp each accent above.

Formation

Dancers form a line in an open circle, facing inward, with the leader at the right end. Hands are on the shoulders of the adjacent dancers.

Dance

Note: Practice segments of the following dance by moving individually in the room until the steps and the rhythm are securely "in the feet." It can help to speak the words used above. (The following chart is based on ideas in *Integrating Music into the Classroom* by William M. Anderson and Joy E. Lawrence [Belmont, Calif.: Wadsworth Publishing Company].)

R means right foot, or to move to the right.

L means left foot, or to move to the left.

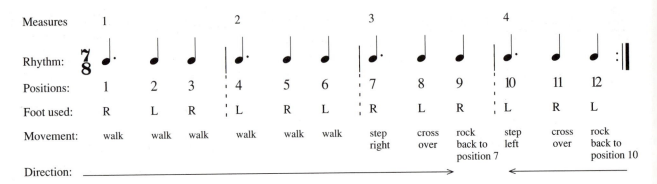

Measures	1			2			3			4		
Positions:	1	2	3	4	5	6	7	8	9	10	11	12
Foot used:	R	L	R	L	R	L	R	L	R	L	R	L
Movement:	walk	walk	walk	walk	walk	walk	step right	cross over	rock back to position 7	step left	cross over	rock back to position 10

Direction: ⟶ ⟵

Measures 1 and 2 are "grapevine steps" that move always *to the right*.

       Position and foot used

Measure 1: 1. R foot walks R.

      2. L foot walks in back of R foot.

      3. R foot walks R.

Measure 2: 4. L foot walks in front of R foot.

      5. R foot walks R.

      6. L foot walks in *back* of R foot.

Measures 3 and 4 involve a kind of "rocking step."

       Position and foot used

Measure 3: 7. R foot steps R.

      8. L toe crosses over the R foot, but *keep weight on R foot.*

      9. "Rock" on R foot back to position 7, above.

Measure 4: 10. L foot steps L.

      11. R toe crosses over the L foot, but *keep weight on L foot.*

      12. "Rock" on L foot back to position 10, above.

GHOST OF JOHN

Martha Grubb

Have you seen the ghost of John? Long white bones with the flesh all gone. _____

Oh, _____ Would-n't it be chil - ly with no skin on?

Guitar, strum 22

Play these patterns on a xylophone with "Ghost of John." Create a rhythm part for wood block or sticks.

GIVE MY REGARDS TO BROADWAY

Words and music by George M. Cohan
(United States, 1878–1942)

Piano, accompaniment pattern XVI

GOLDEN RING AROUND THE SUSAN GIRL

Appalachian Folk Song

Refrain

'Round and a-round, Su - san girl, Round and a-round, Su - san girl,

'Round and a-round, Su - san girl, All the way a-round, Su - san girl.

Autoharp (15-bar) strum E

Formation

Form a single circle of partners, with "Susan" in the middle.

Dance

Verse 1, measures 1–8: The circle walks clockwise around Susan. Measures 9–16: Partners face each other, hold hands, and turn around once back to place. During each refrain: Susan skips around the inside of the circle.

Verse 2, measures 1–8: Partners do-si-do right shoulders. Measures 9–16: Partners do-si-do left shoulders.

Verse 3: Grand right and left. Partners face each other and join right hands. They pull past each other, passing right shoulders. Each moves forward around the circle. (One moves clockwise; the other moves counterclockwise.) Each reaches forward to the next person and gives the left hand; the two pull past each other, passing left shoulders. They alternate right and left hands until each partner returns home. (If there are too many couples to make it home in 16 measures, make several smaller circles.)

Verse 4: Susan chooses a partner, and the new Susan goes to the middle. Partners promenade counterclockwise around the circle and return home.

Goodbye Round

Frederick Silver

Good - bye, fare - well; The time has come for part - ing. Take

care, stay well; I'll see you in a while. We have

had a lot of hap - py mem - o - ries, And I guess we've had a lot of fun; And I

hope the mem - o - ries will lin - ger on Now that we're through and done. Good -

bye, *au re - voir,* *ciao,* fare thee well, We've had a hap - py time. Good -
(oh ruh - vwah chow)

bye, *au re - voir,* *ciao,* fare thee well, See you a - gain.
(oh ruh - vwah chow)

Autoharp, strum J

After one sing-through, perform as a round.

GOOD KING WENCESLAS

John Neale
(England, 1818–1866)

English Carol

= 144–152

Chorus. 1. Good King Wen - ces - las looked out / On the Feast of Ste - phen,
King. 2. "Hith - er, page, and stand by me, / If thou knows't it tell - ing,
King. 3. "Bring me flesh and bring me wine, / Bring me pine logs hith - er;
Page. 4. "Sire, the night is dark - er now, / And the wind blows strong - er;
Chorus. 5. In his mas - ter's steps he trod, / Where the snow lay dint - ed;

When the snow lay round a - bout, / Deep and crisp and e - ven.
Yon - der peas - ant who is he? / Where and what his dwell - ing?"
Thou and I will see him dine / When we bear them thith - er."
Fails my heart, I know not how; / I can go no long - er."
Heat was in the ver - y sod / Which the Saint had print - ed.

Bright - ly shone the moon that night, / Though the frost was cru - el,
Page. "Sire, he lives a good league hence, / Un - der - neath the moun - tain,
Chorus. Page and mon - arch, forth they went, / Forth they went to - geth - er
King. "Mark my foot - steps, my good page, / Tread thou in them bold - ly;
There - fore, peo - ple all, be sure, / Wealth or rank pos - sess - ing,

When a poor man came in sight, / Gath - 'ring win - ter fu - el.
Right a - gainst the for - est fence, / By Saint Ag - nes' foun - tain."
Through the rude wind's wild la - ment / And the bit - ter weath - er.
Thou shalt find the win - ter's rage / Freeze thy blood less cold - ly."
Ye who now will bless the poor / Shall your - selves find bless - ing.

Guitar, brush each chord change or play melody notes
Piano, accompany using chord roots
Soprano recorder

John Neale used the melody of an old spring carol as the vehicle for his story of the "Good King Wenceslas." From about A.D. 924 to A.D. 929, King Vaclav was a Christian king of Bohemia (the present-day Czech Republic). After his murder on the steps of a church, he became a martyr for his religion and was immediately venerated as the patron Saint Wenceslas of Bohemia described in the song.

Go Tell Aunt Rhody

American Lullaby

Simply

| | Go | tell | Aunt | Rho | - | dy, | | Go | tell | Aunt | Rho | - | dy, |

1. Go tell Aunt Rho - dy,
(2.) one she's been sav - in', The one she's been sav - in', The
(3.) broke all the saw teeth, She broke all the saw ___ teeth, She
(4.) gos - lings are cry - in', The gos - lings are cry - in', The
(5.) gan - der is weep - in', The gan - der is weep - in', The

Go tell Aunt Rho - dy, The old gray goose is dead. 2. The
one she's been sav - in', To make a feath - er bed. 3. She
broke all the saw teeth, That old gray goose was tough. 4. The
gos - lings are cry - in', Be - cause their moth - er's dead. 5. The
gan - der is weep - in', Be - cause the goose is dead.

Coda following verse 5

Go tell Aunt Rho - dy, poor old Aunt Rho - dy,

Go tell Aunt Rho - dy, The old gray goose is dead.

Autoharp, strum D
Piano accompaniment pattern II

GO TELL IT ON THE MOUNTAIN

African American Spiritual

Freely

1. 'Twas in a low-ly man-ger that Je-sus Christ was born; The
2. While shep-herds kept their watch-ing o'er wan-d'ring flocks by night; Be-
3. When I was a sin-ner I prayed both night and day; I
4. When I was a seek-er I sought both night and day; I

Lord sent down an an-gel that bright and glo-rious morn. _____
hold! from out the heav-ens there shown a ho-ly light. _____
asked the Lord to help me and He showed me the way. _____
asked the Lord to help me and He taught me to pray. _____

Refrain   a tempo

Go, tell it on the moun-tain, o-ver the hills and ev-'ry-where,

Go, tell it on the moun-tain that Je-sus Christ _ is born.

Guitar, free strum (verse) and strum 9 (refrain)

In post–Civil War years, several African American universities developed choirs that went on fund-raising tours throughout the nation. Audiences familiar only with stereotyped minstrel entertainment finally heard the great African American spirituals—in exciting concert arrangements. But spirituals flowered in rural America. Twentieth-century urban life gave rise to gospel music, a composite of the style of blues, spirituals, and tabernacle songs. The emotional fervor of gospel singing is often backed by strong rhythms on piano, guitar, or other instruments. Hand clapping, shouting, and demonstrative interplay all contribute to the highly religious intensity of Black gospel music. Much of this same energy and excitement can be heard in soul music, the secular equivalent of gospel.

GRANDPA GRIGG

Mother Goose

Doug Goodkin
Arr. Doug Goodkin

Grand-pa Grigg had a pig in a field of clo - ver. Pig - gy died,

Grand-pa cried, "All the fun is o - ver!"

Last time go to ⊕

D.C. al Coda

⊕ Coda

(All)

Guide to abbreviations

AX means alto xylophone.

BX means bass xylophone.

BM means bass metallophone.

AM means alto metallophone.

AX means alto xylophone.

 means the notes sound one octave lower than written.

Doug Goodkin is music teacher for The San Francisco School (San Francisco, California), Orff specialist, composer, author, and clinician.

GREEN, GREEN GRASS OF HOME

Curly Putnam

1. The old home town _ looks the same, as I step down _____ from the
(2.) old house _____ is still stand - ing Though the paint is cracked and

train, And there, to meet me _____ is my ma - ma and my
dry. And there's that old oak tree that I _____ used to

pa - pa. _____ Down the road I look and
play on. _____ Down the lane I walk with

there runs Ma - ry, hair of gold and lips like cher - ries: It's
my sweet Ma - ry, hair of gold and lips like cher - ries;

good to touch the green, green grass of home. _____

Yes, they'll all come to meet me, arms _ reach - ing smil-ing

sweet-ly; Oh, it's good to touch the green, green grass of home. _____ 2. The

green, green grass of home. _____

Autoharp, strum A

GREENSLEEVES
(What Child Is This?)

English Folk Song

1. A - las, my love, ____ you do me wrong ____ To cast me
2. I have been read - y at your hand, ____ To grant what -
3. Thou couldst de - sire ____ no earth - ly thing, ____ But still thou
4. I bought thee ker - chers to thy head, ____ That were wrought

off ____ dis - court - eous - ly; When I have loved ____ you so
ev - er you would crave; I have both wager - ed life and
hadst ____ it read - i - ly; My mu - sic still ____ to play and
fine ____ and gal - lant - ly; I kept thee both ____ at board and

long, ____ De - light - ing in ____ your com - pan - y.
land, ____ Your love and good - will for to have. ____
sing, ____ And yet ____ thou wouldst ___ not love ____ me.
bed, ____ Which cost ____ my purse ____ well fav - oured - ly.

Refrain

Green - - sleeves ____ was all my joy, ____ and Green - -

sleeves ____ was my de - light; Green - sleeves was my

heart of gold, ____ And who but my la - dy Green - sleeves.

Autoharp, strum each downbeat (use harp strum)
Piano, accompaniment pattern VIII

97

| Dm | C | Bb | A7 |
5. Thy gown was of the grassy green, Thy sleeves of satin hanging by,

| Dm | C | Bb | A7 | Dm |
Which made thee be our harvest queen, And yet thou wouldst not love me. (*Refrain*)

| Dm | C | Bb | A7 |
6. Well, I will pray to God on high, That thou my constancy mayst see;

| Dm | C | Bb | A7 | Dm |
And that yet once before I die, Thou will vouchsafe to love me. (*Refrain*)

| Dm | C | Bb | A7 |
7. Oh, Greensleeves, now farewell, adieu, And God I pray to prosper thee;

| Dm | C | Bb | A7 | Dm |
For I am still thy lover true, Come once again and love me. (*Refrain*)

The old English tune "Greensleeves" was mentioned by Shakespeare in The Merry Wives of Windsor *(1601), and many political texts were set to the tune during the seventeenth century. The melody is sometimes varied, perhaps with the fifth note of the tune sung a half step higher, or the third note of the refrain sung a half step lower.*

New Year's version (1642)

| Dm | C | Bb | A7 |
The old year now away is fled, The new year it is enteréd,

| Dm | C | Bb | A7 | Dm |
And let us now our sins downtread, And joyfully all appear.

Refrain:

| F | C | Bb | A7 |
Let's merry be this day, And let us now both sport and play;

| F | C | Bb | A7 | Dm |
Hang grief, cast care away! God send us a happy New Year!

"What Child Is This?" version

| Dm | C | Bb | A7 |
What Child is this, Who, laid to rest On Mary's lap, is sleeping?

| Dm | C | Bb | A7 | Dm |
Whom angels greet with anthems sweet, While shepherds watch are keeping?

Refrain:

| F | C | Bb | A7 |
This, this is Christ the King, Whom shepherds guard and angels sing;

| F | C | Bb | A7 | Dm |
Haste, haste to bring Him laud, The Babe, the Son of Mary.

(Words by William C. Dix, England, 1837–1898)

GUANTANAMO LADY
(*Guantanamera*)

José Marti,
(Cuba, 1853–1895)
English words by
Aura Kontra

Jose Fernandez Dias (Joseito Fernandez)

♩ = 116–120

Refrain

Spanish: Guan - ta - na - me - ra.   gua - ji - ra. Guan - ta - na - me - ra.
Pronunciation: gwahn - tah - nah - may-rah   gwah-hee-rah gwahn - tah-nah-may-rah

Guan - ta - na - me - ra.   gua - ji - ra. Guan - ta - na - me - ra.   - ra.
gwahn-tah-nah-may - rah   gwah-hee-rah gwahn-tah-nah-may - rah   -rah

Verse

1. I'm just a man from the is - lands,   Born in the shade of the palm tree. __
1. Yo soy un hom - bre sin - ce - ro,   De don - de cre - ce la pal - ma. __
   yoh soy oon ome - bray sin-say-roh   day don-day cray - say lah pahl- mah

__   I'm just a man from the is - lands,   Born in the shade __ of the
__   Yo soy un hom - bre sin - ce - ro,   De don - de cre - ce la
    yoh soy oon ome - bray sin-say-roh   day-don-day cray - say lah

palm tree. __ In - spired to tell of my long - ing,   I'll leave my sto - ries be - hind me.
pal - ma. __ Y an - tes de mo - rir - me quie - ro,   E - char mis ver - sos del al - ma.
pahl-mah   ee ahn-tays day moh-reer-may keeaye - roh   aye-chahr mees vare-sohs dehl ahl - mah

Autoharp (15-bar), strum N (refrain) and free strum (verse)
Guitar, strum 21 (refrain) and 23 (verse)

99

Literal translation

1. I'm a sincere man from a land where palms grow.
   I want to pour forth the poems of my soul before I die.

2. My verses are light green and bright red . . .
   Like wounded fawns trying to hide in the mountain forest.

3. Let me be as one with all the humble people of the world.
   And take more pleasure from the mountain stream,
   than from the mighty ocean.

    A7   D   G   A7
2. My words are spo-ken sin-cere-ly   } *sing 2 times*
               D   G   A7
And ring with hope for to-mor-row.

         D   G A7
I speak of life and its pro-mise.

         D   G A7
I know its joy and its sor-row. (*Refrain*)

    A7   D   G   A7
3. I choose the poor as my peo-ple   } *sing 2 times*
               D   G   A7
And share their dreams and their trou-bles.

         D   G A7
I'd rath-er lose ev-'ry com-fort

         D   G A7
Than turn a-way from their strug-gles. (*Refrain*)

    A7   D   G   A7
2. Mi verso es de un verde claro   } *sing 2 times*
               D   G   A7
    Y de un carmín encendido.

         D   GA7
Mi verso es de un ciervo herido,

              D   GA7
Que busca en el monte amparo. (*Refrain*)

    A7   D   G   A7
3. Con los pobres de la tierra,   } *sing 2 times*
               D   G   A7
Quiero yo mi suerte echar.

         D   GA7
El arroyo de la sierra,

         D   GA7
Me complace más que el mar. (*Refrain*)

José Marti was born in Havana, Cuba. Poet, novelist, journalist, and revolutionary, Marti thought of himself as a citizen of the Americas. His dream was of a unified Latin America that would be able to thwart nineteenth-century North American imperialism. Involved in Cuba's struggle to gain independence from Spain, Marti was imprisoned, exiled, and finally killed as he landed with an armed group in Oriente Province—the same province where Fidel Castro's forces landed nearly sixty years later.

THE GYPSY ROVER

Irish Folk Song

Verse

1. The gyp - sy rov - er came o - ver the hill, Bound through the val - ley so shad - y.
2. She left her fa - ther's cas - tle gate. Left her own true lov - er.
3. Her fa - ther sad - dled his fast - est steed, Rode by the riv - er Clay - de.
4. "He's no gyp - sy, my fa-ther," said she, "But lord of the free - lands all o - ver,

He whis - tled and he sang till the green woods rang, ___ And he won the heart of a la — — — dy.
She left ___ her ___ ser - vants and her es - tate ___ To fol - low the gyp - sy ___ rov — — — er.
Drew near ___ to a man - sion ___ with great speed, Found the gyp - sy ___ and his ___ la — — — dy.
And I ___ will ___ stay till my dy - ing day With my whist - ling ___ gyp - sy ___ rov — — — er."

Refrain

Ly - de - o, ly - de - o, da - day, Ly - de - o, Ly - de - ay - de; He whis - tled and he sang till the green woods rang, ___ And he won the heart of a la — — — dy.

Autoharp, strum A

101

Formation

Dancers form groups of four in a circle. Assign a role to each dancer: Gypsy, Father, Lady, and Suitor. Follow the movement instructions below.

VERSE 1

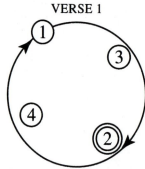

Gypsy (1) circles clockwise, passes Father (3), does two-hand swing with Lady (2), and goes home.

VERSE 2

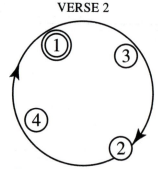

Lady (2) circles clockwise, passes the Suitor (4), does two-hand swing with Gypsy (1), and goes home.

VERSE 3

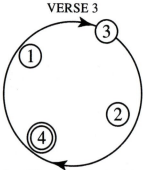

Father (3) circles clockwise, passes Lady (2), does two-hand swing with Suitor (4), and goes home.

VERSE 4

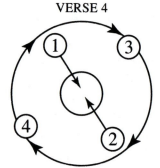

Both (3) and (4) circle clockwise while (1) and (2) do a two-hand swing. All go home.

HABARI GANI

James McBride

1. Win-ter __ is here, so Kwan-zaa __ is near, Cel-e-brat-ing joy and love as a
2. Peace be __ un-to you, good things_ come true When you spread your joy and love in a

hap-py fam-i-ly. Join us in our greet-ing with sev-en days of hol-i-day,
hap-py fam-i-ly. Self de-ter-mi-na-tion, __ liv-ing as a na-tion, too.

Shar-ing all our gifts and love in a hap-py gath-er-ing. Hap-py Kwan-zaa! Hap-py
We're all one re-la-tion and _ live in har-mo-ny.

Kwan-zaa! Love and peace _____ from me to you. Ha-ba-ri
hah - bah - ree

Ga-ni* spreads the news _____ of joy to you and asks "What's new?"
gah - nee

new?" new?" "What's new?" Ha - ba - ri Ga - ni!

Habari Gani is a Swahili greeting that means "What's the good news?"

Autoharp, strum L
Piano, accompaniment pattern XI

Kwanzaa (kwahn-zah) is a Swahili word meaning "first." Kwanzaa is a cultural holiday created in 1966 by Dr. Maulana Karenga. Lasting for seven days, from December 26 to January 1, Kwanzaa is based on African harvest festivals and emphasizes values universal to African Americans. The celebration is a rededication to greater achievement and more meaningful lives.

Decorations feature red, green, and black—traditional Kwanzaa colors. A special Kwanzaa table is set up, containing a straw mat, a holder with seven candles, a unity cup, and a bowl of fruits and vegetables. On each night, families gather to light a candle and to talk about one of the seven values of family life: unity, self-determination, collective work and responsibility, cooperative economics, purpose, creativity, and faith. Finally, each family member drinks from the unity cup.

At the conclusion of the festival on January 1, children receive presents (often homemade or homegrown), and the celebration ends with food, music, dancing, singing, and storytelling.

HALIWA-SAPONI CANOE SONG

Native American Song
Transcribed by J. Bryan Burton

Drums: Drums continue throughout

We ya we we ya we we ya we, ya

we ya o - we; Ya we ya we we ya we we ya we, ya we ya o - we.

Ya we ha ya we ha yo - we; ya we ya o - we. Ya we ha ya we, ha

1. yo - we; ya we ya o - we. Ya we ya o - we.

2. Ya we ya o - we.

Pronunciation guide
a as in f*a*ther
e as in m*e*t
o as in t*oo*t

The dance for "Haliwa-Saponi Canoe Song" imitates the motion of paddling a canoe. Native Americans often use dances and games to teach skills to children, so this type of music is suitable for use with young people in schools.

Formation

Groups of three to five dancers form single-file lines behind a lead dancer. The second and subsequent dancers place hands on the waist, upper arms, or elbows of the preceding dancer. One or more drummers perform near the dancers.

Dance

Elbows and arms move in a rowing motion, as if paddling a canoe. Dancers sing while moving.

Dancers step *sideways,* first to the left (eight beats), then to the right (eight beats); steps correspond to the quarter-note beat. The left–right alternation of direction continues throughout.

When moving left, the left foot leads.

    Left: step-together, step-together, step-together, step-together (8 beats).

When moving right, the right foot leads.

    Right: step-together, step-together, step-together, step-together (8 beats).

While stepping, the lead dancer maneuvers his or her line forward in a generally clockwise circle, taking care not to collide with other lines.

Small bands of Saponi people were located in North Carolina and Virginia in the 1700s but were pressured by white settlement to gradually migrate north as far as New York, where they became part of the Iroquois Confederation in 1753. Haliwa-Saponi now live in North Carolina, and "Haliwa" is derived from "Halifax" and "Warren," the counties where most live. At Hollister, North Carolina, the Haliwa-Saponi have a tribal center and day-care facility. The Haliwa-Saponi often attend and perform at powwows and Native American cultural fairs in the mid-Atlantic states. This "Canoe Song" was performed in Pennsylvania in 1989, where it was recorded and transcribed by J. Bryan Burton, a Native American who teaches at West Chester University. The song is made up of vocables: syllables without specific meaning. (Based on information in Moving within the Circle: Songs and Dances from Native American Traditions *by J. Bryan Burton. Book and tape or CD set from World Music Press.)*

HANUKKAH

Hebrew Melody

♩ = 120

C

Ha - nu - kkah,   Ha - nu - kkah,   hol - i - day   so   fair,

Dm   **G7**   **C**

Glow - ing   light,   can - dles   bright,   hap - pi - ness   we   share.

                                                    F

Gai - ly   dance,   gai - ly   sing   while   the   drey - dl   whirls,

G7   **C**

Round   and   round,   round   and   round,   see   how   fast   it   twirls.

Autoharp, strum C

Hanukkah, or Festival of Lights, is a Jewish celebration commemorating the rededication of the Temple in Jerusalem in 165 B.C. Special candles are lit on each of the eight days, and there are parties and gifts. The dreydl is a top used in children's games.

HAPPILY SINGING
(*Alegria*)

Puerto Rican Carol

Moderately and expressively (♩. = 52)

English: On to Be - lén _____ goes Ma - ri - a, _____ Lov - ing hus - band _____ close be -
Spanish: Ha - cia Be - lén _____ se en - ca - mi - nan, _____ Ma - ría con su a - man - te es -
Pronunciation: ah - syah beh - lehn sehn-kah - mee - nah mah-ryah kohn soo ah - mahn-tehs -

side her, God is with them _____ a com - pan - ion _____ To pro - tect them _____ on their
po - so, Lle - van - do en su _____ com - pa - ñí - a A to - do un Dios _____ po - de -
poh-soh yeh-vahn-dwehn soo koem-pah - nyee - ah ah toh - doon dyohs poh-theh-

Refrain

jour - ney. Oh, re - joice in the joy of this morn - ing, Oh, re -
ro - so. A - le - grí - a, a - le - grí - a, a - le - grí - a, A - le -
roh - soh ah - leh - gree - ah - leh - gree - ah - leh - gree - ah ah - leh -

joice in the joy of this day, On to Bel - én _____ they will
grí - a, a - le - grí - a y pla - cer, Que la Vir - gen va de
gree - ah - leh - gree - ah ee - plah - sehr keh lah veer - hehn va - deh

jour - ney, They will pass us _____ on their way. _____
pa - so Con su es - po - so ha - - cia Be - lén. _____
pah - soh Kohn swehs - poh - soh ah - syah beh - lehn

Autoharp (15-bar), strum S
Guitar, strum 28

108

HAPPINESS RUNS

Traditional American Song

Hap-pi-ness runs in a cir-cu-lar mo-tion. Love is a lit-tle boat up-on the sea. ___ Ev-'ry-one is a part of ev-'ry-thing an-y-way, You can be hap-py if you let your-self be. Pa-pa-pa-pa-pa - pa-pa-pa - pa-pa-pa; Pa - pa-pa-pa - pa - pa-pa-pa-pa; ___ Pa - pa-pa-pa - pa - pa-pa-pa - pa-pa-pa; Pa - pa-pa-pa - pa - pa-pa-pa - pa.

Autoharp, strum A
Piano, accompaniment pattern XVII (play solid chords)

HAPPY ARE THEY
(Hineh Ma Tov)

Israeli Echo Song

Guitar, strum 7 (To sing *Happy Are They* in C major with guitar, place the capo in fret 3 and play the chords shown above.)

Translation

How good it is for brothers to dwell together!

Also see another "Hineh Ma Tov" song that follows (page 123).

Harmony

Norman J. Simon and Artie Kaplan

1. The time has come, let us be - gin __ With all our voice - es
2. Like the shep - herd guards his sheep, _ Watch your child - ren

join - ing in __ To sing of love and broth - er - hood, _
as they sleep, _ And like the pot - ter turns his clay, _

And peo - ple do - ing what they should To make this world a
Help us shape a bet - ter day, __ Let us sing a

fam - i - ly, __ And fill this land with har - mo - ny, __
song of love, _ For there's one thing I'm cer - tain of, __

The young, the old, the rich, the poor, _ Mak - ing sounds _
Love will fill the hearts of men, _ And peace will come on

Refrain

nev - er heard be - fore. _____ La la la la la
earth ___ once a - gain. _____

On the smaller notes, one group can sing "loo" or "la." Or play smaller notes on bars or soprano recorder.

111

Har - mo - ny, ___ har - mo - ny, ___ Let's all join in

har - mo - ny, ___ And sing a - way ___ the hurt and fear, ___ A

great new day will soon ___ be ___ here. _____

Piano, accompaniment pattern XVII, rolled chords (verse) and solid chords (refrain)

Hava Nagila

Moshe Nathanson
(Israeli Dance Song)

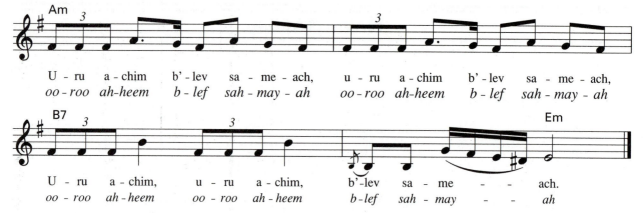

U – ru a – chim b' – lev sa – me – ach, u – ru a – chim b' – lev sa – me – ach,
oo - roo ah-heem b - lef sah – may - ah oo - roo ah-heem b - lef sah – may - ah

U – ru a – chim, u – ru a – chim, b' –lev sa – me – – ach.
oo - roo ah - heem oo - roo ah - heem b - lef sah – may – – ah

Guitar strum 18

Translation

Let us rejoice and be happy;
Let us sing and be happy.
Stir yourselves, friends, with a happy heart.

Formation

The hora is a line or circle dance without partners. Hands are on the neighbor's shoulders.

Dance

Begin with the weight on the right foot; *movement is always to the left.*

Beat 1: Step with the left foot, putting weight on it.

Beat 2: Place the right foot behind the left foot (weight on the *right* foot).

Beat 3: Step, putting weight on the left foot.

Beat 4: Hop on the left foot, swinging the right leg in front.

Beat 5: Step with the right foot, putting weight on it.

Beat 6: Hop on the right foot, swinging the left leg in front.

Repeat movements of beats 1–6, gradually accelerating the tempo.

Note: On beats 1 and 2, travel to the left; on beats 3–6, step-swing in place.

Hawaiian Rainbows

Modern Hawaiian Song

♩ = 60

G

Ha - wai - ian rain - bows,

*Slowly swing arms over the
head from left to right to
show the shape of a rainbow.*

C

White clouds roll by;

*Swing arms back from right to left.
At the same time, roll one hand
over the other to show clouds.*

G   **D7**   **G**

You show your col - ors

*Swing arms from left to right.
At the same time, make a rippling
motion with the fingers as if
pointing to all the colors of
the rainbow.*

A - gainst the sky.

*Raise both hands high to the right
(palms up). Move the left hand
"across the sky" to the left side.*

C

Ha - wai - ian rain - bows.

*Slowly swing arms over the
head from left to right to
show the shape of a rainbow.*

It seems to me.

*Place the right hand under the left
elbow and point the index finger of
the left hand toward the chest ("It
seems to me").*

G   **D7**   **G**

Reach from the moun - tain

*Raise both hands high to
the left.*

Down to the sea.

*Slowly lower hands toward the right
knee and continue moving them out
to the right ("Down to the sea").*

Autoharp, harp strum
Guitar, strum 2

Formation

Dancers kneel and sit low on their heels. To begin, they stretch both arms out to the left, with fingers pointing up and palms facing out. Each motion is smooth and flowing, and is performed slowly so it extends through two measures.

The movements for "Hawaiian Rainbows" resemble those of a traditional *mele hula*. A description of the *mele hula* accompanies "This Beautiful World," also found in this anthology.

HEAD-SHOULDERS, BABY

African American Game Song

Lively

1. Head - shoul - ders, Ba - by, one, two, three; Head -
2. Shoulders - chest, ___ Ba - by, one, two, three; Shoulders -
3. Chest - knees, ___ Ba - by, one, two, three; Chest -

touch touch clap snap clap snap clap snap and so on

shoul - ders, Ba - by one, two, three; Head - shoul - ders, head
chest, ___ Ba - by, one, two, three; Shoulders - chest, __ shoulders
knees, ___ Ba - by, one, two, three; Chest - knees, __ chest

shoul - ders, Head - shoul - ders, Ba - by one, two, three.
chest, __ Shoulders - chest, ___ Ba - by, one, two, three.
knees, ___ Chest - knees, ___ Ba - by, one, two, three.

Use both hands to touch the body parts named in the song. Touch, clap, and snap in a steady beat rhythm.

4. Knees-ankles. Baby, . . .
5. Ankles-knees, Baby, . . .
6. Knees-chest, Baby, . . .
7. Chest-shoulders, Baby, . . .
8. Shoulders-head, Baby, . . .

Coda

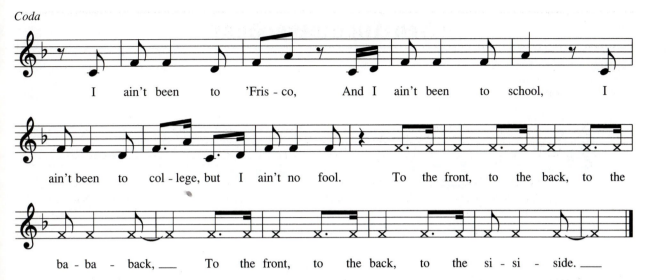

I ain't been to 'Fris - co, And I ain't been to school, I ain't been to col - lege, but I ain't no fool. To the front, to the back, to the ba - ba - back, ___ To the front, to the back, to the si - si - side. ___

Movements for Coda

On sung measures: Create movements.

On spoken measures: Put hands on hips, elbows out. Jump on both feet in the direction of the words "front," "back," and "side."

117

Hello, Ev'rybody

Words by Charity Bailey
(United States, 1904–1978)
and Eunice Holsaert

American Folk Melody

♩ = 160

Hel - lo, ev - 'ry-bod - y, yes, in - deed! _ Yes, in - deed! _

Yes, in - deed! _____ Let's make mu - sic, yes, in - deed! _____ Yes, in-deed, my dar - lin'.

Autoharp, strum N
Piano, accompaniment pattern XI

HEVENU SHALOM A'LEYCHEM

Israeli Song

With accents (♩ = 116)

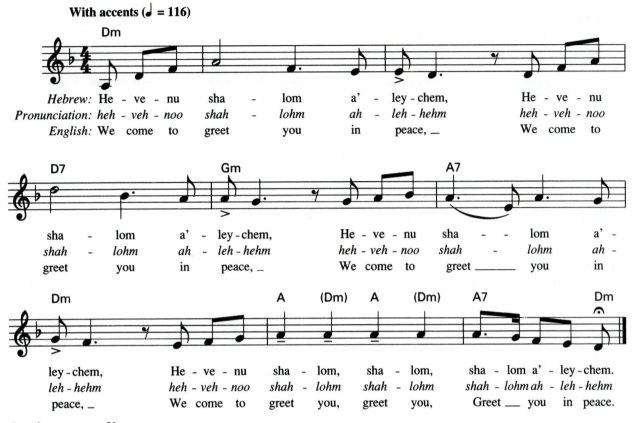

Hebrew: He - ve - nu sha - lom a' - ley - chem, He - ve - nu
Pronunciation: *heh - veh - noo shah - lohm ah - leh - hehm heh - veh - noo*
English: We come to greet you in peace, __ We come to

sha - lom a' - ley - chem, He - ve - nu sha - - lom a' -
shah - lohm ah - leh - hehm heh - veh - noo shah - lohm ah -
greet you in peace, __ We come to greet _____ you in

ley - chem, He - ve - nu sha - lom, sha - lom, sha - lom a' - ley - chem.
leh - hehm heh - veh - noo shah - lohm shah - lohm shah - lohm ah - leh - hehm
peace, __ We come to greet you, greet you, Greet __ you in peace.

Autoharp, strum N

HEY, HO! NOBODY HOME

English Round

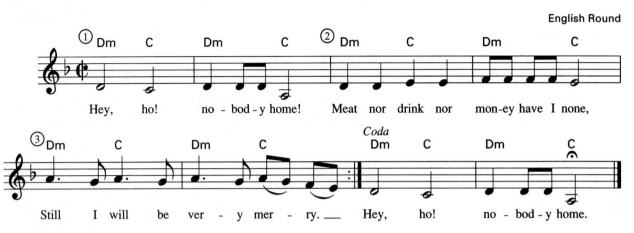

Hey, ho! no - bod - y home! Meat nor drink nor mon-ey have I none,

Still I will be ver - y mer - ry. ___ Hey, ho! no - bod - y home.

Autoharp, strum A

Play one or all of these patterns on a xylophone with "Hey, Ho! Nobody Home." (Use A minor chord in place of C major.)

HEY, LIDEE

American Song

Brightly (♩ = 100)

Refrain

Hey, li-dee, li-dee, li-dee, Hey, li-dee, li-dee-lo, ___

Hey, li-dee, li-dee, li-dee, Hey, li-dee, li-dee-lo. ___

Verse

1. This is a sil-ly kind of song, ___ } Hey, li-dee, li-dee-lo, ___ { You
2. I have a girl she's ten feet tall, ___ } Hey, li-dee, li-dee-lo, ___ { She
3. Ev-'ry-bod-y sing the cho-rus, ___ } ___

make it up as you go a-long, ___ } Hey, li-dee, li-dee-lo. ___
sleeps in the kitchen with her feet in the hall, ___ } Hey, li-dee, li-dee-lo. ___
Eith-er you're a-gainst us ___ or you're for us, ___ }

Autoharp, strum M
Guitar, strum 19
Piano, accompaniment pattern XI

Make up your own verses for this song.

HILLS OF ARIRANG

English words by
Patricia Hackett

Korean Folk Song

Autoharp, play drone (Gmaj + Gmin) on each downbeat
Guitar, strum 13
Soprano recorder

The words of Korea's oldest and most famous folk song speak of "crossing the hills of Arirang." These words have come to suggest that to be truly happy, one must face and overcome life's difficulties.

HINEH MA TOV
(Happy Are They)

Israeli Round

Autoharp, strum B

Florence Harlub

123

HOLD ON

African American Song

With a strong beat (♩ = 80)

1. When you plow, don't lose your track, _____ Can't plow straight and keep a -
2. Want to get to heav'n, I'll tell you how, _____ Keep your hand _ right _
3. Mar - y wore three links _ of chain, _____ Ev - 'ry link _ was _
4. At the moment I thought I was lost, __ The dun - geon shook _ and the
5. Got my hands on the gos - pel plow, _____ Wouldn't take noth - in' for my

look - in' back. _
on _ that plow. _
Je - sus name. _   Keep your hand on _ that plow, _____ Hold on, hold on,
chains . fell off. ___
jour - ney now. _

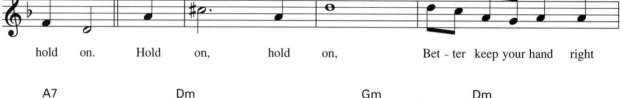

hold on. Hold on, hold on, Bet - ter keep your hand right

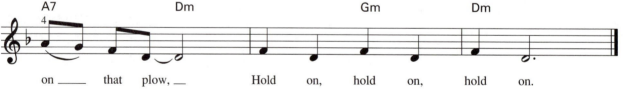

on _____ that plow, _ Hold on, hold on, hold on.

Autoharp, strum A
Piano, accompaniment pattern XI

Because it is originally a social and religious commentary, "Hold On" was easily adapted
to become the "Freedom Rider's Song" by African Americans attempting to desegregate public
transportation in the South. Some of the verses created in the 1960s follow.

Dm
1. Paul and Silas bound in jail,

    A7   Dm
Had no money to go their bail,

Keep your eyes on the prize,

    Gm Dm
Hold on, hold on, hold on. (*Refrain*)

Dm
2. The only chain that man can stand,

    A7   Dm
Is that chain of hand in hand,

Keep your eyes on the prize,

    Gm Dm
Hold on, hold on, hold on. (*Refrain*)

HOME ON THE RANGE

Dr. Brewster Higley
(United States)

Daniel E. Kelley
(United States)

1. Oh, give me a home where the buf - fa - lo roam, Where the
2. How of - ten at night when the heav - ens are bright With the
3. Where the air is so pure and the zeph - yrs so free; And the
4. Oh, give me a land where the bright dia-mond sand Flows __

deer and the an - te - lope play; _____ Where sel - dom is heard a dis -
light of the glit - ter - ing stars, _____ Have I stood there, a - mazed, and __
breez - es so balm - y and light, _____ Oh, I would not ex - change, my __
lei - sure - ly down with the stream, _____ Where the grace - ful white swan glides _

cour - ag - ing word, And the skies are not cloud - y all day. _____
asked as I gazed, If their glo - ry ex - ceeds that of ours. _____
home on the range, For the glit - ter - ing cit - ies so bright. _____
slow - ly a - long, Like a maid in a heav - en - ly dream. _____

Refrain

Home, home on the range, _____ Where the deer and the an - te - lope

play; _____ Where sel - dom is heard a dis -

cour - ag - ing word, And the skies are not cloud - y all day. _____

Autoharp (15-bar), strum Q
Guitar, strum 27 or melody

"Home on the Range" is the state song of Kansas.

125

HUSH, LITTLE BABY

American Folk Song

Gently, with motion

E   B7   E

1. Hush, lit - tle ba - by,   don't say a word,   Pa-pa's gon-na buy you a   mock - ing - bird.
2. If   that _ mock - ing - bird won't   sing,   Pa-pa's gon-na buy you a   dia - mond ring.
3. If   that __ dia-mond   ring turns   brass,   Pa-pa's gon-na buy you a   look - ing glass.
4. If   that __ look - ing   glass gets broke,   Pa-pa's gon-na buy you a   bil - ly goat.

Guitar, strum 8

        E   *B7*
5. If that billy goat don't pull,

                   E
    Papa's gonna buy you a cart and bull.

        E   *B7*
6. If that cart and bull turn over,

                    E
    Papa's gonna buy you a dog named Rover.

        E   *B7*
7. If that dog named Rover don't bark,

                      E
    Papa's gonna buy you a pony cart.

        E   *B7*
8. If that pony cart falls down,

                   E
    You'll be the saddest little child in town.

126

I Bought Me a Cat

Kentucky Folk Song

♩ = 144

1.,2.,3. I bought me a {cat, hen, duck,} and the {cat hen duck} pleased me. I

fed my {cat hen duck} un-der yon-der tree.

1. Cat goes fid-dle-i - fee! _____ *Fine*

2. Hen goes chim-my - chuck, chim-my - chuck! *repeat ending 1.*

3. Duck goes quack, quack! *repeat ending 2, then 1, then proceed to verse 4.*

4. I bought me a goose…

4. Goose goes his - sy, his - sy! *repeat 3,2,1.*

5. I bought me a sheep…

5. Sheep goes baa, baa! *repeat 4,3,2,1.*

6. I bought me a hog…

6. Hog goes grif - fy, grif - fy! *repeat as before*

7. I bought me a cow…

7. Cow goes moo, moo!

8. I bought me a horse…

8. Horse goes neigh, neigh!

9. I bought me a dog…

9. Dog goes bow wow, bow wow!

Autoharp, strum D

127

I'd Like to Teach the World to Sing

Words and music by Bill Backer, Billy Davis,
Roger Cook and Roger Greenaway
(United States)

1. I'd like to teach the world to sing __ in per-fect har-mo-ny, __
2. I'd like to build the world a home __ and fur-nish it with love, __
3. I'd like to see the world for once __ all stand-ing hand in hand, __

I'd like to hold it in my arms __ and
Grow ap-ple trees and hon-ey bees __ and
And hear them e-cho through the hills __ for

keep it com-pa-ny. __
snow white tur-tle doves. __
peace through-out the land. __

That's the song I hear

That's the song I hear

Let the world sing to-day

Let the world sing to-day A song of peace that

D.C. al Fine (sing verse 1)

e-choes on __ and nev-er goes a-way. __

Autoharp (15-bar), strum N
Guitar, strum 24
Piano, accompaniment pattern XV

128

If You're Happy

Traditional American Song

Playfully

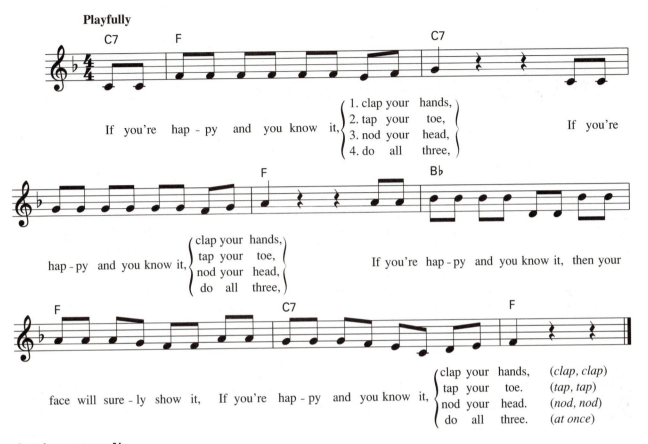

If you're hap-py and you know it,
1. clap your hands,
2. tap your toe,
3. nod your head,
4. do all three,
If you're

hap-py and you know it,
clap your hands,
tap your toe,
nod your head,
do all three,
If you're hap-py and you know it, then your

face will sure-ly show it, If you're hap-py and you know it,
clap your hands,   (clap, clap)
tap your toe.   (tap, tap)
nod your head.   (nod, nod)
do all three.   (at once)

Autoharp, strum N

I Love the Mountains

Traditional American Round

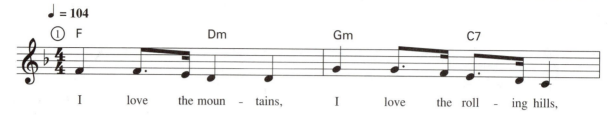

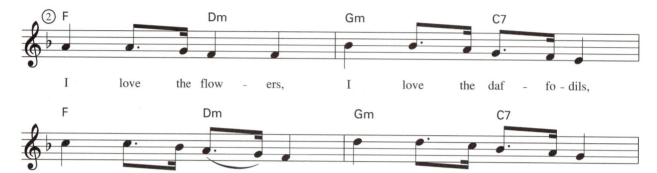

You can sing this part continuously during the song.

Autoharp, strum L or G

I'm on My Way

African American Freedom Song

1. I'm on my way _____ to the free-dom land, _____ I'm on my
2. I'll ask my friends _____ to come with _ me, _____ I'll ask my
3. If they won't go, _____ then I'll go a - lone, _____ If they won't
4. I'm on my way, _____ and I won't turn back, _____ I'm on my

way _____ to the free-dom land; _____ I'm on my way _____ to the free-dom
friends _____ to _ come with me; _____ I'll ask my friends _____ to _ come with
go, _____ then I'll to a - lone; _____ If they won't go, _____ then I'll go a -
way, _____ and I won't turn back; _____ I'm on my way _____ and I won't turn

land; _____
me; _____   } I'm on my way; __ thank God! I'm on my way. _____
lone; _____
back; _____

Autoharp, strum L
Piano, accompaniment pattern XVII (play a chord on each beat)

Divide into two groups and sing "I'm on My Way" as an echo song. After group 1 sings "I'm on my way," group 2 begins.

131

IN THE MOONLIGHT
(*Au clair de la lune*)

D. Auberge

French Folk Song

English: Stand - ing in the moon - light, *Mon a - mi Pier - rot,*
French: Au clair de la lu - ne, Mon a - mi Pier - rot,
Pronunciation: *oh klehr duh la loo - nuh mohn ah - mee pyehr - roh*

I have lost my can - dle, How, I do not know!
Prê - te - moi ta plu - me, Pour é - crire un mot;
preh - tuh - mwah tah plew - muh poor ay - creer uhn moh

If you can - not help me, I will have to stay
Ma chan - delle est mor - te, Je n'ai plus de feu.
mah shahn - dell eh mohr - tuh zhuh nay plew duh fuh

Stand - ing in the dark - ness, 'Til the light of day.
Ou - vre - moi ta por - te, Pour l'a - mour de Dieu.
oo - vruh - mwah tah pohr - tuh poor lah - moor duh dyuh

Autoharp, strum C (play D7 throughout)
Piano, accompaniment pattern I
Soprano recorder

Literal translation

In the light of the moon (I ask) my friend Pierrot:
Give me your pen, just to write a word;
My candle is dead and I have no more fire (light).
Open your door to me, please, for the love of God.

It's a Small World

Words and music by
Richard M. Sherman (United States)
Robert B. Sherman (United States)

1. It's a world of laugh-ter, a world of tears; It's a world of hopes and a world of fears. There's so much that we share that it's time we're a-ware
2. There is just one moon and one gold-en sun, And a smile means friend-ship to ev-'ry-one. Though the moun-tains di-vide and the o-ceans are wide,

It's a small world af-ter all! ___

Refrain

It's a small world af-ter all, It's a small world af-ter all. It's a small world af-ter all. It's a small, small world. ___

Autorharp, strum A
Guitar, strum 2 (verse), and 20 (refrain)
Piano, accompaniment pattern XV

Sing the verse and the refrain simultaneously to create harmony.

353

It's Raining!
(¡Qué llueva!)

Mexican Children's Song

English:	It's	rain - ing,	it's	rain - ing!	The	lit - tle	girl	is	say - ing;	The
Spanish:	¡Qué	llue - va,	qué	llue - va!	La	chi - qui - ta	di - cien - do;	Los
Pronunciation:	kay	yway - vah	kay	yway - vah	lah chee - kee - tah	dee - keeaye - doh	lohss

lit - tle	birds	are	sing - ing,	And	all	the	clouds	are	leav - ing,	Oh,
pa - ja - ri - tos	can - tan,	Las	nu - bes	se	le - van - tan,	¡Qué
pah - hah - ree - toess	kahn - tahn	lahss	noo - behss	say	lay - vahn - tahn	kay

yes!	Oh,	no!	Oh,	let	the	rain	fall	down!	Oh,
si!	¡Qué	no!	¡Qué	cai - ga el	cha - pa - rrón!	¡Qué
see	kay	noe	kay	kahee - gah ehl	chah - pah - rrohn	kay

yes!	Oh,	no!	Oh,	let	the	rain	fall	down!
si!	¡Qué	no!	¡Qué	cai - ga el	cha - pa - rrón!
see	kay	noe	kay	kahee - gah ehl	chah - pah - rrohn

Soprano recorder

I'VE BEEN WORKING ON THE RAILROAD
(Dinah)

United States Folk Song

I've been work-ing on the rail - road, All the live - long day;

I've been work-ing on the rail - road, Just to pass the time a - way.

Don't you hear the whis - tle blow - ing? Rise up so ear - ly in the morn.

Don't you hear the cap - tain shout - ing, "Di - nah, blow your horn!"

Di - nah, won't you blow, Di - nah, won't you blow, Di - nah, won't you blow your

horn? _____ Di - nah, won't you blow, Di - nah won't you blow,

Di - nah, won't you blow your horn? Some-one's in the kitch - en with Di - nah.

Some-one's in the kitch - en I know. _____ Some-one's in the kitch - en with

Di - nah, strum - ming on the old ban - jo. Fee, Fie,

Fid-dle - ee I O, Fee, Fie, Fid-dle - e I O, _____

Fee, Fie, Fid-dle -ee I O, Strum-ming on the old ban - jo.

Autoharp, strums A, L, and O for each different section

JAMAICA FAREWELL

Caribbean Folk Song

♩ = 108

1. Down the way where the folks all play, and the sun - shines dail - y on the
2. Sounds of laugh - ter ___ ev - 'ry-where, and the dan - cing girls ___ sway-ing

moun-tain top. I took a trip on a sail - ing ship, And when I reached Ja-mai - ca I
to and fro; I must de-clare that my heart is there, _ Tho' I've been from Maine _ to

made a stop.} But I'm sad to say ___ I'm on my way, ___
Mex - i - co.}

Won't be back for man - y a - day. ___ My head is down, my heart is

turn - ing a - round, _ I had to leave a lit - tle girl in Kings - ton Town. _

Guitar, strum 18 (To sing in C major with guitar, place the capo in
fret 3, and play the chords shown above.)
Piano, accompaniment pattern XVI

137

JINGLE BELLS

Words and music by James Pierpont
(United States, 1822–1893)

1. Dash - ing through the snow   In a   one - horse o - pen sleigh;
(2.) day   or   two   a - go   I ____ thought I'd   take   a   ride,   And
3. Now   the   ground   is   white,   Go   it   while you're young,

O'er the fields we   go,   laugh-ing all   the way!   Bells on bob - tail ring,   They're
soon Miss Fan - nie Bright, was   seat - ed by my side!   The   horse was lean and lank, Mis -
Take the girls to - night,   and sing this sleigh-ing song!   Just   get a   bob-tailed nag, Two -

mak - ing   spir - its   bright.   What   fun   it   is   to   laugh   and   sing,   A
for - tune seemed his   lot;   He   got   in - to   a   drift - ed   bank,   And
for - ty   for   his   speed,   Then   hitch   him   to   an   o - pen   sleigh,   And

Refrain

sleigh - ing   song   to - night!)
we,   we   got   up - sot!   Jin - gle bells!   Jin - gle bells!   Jin - gle   all   the way!
crack! You'll take   the lead!)

1.   **2.**

Oh, what fun   it   is   to ride in a   one-horse o - pen sleigh! ___   one-horse o - pen sleigh! 2. A

Autoharp (15-bar), strum N
Guitar, strum 21 (To sing in F major with guitar, place the capo in
    fret 3 and play the chords shown above.)
Piano, accompaniment pattern XVI

Joe Turner Blues

American Blues

♩ = 88

A   A7

1. They tell me __ Joe Turn-er's __ come and gone, __   They
2. He came here _ with for-ty __ links of chain, __   He
3. Joe Turn-er, __ he took my __ man a-way, __   Joe

D7   A

tell me __ Joe Turn-er's __ come and gone; __   He
came here _ with for-ty __ links of chain; __
Turn-er __ he took my __ man a-way; __

E7   A

left me __ here to sing _____ this _____ song.

Guitar, strum 26

These subjective sorrow songs called the blues developed in the early twentieth century, with the migration of rural Blacks to the cities. The bluesman was considered a footloose, irresponsible figure. Perhaps his blues songs eased the pain and stress of adjustment to the new urban lifestyle. There has been much research and speculation, but no one has really identified the roots of blues. Whatever their origin, they were considered the devil's music by many faithful churchgoers. Blues are a unique and powerful musical expression of twentieth-century America and had a profound influence on the development of jazz.

JOHNNY, I HARDLY KNEW YOU

♩ = 76

Em   **G**

* 1. With your guns __ and drums and drums and guns,
2. Where _ are __ your legs with which you run?
3. And _ where are your eyes that looked so mild?   Ha - roo, _____   Ha -
4. You __ have-n't an arm and you haven't a leg,
5. 'Tis __ glad __ I am to see you home,

Em   **G**

roo. _____

With your guns __ and drums and drums and guns,
Where _ are __ your legs with which you run?
And _ where are your eyes that looked so mild?   Ha - roo, _____   Ha -
You _ have-n't an arm and you haven't a leg,
'Tis _ glad __ I am __ to see you home,

B7   **Em**   **Am**

roo. _____

With your guns and drums __ and drums and guns, The
Where _ are your legs _____ with which you run When
And _ where are your eyes _____ that looked so mild, When you
You _ haven't an arm and you haven't a leg, You're an
'Tis _ glad I am _____ to see you home,

Em   **B7**   **Em**   **B7**

en - e - my near - ly slew ___ you, Oh John - ny lad, you
first ___ you went ___ to car - ry a gun; I fear your danc - ing
first ___ my in - no - cent heart _ be–guiled; And why did you run from
eye - less, bone - less, chick-en-less egg; You'll have to be put with a
Safe from the is - land of _____ Cey–lon; So low in the flesh, so

Em   **B7**   **Em**

look so bad,
days are done,
me and the child?   John-ny, I hard - ly knew you.
bowl to beg,
high in the bone,

Verse 1 may be sung as a recurring refrain.

Guitar, strum 1 or 27

JOSHUA FOUGHT THE BATTLE OF JERICHO

African American Spiritual

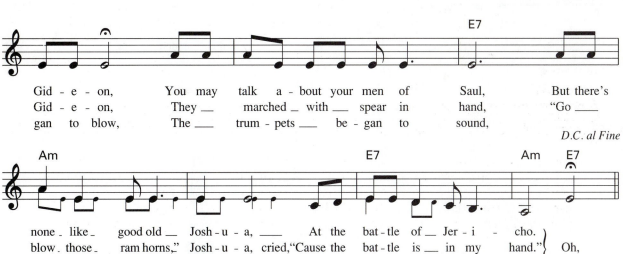

Autoharp, strum L (refrain) and free strum (verse)
Guitar, strum 2 (To sing in C minor with guitar, place the capo in
    fret 3, and play the chords shown above.)

133

JOY TO THE WORLD

Isaac Watts
(England, 1674–1748)

George Frideric Handel
(Germany, 1685–1759)

1. Joy to the world! the Lord is come; Let earth re-ceive her King. _____ Let ev-'ry _____ heart _____ pre-pare _____ Him _____ room, _____ And heav'n and na-ture _____ sing, And _____ heav'n and na-ture sing, And _____ heav'n _____ and heav'n _____ and na-ture sing!

2. Joy to the world! the Sav-ior reigns; Let men their songs em-ploy. _____ While fields _____ and _____ floods, _____ rocks, hills, _____ and _____ plains _____ Re-peat the sound-ing _____ joy, Re-peat the sound-ing _____ joy, Re-peat, _____ re-peat, _____ the sound-ing joy!

Autoharp, strum C

Piano, accompaniment pattern II on each chord symbol

142

JUBILEE

Kentucky Play-Party Song

♩ = 84

Verse

1. All out on the old rail - road, All out on the sea;
2. Hard - est work I ev - er did, Work - ing on the farm.
3. If I had no horse at all, I'd be found a - crawl - in',
4. Some will come on Sat—ur - day night, Some will come on Sun—day;

All out on the old rail - road, Far as I could see.
Eas - i—est work I ev - er did was Swing—in' my true love's arm.
Up and down this rock - y road, Look - in' for my dar—lin'.
If you give 'em half a chance, They'll be back on Mon—day.

Refrain

Swing and turn, Ju - bi - lee, Live and learn, Ju - bi - lee.

Autoharp, banjo strum in different rhythms (such as strums D and E)

Play these patterns on xylophones of different pitch and timbre.

Verses 1 and 3

Verses 2 and 4

Refrain

Formation

Two lines of partners face each other.

Dance

On verse 1, the head couple join hands. Using running steps, the head couple lead everyone to the left, in a circle. On the *refrain* "Swing and turn," all quickly form two lines again. The head couple link right arms, turn (swing) once, then left arm swing once.

On verse 2, the head couple reel down the line. They link right arms to swing each person in line, then give *left* hands to partner as they swing in the center. (During the reel, repeat some verses if more music is needed for head couple to reach the end of the line. But don't repeat verse 1.) When the head couple reach the end of the line (the foot), they remain there, and as result, there is a new couple at the head.

On all following verses, the head couple reel down the line (as in verse 2 movements) until everyone has had a turn being a member of the head couple.

When the first head couple are back in place, sing verse 1 again with movements.

KAGOME
(Bird in the Cage)

Japanese Singing Game

Walking tempo

English:	Ka	-	go	-	me,	ka - go - me,	Poor lit - tle bird in a
Japanese:	Ka	-	go	-	me,	ka - go - me,	Ka - go - no na - ka - no
Pronunciation:	kah	-	goh	-	meh	kah - goh - meh	kah - goh - noh nah - kah - noh

bam - boo ___ cage;   Cap - tive eyes and sil - ent ___ wings.
to - ri - wa.   I - tsu i - tsu de - ya - ru?
toh - ree - wah   ih - tsoo ih - tsoo deh - yah - roo

'Round and 'round the wild birds fly,   Cal - ling and cry - ing to
Yo - a - ke - no ba - (n) - ni,   Tsu - ru to ka - me to
yoh - ah - keh - noh bah - (n) - nee   tsoo - roo toh kah - meh toh

ka - go - me.   Guess my name and you can fly ___ free!
su - be - ta.   U - shi - ro - no sho - men da - - re?
soo - beh - tah   oo - shee - roh - noh show - mehn dah - - reh

Soprano recorder

Play one or both of these patterns on a xylophone with "Kagome." Use one pattern for an introduction.

Formation

Players form a circle and join hands. One player depicts the bird and sits or crouches in the center.

Game

Players walk in a circle while singing, stopping on the last word of phrase 4, "fly" ("ni"). During phrase 5, the teacher identifies one player, who sings phrase 6 as a solo. If the soloist's identity is correctly guessed by the bird, the two exchange roles. In case of an incorrect guess, the same bird remains in the center as the game is repeated.

145

KA MATE

Maori Action Round
(New Zealand)

Maori: Ka ma-te ka ma-te Ka o-ra ka o-ra
Pronunciation: kah mah-teh kah mah-teh kah oh-rah kah oh-rah

Te-nei te ta-nga-ta Pu-hu-ru-hu-ru
teh-nay teh tah-ngah-tah poo-hoo-roo-hoo-roo

Na-na nei i ti-ki mai Wha-ka whi-ti te ra
nah-nah neh ih tih-kih mahih wah-kah whih-tih teh rah

U-pa-ne kau-pa-ne Whi-ti te ra.
oo-pah-neh kah-pah-neh whih-tih teh rah

Literal translation

Chief Te Rauparaha of New Zealand exults that instead of death (*mate*), the prospect of life (*ora*) is given him, because the hairy man (*tangata puhuruhuru*) brought the sunshine (*ra*) and saved him. When Te Rauparaha climbed to the top of the pit (*kaupane*), the sun was shining (*whiti te ra.*)

Choreography for "Ka Mate" follows.

Dancers form a row.

Actions: All actions are performed crisply. Perform foot movements throughout. The weight is on the left foot, while the right foot stamps the ground, the left knee bending slightly. Stamp on each beat. Keep the back straight during all movements.

Wiri: Bend the arms at the elbow, angling the forearms slightly forward, with palms facing. Perform a quivering motion; move the wrist and palm, not the fingers. The fingers move as extensions of the quivering palm. (ma-te)

Ka ma-te, ka   ma-te.   Ka o - ra, ka   o - ra

slap thighs   *wiri*   *slap thighs*   *wiri*

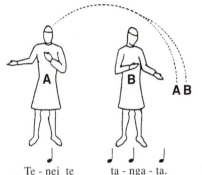

Drop the forearm so that the fingers point straight ahead. Move the hand forward and backward alternately, beginning with the right hand. (Te-nei-te ta-nga-ta)

Feet: Make a quarter turn to the left, pivoting on the left foot, stamping 4 times with the right foot (Pu-hu-ru-hu-ru)

Arms: Close the right fist: bend the elbow and bring the forearm up. Slap the forearm and the outside with the left hand 4 times, coinciding with the foot stamps (Pu-hu-ru-hu-ru)

Te - nei te   ta - nga - ta.   Pu - hu - ru - hu - ru

While still facing left repeat motions A and B above using the fourth stamp (on the rest) to pivot

  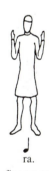

Nan - na   nei i   ti - ki mai,   Wha - ka - whi - ti   te   ra.

    (pivot)   *slap thighs*   *slap chest*   *fingers up,*

       once   *once*   *palms facing*

                       each other

U - pa - ne   kau - pa - ne   Whi - ti   te   ra.

Drop both arms to the left. Push back with both hands (palms back); repeat on right side and then left.   *slap thighs*   *slap chest*   *clap hands*   *fingers up, palms*

                                               once   *once*   *once*   *facing each other*

"Ka Mate" action song is based on a famous Maori haka *(meaning dance or song). The words and gestures of this action song are similar to a traditional haka, but the melody is not. It honors and recounts an event in the life of Maori[2] Chief Te Rauparaha, who lived over one hundred years ago.*

"Ka Mate" action song tells how Chief Te Rauparaha, when seeking safety from his enemies, was hidden in a sweet potato storage pit by an ally. This friend, another chief, covered the hiding place by putting a mat over the top and having his wife sit upon it. The "Ka Mate" haka was chanted by Te Rauparaha as he emerged from the pit.

A traditional haka is a shouted chant in speech-song style. Splendid musicians and orators, Maori men (women also, in earlier days) keep time by stamping a foot while gesturing with the hands, face, arms, and torso. A raucous voice accompanies fierce facial expressions, distorted mouth positions (including showing the tongue), and rolling the eyes. (Based on information in Comprehensive Musicianship Through Classroom Music *by Dorothy Gillett [Addison-Wesley].)*

Maori music is related to music of their Polynesian cousins in Samoa, Tahiti, and the Cook Islands—probably the original home of the Maoris. Vocal music is performed throughout all of Polynesia, where music was traditionally associated with lineage and religious ceremonies. Music continues to be important in life and culture; choral singing thrives in schools and churches, and new pieces are composed. For example, when Prince Charles visited the Maori, a haka was composed in his honor that mentioned his visit and the occasion being celebrated.

---

[2] Maori ("MAOO-ree") are the indigenous people of New Zealand.

KANG DING CITY
(Kang Ding Ching Ge)

English words by
Patricia Hackett

Chinese Folk Song

Gently (♪ = 92)

English:	Cres - cent moon float-ing in the sky,	Sil - ver clouds on the
Mandarin:	Pau ma lyou, lyou de shan ___ shang,	Yi dwo lyou, lyou de
Pronunciation:	pow mah leeoh leeoh duh shahn shahng	yee dwoh leeoh leeoh duh

moun - tain,	Bright, bright stars in a night of calm,
yun, Ah!	Dwan, dwan lyou, lyou de jau ___ dzai,
yuhn ah	*dwahn dwahn leeoh leeoh duh jahaoo dsigh*

Kang Ding, ci - ty of the moon, Ah!	Kang Ding,	Kang Ding,
Kang Ding lyou, ___ lyou de cheng, Ah!	Ywe lyang,	wan, ___
kahng dihng leeoh leeoh duh chuhng ah	*yooeh leeahng*	*wahn*

shin - ing home, ___	Kang Ding, ci - ty of the moon, Ah!
wan, ___	Kang Ding lyou, ___ lyou de cheng, Ah!
wahn	*kahng dihng leeoh leeoh duh chuhng ah*

Play patterns 1 and 2 on a xylophone for "Kang Ding City." Play pattern 3 on a wood block. Choose one pattern for an introduction or a coda.

KIOWA BUFFALO DANCE

Native American Song
(Southern Plains)
Transcribed by Patricia Hackett

Strongly accented (♩ = 80)

Soloist initially on measures 1 & 2; all singers join on repetition   All:

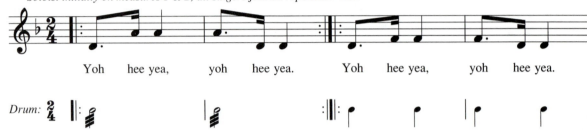

Yoh   hee yea,   yoh   hee yea.   Yoh   hee yea,   yoh   hee yea.

Drum:

Yoh   hee yea,   yoh   hee yea.   Yoh   hee yea,   yoh   hee yea,   yoh   hee yea.

Perform song three times.
After one sing-through, play a 4- to 8-beat drumroll
"interlude" before the second and third song repetitions.

Traditional Native American music consisted almost entirely of song and was vital to Indian life. Music was associated with an individual's birth, coming of age, marriage, and so forth, and with the round of tribal events for the group. It was religious music with important ritual functions.

A buffalo dance was performed to honor the spirit of the buffalo, either before or after the hunt. Today, "Kiowa Buffalo Dance" is popular at Native American powwows and cultural fairs in Oklahoma and in the western states.

Equipment

One large drum, padded mallets, and chairs for six to eight drummers; large sleigh bells (tied to the ankles of the dancers).

Formation

Drummers sit in a circle around the drum, and the dancers form a large circle around them. Only the drummers sing the "Buffalo Dance"; dancers do not sing.

Dance

On the drum roll of measures 1 and 2, the dancers individually meander, as if they were bison grazing. During measures 3–9, the dancers face center, stand in place, and bounce on their heels. On the repeat of measures 3–9, the dancers move quickly to the center to form a tight circle around the drummers, and continue the bouncing movement.

Before the dance is repeated, a drum roll gives the dancers time to move away from the drum and back into a large circle.

KIOWA HANDGAME SONG

Native American Song
(Southern Plains)
Transcribed by Patricia Hackett

Aye kuh boo _ duh, aye kuh boo _ duh, Hay yah aye kuh boo _ duh.

Drum: (continue throughout)

The text of the handgame song is Kiowa "song words"; their meaning is unknown or forgotten.

To perform the "Kiowa Handgame Song," form two teams of 10–12 members. Each team consists of

2 hiders

1 guesser

1 drummer

a group of 4–6 singers

1 scorekeeper

Shared equipment

Two pairs of sticks. One stick of each pair is marked with paint (or rubber bands) around the middle.

Equipment for each team

1 guessing wand about 15 inches long. The wand can have strips of fabric or feathers attached at the tip.

1 drum and mallet.

10 scoring sticks (a different color for each team).

Game

The two teams sit opposite each other in an informal arrangement. The scorekeepers are in a central location where both teams can see them.

Two members of the hiding team sit (or stand) at the front of their team, holding a pair of sticks behind their backs. Their hands grasp (and cover) the middle of both sticks, which they then display to the guessing team. Musicians on the hiding team sing and play the drum during the guessing.

Members of the guessing team consult with one another. When they have decided where the marked sticks are located (see the following illustration), the team's guesser prominently displays the wand in one of the positions indicated in the illustration.

Hiding positions with corresponding wand positions

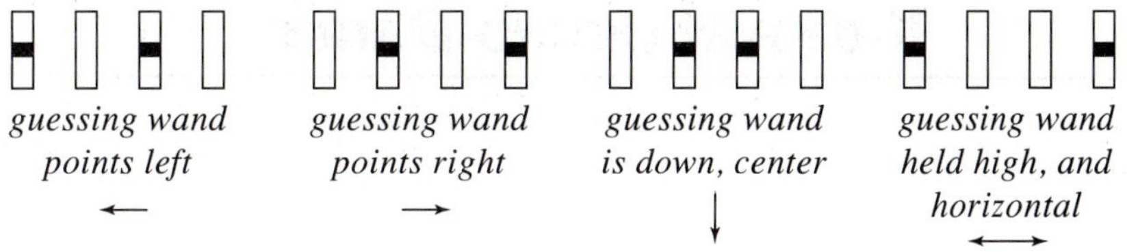

guessing wand
points left

$\leftarrow$

guessing wand
points right

$\rightarrow$

guessing wand
is down, center

$\downarrow$

guessing wand
held high, and
horizontal

$\leftrightarrow$

Scoring

One point is scored each time the hiding team deceives the guessing team.

Only the team with possession of the sticks can score points.

To get possession of the sticks, the guessing team must make a correct guess.

The scorekeeper places a stick on a tabletop each time his or her team scores.

The game ends when ten points (sticks) have been scored by one team.

Kiowa Round Dance

Native American Song
(Southern Plains)
Transcribed by Patricia Hackett

Yah yah yah yah yoh _ hai yah, Yah, _ yah hay yah hay

Drums: (continue throughout)

yah hay yo'oh _ hai yah, Yah yah yah hay yoh _ hai yah hay

yah hay yo'oh _ hai yah. Aye yah hai aye yah hai yah.

Yah yah yah hay yoh _ hai yah, Yah yah yah hay yoh _ hai yah hay

yah hay yo'oh _ hai yah Aye yah hai aye yah hay yah.

Formation

Four or five drummers, each with a large, padded mallet, sit around a big drum. The drummers sing, but the dancers do not. Dancers form an inward-facing circle. Women hold their arms at waist level, one hand resting on the other. Men's arms hang in a natural position by their sides. (Children take the position of their same-sex adult.)

Dance

Dancers move sideways, clockwise, sliding with the dotted quarter-note beat of the song. Slide the left foot to the left, then slide the right foot next to it, using just a little lift to do so. Alternate this footwork throughout.

Repeat the song three times, and on the last repetition both dancers and drummers stop exactly on the last word of the song.

The "Kiowa Round Dance" is popular throughout the western states and is used in several ways: as a mixer, as a friendship dance, and to honor selected tribal members, such as war veterans. The Kiowas' modern location is in southwest Oklahoma, but they probably originated farther northwest in the Great Plains. Kiowa traditional culture was similar to that of other Plains groups because they were buffalo-hunting horsemen who lived in skin teepees that could be dismantled and moved from place to place.

Today, Indian music is still a lively art, though it serves a different function than in earlier times. Many traditional ceremonies have become anachronistic in the modern world. When songs from these ceremonies are sung, they reflect the desire to retain the culture and to affirm a Native American identity. Many Native Americans share a modern musical tradition that reflects the style of Plains music. (See "Kiowa Handgame Song," "Kiowa Buffalo Dance," and "War Dance," found in this anthology.)

KOOKABURRA

Australian Round

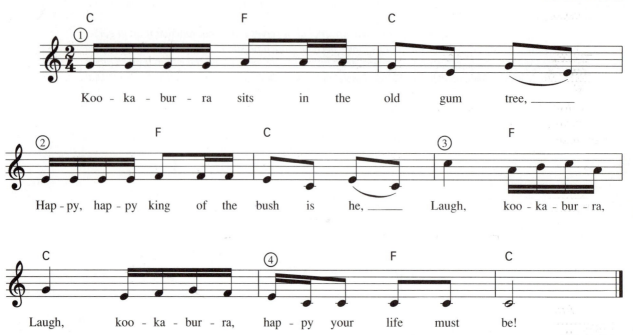

Koo - ka - bur - ra   sits   in   the   old   gum   tree, _____

Hap - py,   hap - py   king   of   the   bush   is   he, _____   Laugh,   koo - ka - bur - ra,

Laugh,   koo - ka - bur - ra,   hap - py   your   life   must   be!

Autoharp, strum C

The kookaburra is an Australian bird with a raucous cry that sits in eucalyptus trees and "laughs" noisily.

KOROBUSHKA

Words by
Nickolay Kekrasov

Russian Folk Song

English: "See what I have here in my ko - ro - bush - ka!"
Russian: Oi pol - - na pol - - na ko - ro - bush - ka;
Pronunciation: *ahee* *pawl* - *nah* *pawl* - *nah* *kah* - *rrah* - *bush* - *kuh*

We can hear the ped - dler's cry.
Est' i sit - sy i par - cha.
yehst *ee* *see* *tsih* *ee* *parr* *chah*

"I am on - ly a rag - ged ped - dler, but
"Lace and sat - in and col - ored rib - bon, and
Po - zha - lei ma - - ia za zno - bush - ka,
paw - *zjuh* - *lay* *mah* - - *yah* *zah* - *znoe* - *bush* - *kuh*

I have treas - ures you can buy:
shin - - y beads to catch your eye!"
Mo - - lo - dets ko - go - ple - cha!
mah - - *lah* *dyets* - *kah* - *vaw* *plyeh* - *chah*

English lyrics used by permission of The McGraw–Hill Companies,
from *Share the Music*, Grade 4. Copyright © 1995.

Guitar, strum 7

Literal translation

Oh, I have a full, full korobushka;
In it, I have cotton and brocade.
Please feel sorry for me, sweetheart,
As my shoulders are already tired.

A korobushka is a basket woven of wicker or other plant materials.

Kum-bah-yah

African American Song

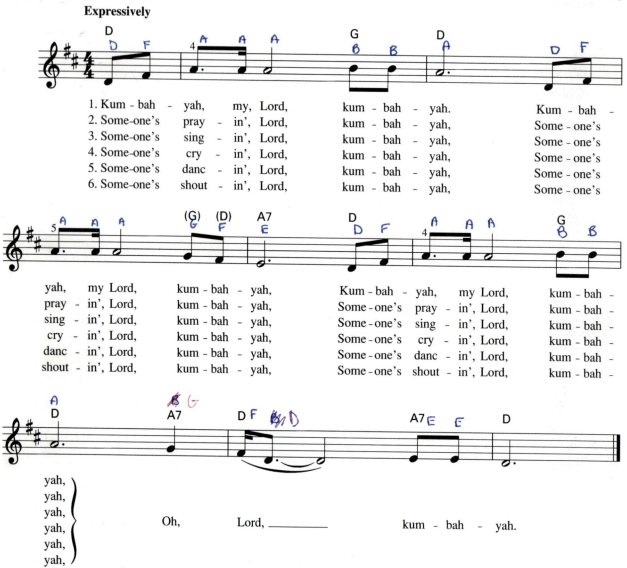

Expressively

1. Kum - bah - yah, my, Lord, kum - bah - yah. Kum - bah
2. Some-one's pray - in', Lord, kum - bah - yah, Some - one's
3. Some-one's sing - in', Lord, kum - bah - yah, Some - one's
4. Some-one's cry - in', Lord, kum - bah - yah, Some - one's
5. Some-one's danc - in', Lord, kum - bah - yah, Some - one's
6. Some-one's shout - in', Lord, kum - bah - yah, Some - one's

yah, my Lord, kum - bah - yah, Kum - bah - yah, my Lord, kum - bah -
pray - in', Lord, kum - bah - yah, Some-one's pray - in', Lord, kum - bah -
sing - in', Lord, kum - bah - yah, Some-one's sing - in', Lord, kum - bah -
cry - in', Lord, kum - bah - yah, Some-one's cry - in', Lord, kum - bah -
danc - in', Lord, kum - bah - yah, Some-one's danc - in', Lord, kum - bah -
shout - in', Lord, kum - bah - yah, Some-one's shout - in', Lord, kum - bah -

yah,
yah,
yah,
yah,
yah,
yah,

Oh, Lord, _____ kum - bah - yah.

Autoharp (15-bar), strum L
Guitar, strum 18 or play melody notes
Piano, accompaniment pattern XI

60

158

La Bamba

English words by
Patricia Hackett

Mexican Folk Song
Arr. Patricia Hackett

ré, por ti se - ré, por ti se - ré!
ray pawr tee seh - ray pawr tee seh - ray
sing, sing, sing, Just sing the Bam - ba song!

Group 1, only: *sing six times*

¡Bam - ba, bam - ba!   ¡Bam - ba, bam - ba!

Group 2 enters: *sing four times*

¡Bam - ba, bam - ba!   ¡Bam - ba, bam - ba!

Group 3 enters: *sing two times*   *All groups:*

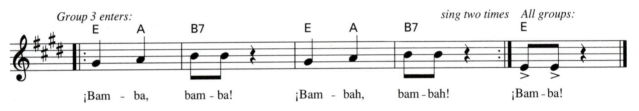

¡Bam - ba, bam - ba!   ¡Bam - bah, bam - bah!   ¡Bam - ba!

Guitar, strum 3

Divide into three groups to sing "La Bamba." Group 1 begins and continues throughout.

THE LAMB
(*Mielule*)

English words by
Michaela Codrescu
and Patricia Hackett

Romanian Folk Song
as sung by Ion Codrescu
Transcribed by Patricia Hackett

Lyrically, without accents (♪ = 200)

Shepherd:

English:	1. Where	do	you _____	go,		mie	– lu	– le?
Romanian:	1. Un'	te	duci _____	tu,		mie	– lu	– le?
Pronunciation:	oon	tay	dooch	too		mihyeh	– loo	– lay

Lamb:

On	to	pas – – ture,		dom	– – nu	– le.
La	pă	– şu – – ne,		dom	– – nu	– le.
lah	puh	– shoo – – nay		dome	– noo	– lay

Pronunciation guide

ă as in s*i*r

ş as in *sh*ut

2. What will you do, *mielule?* (*2 times*)
   Eat the green grass, *domnule.* (*2 times*)

3. Who comes with you, *mielule?* (*2 times*)
   Humble shepherd boy, *domnule.* (*2 times*)

4. What do you hear, *mielule?* (*2 times*).
   Blades[3] to cut grass, *domnule.* (*2 times*)

5. Who will cut you, *mielule?* (*2 times*)
   Butcher cuts me, *domnule.* (*2 times*)

6. Who will eat you, *mielule?* (*2 times*)
   You will eat me, *domnule.* (*2 times*)

Although Ion Codrescu understands that verses 5 and 6 suggest the round of life within our global food chain, young singers may be upset by the lamb's sad ending. The following verse can replace verses 5 and 6.

Substitute verse

5. *Shepherd:* Do you leave me, *mielule?* (*2 times*)
   Lamb: Yes, I'll leave you, *domnule.* (*2 times*)

End the song with verse 7 as shown on the next page.

[3] *Scythe*

Shepherd: What re - mains ___ then, *mie - lu - le?*
Ce ră - mâ - ne, mie - lu - le?
chay ruh - muuh - nay mihyeh - loo - lay

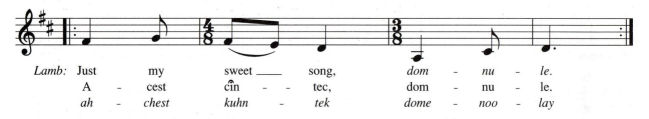

Lamb: Just my sweet ___ song, *dom - nu - le.*
A - cest cîn - tec, dom - nu - le.
ah - chest kuhn - tek dome - noo - lay

Autoharp (15-bar), strum each downbeat
Guitar, brush stroke on each downbeat

Romanian verses 2–6

2. Ce să faci tu, mielule? (*2 times*)
chay suh fach too mih-yeh-loo-lay
Să pasc iarbă, domnule. (*2 times*)
suh pahsk ih-ar-buh dome-noo-lay

3. Cin'te mînă, mielule? (*2 times*)
chin teh muu-nuh mih-yeh-loo-lay
Ciobănasul, domnule. (*2 times*)
chee-oh-buhn-ah-shool dome-noo lay

4. Ce s-aude, mielule? (*2 times*)
chay sah-auoo-day mih-yeh-loo-lay
Coasa-n iarbă, domnule. (*2 times*)
Kwah-sah ih-ar-buh dome-noo-lay

5. Cin' te taie, mielule? (*2 times*)
chin tay tah-ee-aye mih-yeh-loo-lay
Măcelarul, domnule. (*2 times*)
muh-cheh-lah-rool dome-noo-lay

6. Cin' te mîncă, mielule? (*2 times*)
chin teh muun-kuh mih-yeh-loo-lay
Dumnea voastră, domnule. (*2 times*)
doom-nea[4]-voh-ahs-truh dome-noo-lay

Substitute for verses 5 and 6

5. Mă lasi singur, mielule? (*2 times*)
muh lah-sh sihn-goor mih-yeh-loo-lay
Te las singur, domnule. (*2 times*)
tay lahs sihn-goor dome-noo-lay
(Conclude with verse 7)

*This Romanian children's song is a dialogue between a lamb (*mielule*) and a shepherd, whom the lamb addresses as "sir" (*domnule*). Poet and painter Ion Codrescu, of Constanţa, Romania, remembers learning this song from his mother and singing it frequently when a small child. Ion's childhood home was in the village of Viişoara, near the Black Sea. Viişoara means "little [grape] vine.") Ion's mother grew up in the central mountain area of Romania and brought many of her childhood songs with her to Viişoara, where she moved as a young married woman and where Ion was born in 1951. Although some children learned folk songs from their mothers in the home, many Romanian children of that period learned songs and heard music through government-run radio and schools.*

[4] Pronounce *ea* as in h*a*t.

La Raspa

Mexican Folk Song

Autoharp, strum B
Guitar, strum 1

Formation

Students form two circles, one inside the other. The inner circle faces the outer circle. Partners face each other, holding both hands.

R means right foot; L means left foot

Section A

Measure 1: Hop on L foot while tapping R heel forward, reverse, reverse again, then hold for 1 beat.

Measure 2: Repeat, beginning with a hop on the R foot while tapping L heel forward.

Measures 3–4: Repeat previous measures.

Section A (repeat)

Repeat steps for Section A, above.

Section B

Measures 9–12: Clasping their own hands behind backs, partners continue to face each other, taking 4 side steps counterclockwise, then moving right, taking 4 side steps clockwise.

Measures 13–16: Repeat measures 9–12.

Repeat steps for Section A above. (Don't repeat the A section.)

LAREDO

English words by
Margaret Marks

Mexican Folk Song

Guitar, strum 24

2. I've brought you a hand-sewn saddle, my love,

    E

  B7   *E*
A blanket and bridle fine;

So when you go past the bunkhouse, my love,

  B7   *E*
The cowboys will know you're mine.

   A   *E*
I've brought you a key of silver, my love,

  B7   *E*
Attached to a golden chain,

   A   *E*
To lock up your heart forever, my love,

  B7   *E*
If never we meet again.

Mexican folk music has special characteristics. Melodies often emphasize the first and third scale tones, and are frequently harmonized in thirds or sixths. There is no ornamentation or improvisation. Triple meter is frequently used. A composition often begins slowly, gradually accelerating to the main body of the composition, and accelerating again at the end. The vocal style is also distinctive, because the voice is tense and nasalized, and at a high pitch—often going into falsetto.

LET MUSIC SURROUND YOU

Fran Smartt Addicott

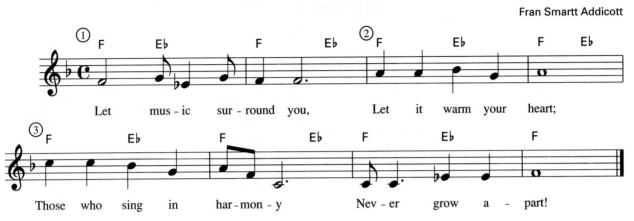

Let mus - ic sur - round you, Let it warm your heart;

Those who sing in har - mon - y Nev - er grow a - part!

Autoharp (15-bar), strum A

Fran Smartt Addicott is Orff-Schulwerk supervisor for the Memphis, Tennessee, schools.

LET'S GO TO THE SEA
(*Vamos al mar*)

Guatemalan Folk Song

English: 1. Let's go to the sea, ___ tum tum, Hook some fish and
Spanish: 1. Va - mos al ___ mar, ___ tum tum, a co - mer pes -
Pronunciation: vah - mohs ahl mahr toom toom ah coe - mehr pehs -
2. Af - ter we have caught it, tum tum, In a pan we'll

fry 'em, tum tum, Mouth as red as ru - by, tum tum,
ca - do, tum tum, Bo - ca co - lo - ra - da, tum tum,
kah - do toom toom boe - kah coe - loh - rah - dah toom toom
toss it, tum tum, Fry it in some but - ter, tum tum,

Bar - be - que or fry 'em, tum tum. ___
Fri - ti - to y a - sa - do, tum tum. ___
free - tee - toe ee ah - sah - doh toom toom
For a tast - y sup - per, tum tum. ___

Autoharp, strum K
Piano, accompaniment pattern VI

Spanish

    F   C7
2. Vamos al mar, tum tum,
   vah-mohs ahl marh toom toom

                 F
A comer pescado, tum tum,
ah koh-mehr pehs-kah-doh toom toom

            C7
Fritito y asado, tum tum,
free-tee-toh ee ah-sah-doh toom toom

              F
En sartén de palo, tum tum.
en sahr-tehn deh pah-loh toom toom

THE LION
(*Mbube*)

Solomon Linda
(South Africa)

♩ = 104

mf

1., 2. In the jun - gle ___ the { qui - et / might - y } jun - gle ___ The

mp

Wim - o - weh, o wim - o - weh, o wim - o - weh, o wim - o - weh, O

mp

Wim - o - weh, o wim - o - weh, o wim - o - weh, o wim - o - weh, O

mp

Wim - o - weh, o wim - o - weh, o wim - o - weh, o wim - o - weh, O

Coda

li - on sleeps to - night.

Wim - o - weh, o wim - o - weh, o wim - o - weh, o wim - o - weh, o wim - o - weh.

Wim - o - weh, o wim - o - weh, o wim - o - weh, o wim - o - weh, o wim - o - weh.

Wim - o - weh, o wim - o - weh, o wim - o - weh, o wim - o - weh, o wim - o - weh.

Pronunciation guide
wihm-oh-way

"The Lion" can be performed as follows.
Introduction (4 measures): Parts 2, 3, 4 only
Verse 1 (4 measures): Part 1 and Parts 2, 3, 4
Verse 2 (4 measures): Part 1 and Parts 2, 3, 4
Ending (4 measures): Parts 2, 3, 4 only
Coda ("Wim-o-weh"): Parts 2, 3, 4 only

In 1939, a Zulu choral group led by Solomon Linda recorded Linda's composition "Mbube" ("The Lion"). It was the first recording in Africa to sell 100,000 copies, and the song later provided the basis for two hit records in America: "Wimoweh" in 1950 and "The Lion Sleeps Tonight" in 1961. Linda's group introduced techniques that included a high-voiced leader and softly executed dance routines performed in uniform. (For additional information on South African popular music, see the song "Siyahamba.")

LITTLE BIRD
(*Pateachka*)

English words by
Patricia Hackett

Russian Game Song
Transcribed by Patricia Hackett

Autoharp, strum C (verse) and strum H (refrain)
Piano, accompaniment pattterns III (verse) and VII (refrain)

Game

Children form a circle around one child, who is the bird. On the first verse, the children walk in a circle around the bird. During the refrain, the circle children stand in place and the bird faces a selected child in the circle. These two players exchange places so that there is a new bird in the center for the second verse.

English

C
2. Oh, Pateachka, stay with us,

   G   C
Take our tea and candy!

Oh, Pateachka, stay with us,

   G   C
Take our tea and candy!

Refrain

                  G
"Oh, I don't want any sweets,

      F   C
And I don't want your tea!

               G
Let me go now, set me free,

            C
As a wild bird must be!"

Russian

C
2. Nyt′ ny poo stem pateachka   nyt′,
nnyeh voo poo stehm puh-teech-ka nnyeh

G   C
Ost te   vis sah snei̅ me̅,
ah steh vee so snee mee

Mea dah deam teabeer confet,
mwee dah dehm key-syah cohn-feht

G   C
Chah you suharyahme.
chah yoo sah-kha-ryah-mee

Refrain

                      G
"Ach confet   ya neit cluyou;
ach cohn-fyeht yah nyeht chloo-you

          F   C
Ny lu blu̅   ya chi̅ you,
nnyeh lyoo blyoo yah chay yoo

                       G
Vaul lea maulshik   yah lou lou,
voh lee mahl-chick yah lyoo lyoo

                    C
Zornshke̅   spe̅bryeyou."
zore-nsh-keh spehb-rye-yoo

**Cathedral of
St. Basil**

LITTLE DONKEY
(*Shau Mau Lyu*)

English words by
Patricia Hackett

Taiwan Children's Song

English: Walk - ing, walk - ing by my side, A don - key, grey and brown;
Mandarin: Wo you yi jr syau mau lyu, wo tsung lai ye bu chi,
Pronunciation: woh you ee jer ssyow mahoo leeoo woe tssong lye yay boo chee

Rid - ing, rid - ing on his back, I'm go - ing in - to town. He's
You yi tyan wo syin sye lai Chau chi je chyu gan ji, Wo
yo ee tyehn woh seeihn syey lye chaoo chee juh chuh gahn jee woh

run - ning, run - ning craz - y brute: Be care - ful or I'm downed;
shou li na je syau pi byan Wo syin li jen de yi,
show lee nah juh sheeaou pee byahn woh sshihn lee jehn deh yee

Fal - ling, fal - ling, *Hwa la la la la!* I'm dumped on - to the ground!
Bu jr dzen me, hwa la la la la, Wo shwai le yi shen ni.
boo jer tzuhn muh hwah lah lah lah lah woh shwye luh yee shuhn nee

Autoharp, strum E

Traditional Chinese performance styles continue on Taiwan, as well as in Chinese American communities in the United States. In mainland China, many old folk tunes are used in choral settings, with new texts promoting national values. This extramusical function for music is at least as ancient as Confucius (500 B.C.). Chinese music has long been valued as a vehicle for social and political education, but enjoyed for its programmatic and allegorical qualities.

A LITTLE NIGHT MUSIC
(*Eine kleine Nachtmusik,* K. 525)
Second movement: Romanza
(excerpt)

Wolfgang Amadeus Mozart
(Austria, 1756–1791)

Andante (♩ = 76)

Play one octave higher

(violin)

The "Romanza"[5] theme shown above alternates with two different sections of music in Mozart's *Eine kleine Nachtmusik,* resulting in a form called rondo.

The term Classical was never meant to distinguish art music from popular music. Instead, it specifically designates the music of the Viennese Classical period, from about 1700 to about 1830. During this era, Haydn, Mozart, and Beethoven greatly expanded the repertoire of instrumental music with works of exceptional clarity, balance, and constraint. These eighteenth-century classical ideals were brilliantly synthesized by Mozart, who as a child prodigy was exhibited by his teacher-father throughout the capitals and courts of Europe. As a mature composer, Mozart was versatile, using his creative genius to fashion operas and symphonies as well as chamber and choral music of luminous grace.

[5] Found in *Bowmar Orchestral Library,* Series 2, "Fashions in Music."

LONDON BRIDGE

Traditional Singing Game

1. Lon - don bridge is fall - ing down, fall - ing down, fall - ing down,
2. Take the key and lock her up, lock her up, lock her up,
3. Build it up with silver and gold, silver and gold, silver and gold,

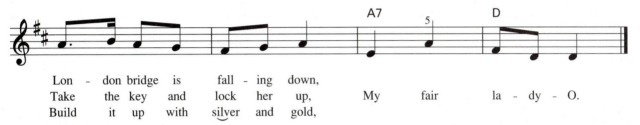

Lon - don bridge is fall - ing down,
Take the key and lock her up, My fair la - dy - O.
Build it up with silver and gold,

Autoharp (15-bar), strum E
Guitar, strum 4
Piano accompaniment pattern III

Formation

Two players face each other, join hands, and raise their arms to form a bridge (arch). One player represents gold, the other, silver. Remaining players make a line, each placing arms on the waist or shoulders of the person ahead.

Game

As they sing verse 1, players in line walk under the bridge. On the words "lady-O," the bridge is lowered over the player underneath.

During verse 2, the players forming the bridge sway gently from side to side, arms encircling their captive.

During verse 3, there is a whispered conference in which the captive chooses silver or gold; the captive then goes to stand behind the player representing this choice.

The song and the game repeat until all players are captured. A tug-of-war is the traditional conclusion to the game, and it determines the victorious group.

LONDON'S BURNING

Traditional Round

Play these patterns on a xylophone for "London's Burning," or create your own. Play one pattern as an introduction.

LOOBY LOO

American Singing Game

Refrain

Here we go loo - by loo, _____ Here we go loo - by light, _____ Here we go loo - by loo, _____ All on a Sat - ur - day night. _____

Verse

1. I put my right hand in, _____ I take my
2. I put my left hand in, _____ I take my
3. I put my right foot in, _____ I take my
4. I put my left foot in, _____ I take my
5. I put my big head in, _____ I take my
6. I put my whole self in, _____ I take my

right hand out; _____ I give my right hand a
left hand out; _____ I give my left hand a
right foot out; _____ I give my right foot a
left foot out; _____ I give my left foot a
big head out; _____ I give my big head a
whole self out; _____ I give my whole self a

shake, shake, shake! And turn my self a - bout! _____

D.C. al Fine

Guitar, brush each downbeat

177

Dance

Form a circle and join hands.

During the refrain, dancers skip around the circle, stopping when the verse begins, and drop hands.

On each verse, dancers pantomime the actions indicated by the lyrics. For example, on "I put my right hand in," dancers hold their right hands toward the center of the circle and shake them several times during "shake, shake, shake." After turning around in place, dancers join hands and prepare to skip once again in a circle.

Los Patitos
(The Ducklings)

English words by
Patricia Hackett

Salvadoran Folk Song
Transcribed by Patricia Hackett

♩ = 76

G   **C**   **G**

English: Los pa - ti - tos in the wa - ter, How they love to

Spanish: Los pa - ti - tos van al a - gua, Tien - en ga - na

Pronunciation: lohs pah - tee - tohs bahn ahl ah - wah tyehn - ehn gah - nah

dive and play; Hear the moth - er call, **C** pa - ti - tos, **G**

de na - dar; En i - le - ras bien for - ma - das,

day nah - dahr ehn ee - lay - rahs b'yehn fohr - mah - dahss

Now it's time to swim a - way. Moth - er leads and

Co - mo sa - ben ca - mi - nar. Va la pa - ta

coh - moh sah - behn cah - mee - nahr vah lah pah - tah

D   **G**   **D(7)**   **G**

they will fol - low, Los pa - ti - tos all in line,

por de - lan - te, Los pa - ti - tos van de - tras.

pohr dee - lahn - tay lohs pah - tee - tohs bahn day - trahss

C   **G**

Four, and five, and six pa - ti - tos, Los pa - ti - tos look so fine!

Qua - tro, cin - co, seis pa - ti - tos, Ni u - no me - nos ni u - no mas.

kwah - troh sin - koh sayees pah - tee - tohss nee oo - noh meh - nohs nee oo - noh mahss

Autoharp, strum C
Guitar, strum 3

LOST MY GOLD RING

Jamaican Game Song

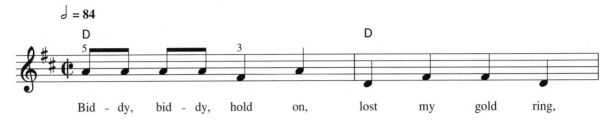

Bid - dy, bid - dy, hold on, lost my gold ring,

One go to Kings - ton, come back a - gain. Bid - dy, bid - dy, hold on,

lost my gold ring, One go to Kings - ton, come back a - gain.

Autoharp (15-bar), strum A
Piano, play a chord root on each downbeat

Formation

Players stand in a circle. Each player's hands are held cupped together at waist level. A hider (called "master") stands in the center of the circle, and a guesser outside the circle.

Game

The master goes from player to player with hands cupped, concealing a gold ring. The guesser moves around the outside of the circle, following the master from player to player. The master pretends to pass the ring to each player, and at some point does so. If the guesser correctly discovers who has received the ring, the player holding the ring becomes the new guesser, and the guesser becomes the master.

THE MANGO
(*Isang Butong Mangga*)

English words by
Patricia Hackett

Philippine Folk Song
Collected and transcribed by
Miriam B. Factora

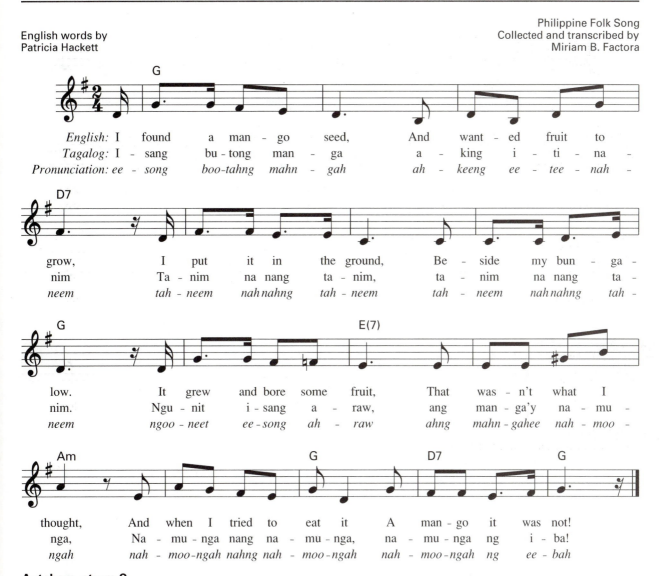

English:	I	found	a	man – go	seed,	And	want – ed	fruit	to
Tagalog:	I – sang		bu – tong	man – ga		a – king	i – ti	na	
Pronunciation:	ee – song		boo-tahng	mahn – gah		ah – keeng	ee – tee	nah –	

grow,	I	put	it	in	the ground,	Be – side	my bun – ga
nim	Ta – nim	na nang	ta – nim,		ta – nim	na nang	ta –
neem	tah – neem	nah nahng	tah – neem		tah – neem	nah nahng	tah –

low.	It	grew	and bore	some	fruit,	That	was – n't	what	I
nim.	Ngu – nit	i – sang	a – raw,		ang	man – ga'y	na – mu –
neem	ngoo – neet	ee – song	ah – raw		ahng	mahn – gahee	nah – moo –

thought,	And	when I	tried	to	eat it	A	man – go	it	was not!
nga,	Na – mu – nga nang na – mu – nga,				na – mu – nga ng	i – ba!		
ngah	nah – moo-ngah nahng nah – moo-ngah				nah – moo-ngah ng	ee – bah		

Autoharp, strum C
Guitar, strum 3

The mango is the national fruit of the Philippines.

MANGO WALK

Jamaican Calypso

With an easy swing

I think my ma-ma deed-a tell me that you go man - go walk, You

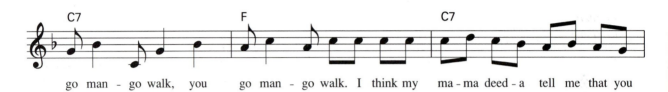

go man - go walk, you go man - go walk. I think my ma-ma deed-a tell me that you

go man - go walk And eat all the num - ber 'lev - en.

Autoharp, strum P

Perform on xylophones, maracas, or wood block, or all three.

Play 4 times

Play 4 times

184

MAYO NAFWA

African Folk Song
(Zambia)

Call

Na - po pa - nshi, Na - po pa - nshi na - ma - ten - ge.
nah - poh pah - nshee nah - poh pah - nshee nah-mah-teeh-ngay

Response

Call

Pa - li nye - le - le, Pa - li nye - le - le na - ma - ten - ge.
pah - lee nyah-lay - lay pah - lee nyay-lay - lay nah-mah-teeh-ngay

Response

Call Response All

Nan - dan da yi - la na - ma - ten - ge. Nan - dan da yi - la na - ma - ten - ge.
nahn - dahn day yee-lah nah-mah-teeh-ngay nahn - dahn dah yee-lah nah-mah-teeh-ngay

African musicians are renowned for their metronomic sense, their ability to maintain a beat and tempo throughout performance. The beats may be accented regularly—ONE, two, three, ONE, two, three—but African music often moves in irregular meters, as in "Mayo Nafwa": ONE, two, ONE, two, ONE, two, three, ONE, two, three, ONE, two, ONE, two. "Mayo Nafwa" incorporates many other traits of African musical style: A single melodic phrase is repeated again and again; the phrase descends through a wide range; it ends on the lowest sung tone. "Mayo Nafwa" is sung by a group, responding to a leader's call; the group often sings in harmony. The Bemba people sing this song about a child who has lost his mother. The singers ask what they can do to help the child.

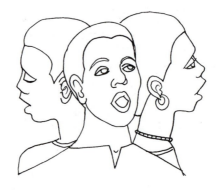

MICHAEL, ROW THE BOAT ASHORE

African American Spiritual

Sustained

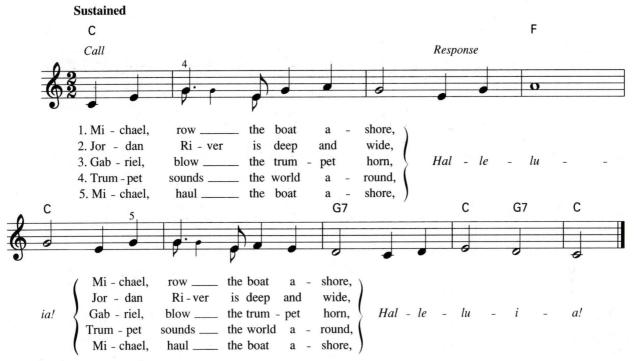

1. Mi - chael, row _____ the boat a - shore,
2. Jor - dan Ri - ver is deep and wide,
3. Gab - riel, blow _____ the trum - pet horn,
4. Trum - pet sounds _____ the world a - round,
5. Mi - chael, haul _____ the boat a - shore,

Hal - le - lu -

Mi - chael, row _____ the boat a - shore,
Jor - dan Ri - ver is deep and wide,
Gab - riel, blow _____ the trum - pet horn,
Trum - pet sounds _____ the world a - round,
Mi - chael, haul _____ the boat a - shore,

ia!

Hal - le - lu - i - a!

Autoharp, play melody rhythm
Piano, accompaniment pattern XIII

187

MISS MARY MACK

African American Play Song

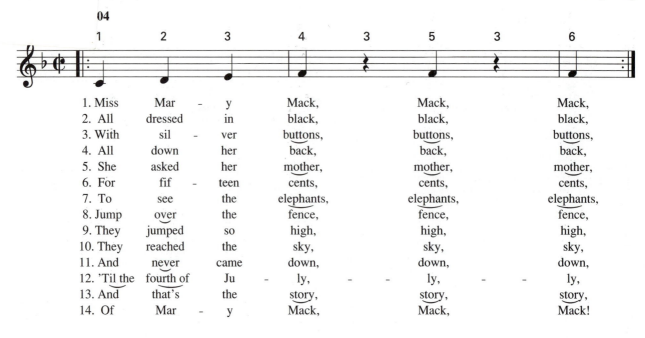

04

	1	2	3	4	3	5	3	6
1. Miss	Mar - y			Mack,		Mack,		Mack,
2. All	dressed	in	black,		black,		black,
3. With	sil - ver		buttons,		buttons,		buttons,
4. All	down	her	back,		back,		back,
5. She	asked	her	mother,		mother,		mother,
6. For	fif - teen		cents,		cents,		cents,
7. To	see	the	elephants,		elephants,		elephants,
8. Jump	over	the	fence,		fence,		fence,
9. They	jumped	so	high,		high,		high,
10. They	reached	the	sky,		sky,		sky,
11. And	never	came	down,		down,		down,
12. 'Til the	fourth of	Ju - ly,	-	-	ly,	-	-	ly,
13. And	that's	the	story,		story,		story,
14. Of	Mar - y		Mack,		Mack,		Mack!

Motions for each beat

1. Cross own hands across chest, hit own shoulders.

2. Slap thighs.

3. Clap own hands.

4. Clap partner's right hand.

5. Clap partner's left hand.

6. Clap both partner's hands.

MISTER FROG WENT A-COURTIN'

Anglo-American Ballad

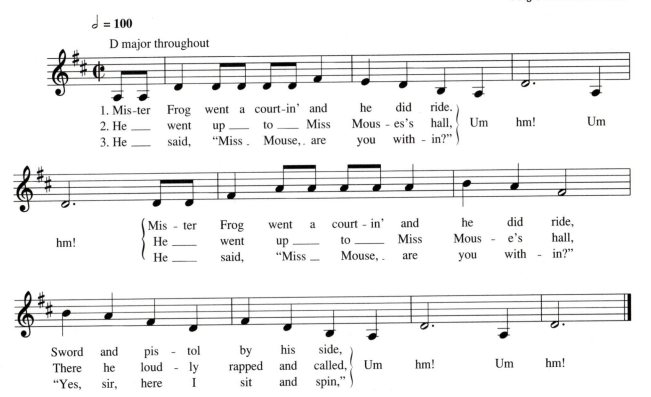

$\textdollar = 100$

D major throughout

1. Mis-ter Frog went a court-in' and he did ride.
2. He ___ went up ___ to ___ Miss Mous-es's hall, Um hm! Um
3. He ___ said, "Miss Mouse, are you with-in?"

hm!

Mis - ter Frog went a court - in' and he did ride,
He ___ went up ___ to ___ Miss Mous - e's hall,
He ___ said, "Miss ___ Mouse, are you with - in?"

Sword and pis - tol by his side,
There he loud - ly rapped and called, Um hm! Um hm!
"Yes, sir, here I sit and spin,"

Autoharp (15-bar), play drone (Dmaj and Dm); strum each downbeat
Guitar, strum 22

In English-speaking lands, songs of the nursery are often related to the ballad tradition. The marriage of frog and mouse is a narrative folk song from the reign of Elizabeth I, originally a biting satire that made use of the queen's habit of referring to her ministers by animal nick-names. After losing its popularity and timeliness, modified versions of "Mister Frog Went A-Courtin' " joined other tunes in the nursery. It resides there with many animal tales and fables, as well as songs about once current events. Children continue to sing counting-out songs and games: ancient rituals reenacted, with their ceremonial texts now tangled and garbled, the orig-inal meanings obscured or forgotten in naive transformations.

4. He took Miss Mouse upon his knee, Um-hm! Um-hm!
   He took Miss Mouse upon his knee,
   Said, "Miss Mouse, will you marry me?" Um-hm! Um-hm!

5. She said "I cannot tell you, Sir," Um-hm! Um-hm!
   She said "I cannot tell you, Sir,
   Till my Uncle Rat comes home," Um-hm! Um-hm!

6. So Uncle Rat gave his consent, Um-hm! Um-hm!
   So Uncle Rat gave his consent,
   And made a handsome settlement, Um-hm! Um-hm!

7. Then Uncle Rat, he went to town, Um-hm! Um-hm!
   Then Uncle Rat, he went to town,
   To buy Miss Mouse a wedding gown, Um-hm! Um-hm!

8. Oh, where will the wedding supper be? Um-hm! Um-hm!
   Oh, where will the wedding supper be?
   Away down yonder in a hollow tree, Um-hm! Um-hm!

9. The first to come was a little bee, Um-hm! Um-hm!
   The first to come was a little bee,
   He carried a Bible on his knee, Um-hm! Um-hm!

10. The next to come was a little white moth, Um-hm! Um-hm!
    The next to come was a little white moth,
    She spread out the tablecloth, Um-hm! Um-hm!

11. The next to come was a great big snail, Um-hm! Um-hm!
    The next to come was a great big snail,
    Carried a fiddle on his tail, Um-hm! Um-hm!

12. Mister Frog came swimming across the lake, Um-hm! Um-hm!
    Mister Frog came swimming across the lake,
    He got swallowed up by a big black snake, Um-hm! Um-hm!

13. There's bread and cheese upon the shelf, Um-hm! Um-hm!
    There's bread and cheese upon the shelf,
    If you want any more you can sing it yourself, Um-hm! Um-hm!

MISTER SUN

Traditional A

Autoharp, banjo strum
Piano, accompaniment pattern XVI

* Perform this song three times. The first two times, perform the melody as written. The last time, sing the second-to-last measure three times before going on to the final measure.

Invent a pantomime to depict the song's words, such as "sun" and "hiding."

MISTY

Johnny Burke
(United States, 1908–1964)

Erroll Garner
(United States, 1921–1977)

Look at me, I'm as help-less as a kit-ten up a tree, _____ And I feel like I'm cling-ing to a cloud, I can't _____ un-der-stand, _____ I get mist-y just hold-ing your hand. _____ Walk my

way and a thou-sand vi-o-lins be-gin to play, _____ Or it might be the sound of your "hel-lo," That mu-sic I hear _____ I get mist-y the mo-ment you're near.

You can say that you're lead-ing me on, _____ but it's just what I want you to do, _____ Don't you no-tice how

E7(G#m7)

hope-less-ly I'm lost, That's why I'm fol-low-ing you. _____ On my

25 *mf* D | Am(7) | D7 | G

own would I wan-der through this won-der-land a - lone? _____ Nev-er know-ing my

Gm | D Bm | Em | A7

right foot from my left, my hat ___ from my glove? _ I'm too mist-y and too much in

D B7 | Em | A7 D

love. _____ I'm just too mist - y, _____ and too much in love. _____

**Piano, accompaniment pattern XVII, rolled chords (measures 1–15 and 25–end)
   and solid chords (measures 16–24)**

MOON, MOON
(Nila, Nila)

South Indian Folk Song
Collected by Gloria Kiester

Not too fast

English: Love - ly, love - ly moon I see, Come down and live with me,
Tamil Pronunciation: nee - lah nee - lah oh - dee - vah nee - lah - mahl oh - dee - vah

Slide the moun - tain to the seas, Bring me jas - mine flow - ers, please.
mah - lay mat - lay ah - ree - vah mah - lee gah-ee poo kawn - doo vah

Love - ly, love - ly moon I see, Come down and
nee - lah nee - lah oh dee vah nee - lah mahl

Coda

live with me. Love - ly, love - ly moon I see.
oh - dee - vah nee - lah nee - lah oh - dee - vah

Soprano recorder

The gestures on the following page are based on bharata-natyam, and can be used with "Moon, Moon."

Bharata-natyam ("BAHraht-NAHTyahm") is a classical dance style of south India. This solo dance can be abstract, can tell a story, or can be a combination of the two. To tell a story, specific gestures and the entire body are used, such as eyes, fingers, hands, and feet. The ancient Hindu scriptures are an important source for bharata-natyam that tell stories. The dancers, who are nearly always women, wear bells on the ankles; the dance is accompanied by a group that includes a drummer and the dancer's teacher, who sings and plays small cymbals. Bharata-natyam was probably developed by the professional dancers attached to temples and courts. In the 1930s, the dance style was renamed bharata-natyam, was shifted to the stage, and was practiced by the educated elite of India. Dance classes now make the style widely available to girls and young women. Group recitals are frequent, and proud parents often urge their daughters to perform for guests in the home.

DANCE DIRECTIONS FOR "MOON, MOON"

Lovely, lovely,   moon . . .   I . . .   see.

Come down and . . .   live with me.

Slide the mountain . . .   to the seas.   Bring me Jasmine   please.
flowers . . .

MOON REFLECTIONS
(*Kojo Notsuki*)

Doi Bansui (Japan)
English words by
Patricia Hackett

Taki Rentaro
(Japan)

With movement

	English:	Bran - ches	sway, __	moon __	shines,	Blos - soms	twist	and	climb,
	Japanese:	Ha - ru	ko - - ro -	no,		Ha	na	no - -	en,
	Pronunciation:	hah - roo	koh - roh - noh			hah	nah	no -	ehn

'Round   an   an - cient   cas - tle   wall,   Where   we   pause   to - night.
Me - gu - ru - sa   ka - zu - ki,   Ka - ge - sa - shi - ta.
meh - goo - roo - sah   kah - zoo - kee   kah - gay - sah - shee - tah

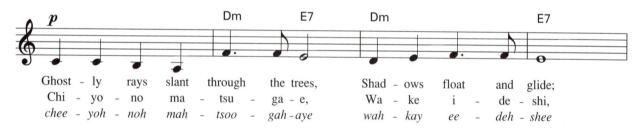

Ghost - ly   rays   slant   through   the   trees,   Shad - ows   float   and   glide;
Chi - yo - no   ma - tsu - ga - e,   Wa - ke   i - de - shi,
chee - yoh - noh   mah - tsoo - gah - aye   wah - kay   ee - deh - shee

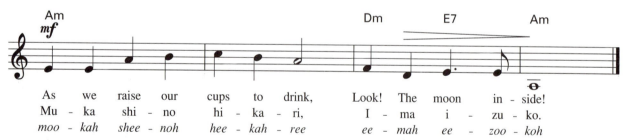

As   we   raise   our   cups   to   drink,   Look!   The   moon   in - side!
Mu - ka   shi - no   hi - ka - ri,   I - ma   i - zu - ko.
moo - kah   shee - noh   hee - kah - ree   ee - mah   ee - zoo - koh

Autoharp, strum A (use only upper- and middle-octave strings, brushed from high to low)
Guitar, strum 23

Play these patterns on a xylophone for "Moon Reflections."

Create a pantomime to fit the words of each phrase; use slow, graceful movements.

MORNING HAS BROKEN

Eleanor Farjeon
(United States, 1881–1965)

Welsh Melody

With movement

1. Morn-ing has bro - ken / Like the first morn - ing, / Black-bird has
2. Sweet the rain's new fall, / Sun - lit from heav - en, / Like the first
3. Mine is the sun light! / Mine is the morn - ing, / Born of the

spo - ken / Like the first bird. _____ / Praise for the sing - ing! / Praise for the
dew fall / On the first grass. _____ / Praise for the sweet - ness / Of the wet
one light / E - den saw play! _____ / Praise with e - la - tion, / Praise ev - 'ry

morn - ing! / Praise for them, spring - ing / Fresh from the Word! _____
gar - den, / Sprung in com - plete - ness / Where His feet pass. _____
morn - ing, / God's re - cre - a - tion / Of the new day! _____

Autoharp, strum three steady beats each measure
Piano, accompany using chord roots

197

MORNING SONG
(*Las Mañanitas*)

English words by
Lupe Allegria

Mexican Folk Song

English: Hear us sing las ma-ña-ni-tas, As the
Spanish: És-tas son las ma-ña-ni-tas, Que can-
Pronunciation: ehs-tahs sohn lahs mah-nyah-nee-tahs keh cahn-

morn-ing light ap-pears, And the gen-tle bird will
ta ba el Rey Da-vid, A las mu-cha-chas bo-
tah bah ehl roy dah-veed ah lahs moo-chah-chahs boh-

join In the hap-py mu-sic he hears. Oh,
ni-tas Se las can-ta-mos a-si: Des-
nee-tahs seh lahs cahn-tah-mohs ah-see dehs-

Refrain

wake up and see the sun-shine, Oh, wake up and meet the day, Hear, the
pier-ta, mi bien,* des-pier-ta Mi-ra que ya a man-ne-ció; Ya los
pyehr-tah mee byehn dehs-pyehr-tah mee-rah keh yah ah mahn-nah-seeoh yah lohs

morn-ing bird is sing-ing, The sil-ver moon's gone a-way.
pa-ja-ri-tos can-tan, La lu-na ya se me-tió.
pah-hah-ree-tohs cahn-yahn lah loo-nah yah seh meh-tyeeoh

* On *mi bien*, substitute the name of the person being honored.

Guitar, strum 13

"Las Mañanitas" is a traditional birthday song that is popular in Mexico and in Latino communities everywhere. In Mexico it is often sung, as in the old days, outside a home as a serenade (between midnight and 2 A.M.) for someone who is celebrating a birthday. "Las Mañanitas" is also performed at birthday parties, where it has become a custom to sing also the American "Happy Birthday to You" song.

Pre-Hispanic music of Mexico was always associated with ritual and ceremony, and was a communal expression rather than an individual one. Instrumental performance was always combined with singing, and certain instruments (such as the four-hole flute) were thought to have supernatural powers. The defeat of the Aztec chief Cuauhtemoc by Cortez (1521) marked the end of the pre-Hispanic period.

The arrival of the Spaniards profoundly changed music in Mexico. During the colonial period (1521–1810), music was used to help convert the people to Christianity. Very soon, European musical instruments and music education were introduced. During this period, Mexican composers wrote much religious music based on European models.

After independence from Spain in 1810, music in Mexico was still influenced by European music—particularly Italian opera. Composers such as Tomás Leon (1826–93) adapted European techniques and forms. However, in the twentieth century, Carlos Chávez (1899–1978) and other composers have developed a classical style deeply rooted in Mexican folk music.

MUSIC ALONE SHALL LIVE
(*Himmel und Erde*)

German Round

Autoharp, strum J

Literal translation

Heaven and earth may end,
But music will still be here.

My Body
(Mi cuerpo)

Hispanic Folk Song

English: My bod - y makes mu - sic, it's eas - y, you will see, My
Spanish: Mi cuer - po, mi cuer - po ___ ha - ce mú - si - ca, Mi
Pronunciation: mee kware - poe mee kware - poe ah - see moo - zee - kah mee

bod - y makes mu - sic, it's eas - y, you will see. My
cuer - po, mi cuer - po ___ ha - ce mú - si - ca. Mis
kware - poe mee kware - poe ah - see moo - zee - kah mees

hands, my hands go (clap clap clap), my feet, my feet go (tap tap tap), My
ma - nos ha - cen (clap clap clap), mis pi - es ha - cen (tap tap tap), Mi
mah - noes ah - sehn mees pee - ehs ah - sehn mee

mouth, my mouth goes "La la la," my bod - y does the "Cha cha cha."
bo - ca ha - ce "La la la," mi cuer - po ha - ce "Cha cha cha."
boh - kuh ah - sehn mee kware - poe ah - say

Autoharp, strum D
Piano, accompaniment pattern IV

MY NIPA HOME
(*Bahay Kubo*)

Philippine Folk Song

English: My ni-pa home is ve-ry small, But it hous-es the
Tagalog: Ba-hay ku-bo ka-hit mun-ti, Ang ha-la-man do-
Pronunciation: bah-high koo-boh kah-hiht moon-tee ahng hah-lah-mahn doh-

foods that I grow, one and all; There is room for the beans, For the
on ay__ sa-ri-sa-ri. Sin-ka mas at 'ta-long, si-ga-
oin oye tsah-ree-tsah-ree seen-kah mahs aht tah-loeng say-gah-

corn and for the rice, And lots of co-co-nut, too._____
ri-las at 'ma-ni, si-taw, ba-taw__ pa-ta-ni!_____
ree-yas aht mah-nee see-taoo bah-taoo__ pah-tah-nee

Guitar, strum 10
Piano, accompaniment pattern VII

The people of the Philippines have been in contact with Spanish culture for more than three hundred years, and today nearly all of their music reflects that Iberian influence. Guitars, pianos, and ensembles of steel strings (rondella) play Philippine folk melodies with harmonies and rhythms borrowed from the music of western Europe. "Bahay Kubo," for example, uses the major chords and triple meter of Spanish music, yet it is considered a typical Philippine folk song. In contrast, there are Moslem peoples in the southern Philippine Islands who retain a distinctive, florid song style, along with ensembles of flutes, zithers, and gongs that resemble Indonesian orchestras. In a few mountain regions, isolated groups still preserve a folk music that has origins in remote and ancient hills of the Malaysian mainland.

MY ROOSTER
(Mi Gallo)

Traditional Round

English:	My	hap - py	roost - er	died to - day,	My hap - py
Spanish:	Mi	gal - lo	se mu - ri ó	a - yer,	Mi gal - lo
Pronunciation:	mee	gahl - loe	say moo - treeoh	ah - yare	mee gahl - loe

roost - er died to - day. He will nev - er sing co - co - rí, co - co -
se mu - ri ó a - yer. Ya no can - ta - rá co - co - rí, co - co -
say moo - reeoh ah - yare yah noh cahn - tah - rah coe - coe - ree coe - coe -

rá. He will nev - er sing co - co - rí, co - co - rá.
rá. Ya no can - ta - rá co - co - rí, co - co - rá.
rah yah noh cahn - tah - rah coe - coe - ree coe - coe - rah

Co - co - co - co -

rí. co - rá, _____ co - co - co - co - rí, co - rá. _____

Autoharp, strum D

MY WHITE HORSE
(Mi Caballo Blanco)

English words by
Samuel Maqui

Francisco Flores del Campo
(Chile)

English: My horse is like the sun-rise, My horse is white as dawn,
Spanish: Es mi ca-ba-llo blan-co, com-o un a-man-e-cer,
Pronunciation: ehs mee cah-bahl-yoh blahn-coh coh-mo oon ah-mahn-eh-sare

We al-ways ride to-geth-er, Sing-ing as we ride a-long.
Siem-pre jun-ti-tos va-mos, es mi a-mi-go mas fi-el.
Syem-pray hoon-tee-tohs bah-mohs ehs mee ah-mee-goh mahs fee-ehl

Mi ca-ba-llo, mi ca-ba-llo, He is trot-ting on,
Mi ca-ba-llo, mi ca-ba-llo, se va y se va.
mee cah-bahl-yoh mee cah-bahl-yoh say vah ee say vah

Mi ca-ba-llo, mi ca-ba-llo, Right in-to the dawn.
Mi ca-ba-llo, mi ca-ba-llo, se va y se va.
mee cah-bahl-yoh mee cah-bahl-yoh say vah ee say vah

Ah, ah, ah, ah.

Ah, ah, ah, ah.

Guitar, strum 10
Piano, accompaniment pattern VII

Navajo Riding Song

Native American Song
Transcribed by Patricia Hackett

H'yoh ee yah, H'yoh ee yoh, yah, Ee

Drum: (Drum continues until measure 21)

yoh ee yoh ee yah nah aye aye yae aye yah ah.

H'way yah _____ nay yoh ee yoh ee yah hay

nah. H'way yah _____ nay yoh ee yoh ee yah.

Drum:

Music has always been important in Navajo culture, where it has many ritual, social, and personal uses. The men and boys might sing "Navajo Riding Song" while herding sheep from the back of a horse or a donkey. (The drum would be added for performance at a cultural fair.) Navajos are dynamic singers who cultivate a strong, rather nasal, high voice that has a kind of wild freedom about it—as if reflecting the wide-open spaces of their large reservation. Navajos are the most populous Native American group, with about 165,000 people who live on the reservation that includes land in Arizona, New Mexico, and Utah. Navajos were traditionally hunters and gatherers but later became sheepherders. Today their distinctive wool rugs and silver jewelry have made Navajo art famous around the world.

THE NOBLE DUKE OF YORK

Play-Party Game

1. Oh, the no - ble Duke of York, He
2. Now, _____ when we're up, we're up; And

had ten thou - sand men; He led them up to the
when we're down, we're down; And when we're on - ly _____

top of the hill, And he led them down a - gain.
half - way up, We're __ nei - ther up nor down.

Autoharp, strum A

Formation

Two lines face each other. The last child in each of the two lines joins hands with the other and together they become the head couple.

Game

On verse 1, the head couple march inside the lines to the opposite end (the foot) and back to place. On verse 2, each of the head-couple partners leads his or her own line outside, back on itself, so that the partners meet at the *foot* of the line. At the foot, the head couple make an arch, which the children of both sides pass through, bringing a new couple to the head. The game continues until everyone has had a turn as a member of the head couple.

Number One

Verse ... *Refrain*

1. Num-ber one, num-ber one, now my song has just be-gun, With a
2. Num-ber two, num-ber two, roost-ers crow; cock-a-doo-dle-doo, With a
3. Num-ber three, num-ber three, three lit-tle mon-keys in a tree, With a
4. Num-ber four, num-ber four, two plus one, then add one more, With a
5. Num-ber five, num-ber five, bees make hon-ey in a hive, With a

rum tum tad-dle-um, Old John Bad-dle-um, Hey, what coun-try folk we are!

Autoharp (15-bar), banjo strum (verse) and strum L (refrain)

        D   G   D   A7
6. Number six, number six, three little ducks and three little chicks. (*Refrain*)

        D   G   D   A7
7. Number seven, number seven, add four more and make eleven. (*Refrain*)

        D   G   D   A7
8. Number eight, number eight, four through the window and four through the gate. (*Refrain*)

        D   G   D   A7
9. Number nine, number nine, nine little ants march in a line. (*Refrain*)

       D   G   D   A7
10. Number ten, number ten, five were women and five were men. (*Refrain*)

       D   G   D   A7
11. Number eleven, number eleven, always rhymes with number seven. (*Refrain*)

       D   G   D   A7
12. Number twelve, number twelve, if you want more, you can sing it yourself! (*Refrain*)

O CHRISTMAS TREE
(O Tannenbaum)

Traditional German Carol

Moderately

English: O Christ - mas tree, O Christ - mas tree, With faith - ful leaves un -
German: O Tan - nen - baum, O Tan - nen - baum, Wie treu sind dei - ne
Pronunciation: o tah - nehn - baoom o tah - nehn - baoom vee troy zihndt die - nuh

chang - ing; O Christ - mas tree, O Christ - mas tree, With
Blät - ter! O Tan - nen - baum. O Tan - nen - baum, Wie
bleh - tehr o tah - nehn - baoom o tah - nehn - baoom vee

faith - ful leaves un - chang - ing. Not on - ly green in
treu sind dei - ne Blät - ter! Du grünst nicht nur zur
troy zihdt die - nuh bleh - tehr doo gruenst nihkt noor tzoor

sum - mer's heat, But al - so win - ter's snow and sleet. O
Som - mer - zeit, Nein, auch im Win - ter wenn es schneit. O
zuhm - mehr - tsite nine aook ihm vihn - tehr vehn ehs shnite o

Christ - mas tree, O Christ - mas tree, With faith - ful leaves un - chang - ing.
Tan - nen - baum, O Tan - nen - baum, Wie treu sind dei - ne Blät - ter!
tah - nehn - baoom o tah - nehn - baoom vee troy zihndt die - nuh bleh - tehr

Autoharp, strum H

208

O Come, All Ye Faithful
(*Adeste Fideles*)

John Francis Wade
Oxford, England
Composed 1740–1743

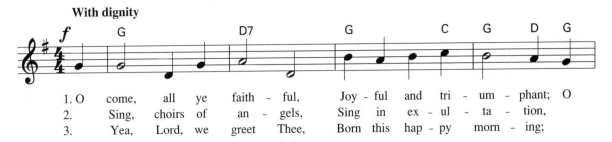

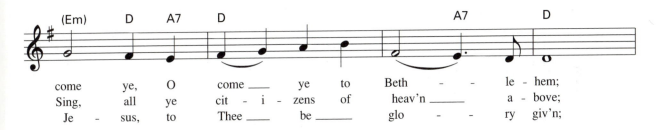

1. O come, all ye faith - ful, Joy - ful and tri - um - phant; O
2. Sing, choirs of an - gels, Sing in ex - ul - ta - tion,
3. Yea, Lord, we greet Thee, Born this hap - py morn - ing;

come ye, O come ___ ye to Beth - - le - hem;
Sing, all ye cit - i - zens of heav'n ___ a - bove;
Je - sus, to Thee ___ be ___ glo - - ry giv'n;

Come and be - hold Him Born the King of an - gels;
Glo - ry to God ___ In ___ the ___ high - est; O
Word of the Fa - ther, Now in flesh ap - pear - ing;

come, let us a - dore Him, O come, let us a - dore Him, O

come, let us a - dore Him, ___ Christ, ___ the Lord.

Autoharp (15-bar), strum A
Piano, accompaniment pattern XVII (solid chords)

209

Latin lyrics and pronunciation

```
G              D7          G          C  G  D
Adeste,        fideles,    laeti      triumphantes,
```
uh-dehs-teh fee-deh-lehs lay-tee tree-oom-phan-tehs


```
G   D        A7 D            A7 D
Venite,      venite    in    Bethlehem!
```
veh-nee-tay veh-nee-tay in   beth-leh-hehm


```
G            C G         D          A7  D
Natum        videte,     Regem      Angelorum,
```
nah-toom   vee-deh-tay reh-jehm   ahn-jeh-loh-ruhm


```
G                                              D7
Venite,       adoremus!        Venite       adoremus!
```
veh-nee-tay ad-doh-reh-moos veh-nee-tay ah-dor-reh-moos


```
G  C         A7 D C          G  D7 G
Venite        adoremus        Dominum.
```
ven-nee-tay ah-doh-reh-moos doh-mee-noom

ODE TO JOY
(from Symphony No. 9 in D major)

English words by
Henry van Dyke

Ludwig van Beethoven
(Germany, 1770–1827)

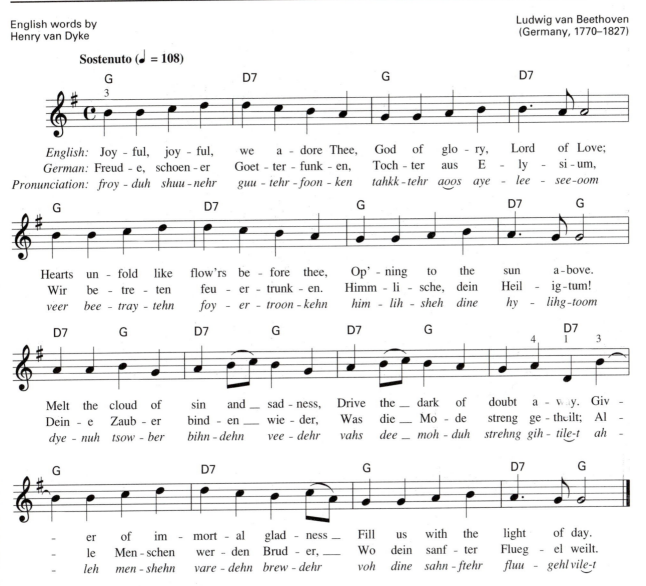

Sostenuto (♩ = 108)

English: Joy - ful, joy - ful, we a - dore Thee, God of glo - ry, Lord of Love;
German: Freud - e, schoen - er Goet - ter - funk - en, Toch - ter aus E - ly - si - um,
Pronunciation: froy - duh shuu - nehr guu - tehr - foon - ken tahkk - tehr aoos aye - lee - see-oom

Hearts un - fold like flow'rs be - fore thee, Op' - ning to the sun a - bove.
Wir be - tre - ten feu - er - trunk - en. Himm - li - sche, dein Heil - ig - tum!
veer bee - tray - tehn foy - er - troon - kehn him - lih - sheh dine hy - lihg - toom

Melt the cloud of sin and _ sad - ness, Drive the _ dark of doubt a - way. Giv -
Dein - e Zaub - er bind - en _ wie - der, Was die _ Mo - de streng ge - theilt; Al -
dye - nuh tsow - ber bihn - dehn vee - dehr vahs dee _ moh - duh strehng gih - tile-t ah -

- er of im - mort - al glad - ness _ Fill us with the light of day.
- le Men - schen wer - den Brud - er, _ Wo dein sanf - ter Flueg - el weilt.
- leh men - shehn vare - dehn brew - dehr voh dine sahn - ftehr fluu - gehl vile-t

Piano, accompaniment pattern XI
Soprano recorder

Two ideas from Schiller's Ode are expressed in the original German text: that joy unites all humankind and that the basis of joy is the love of God.

The genius of Ludwig van Beethoven bridged the eighteenth and nineteenth centuries. As a musical architect, he not only brought eighteenth-century forms to perfection but also infused them with the dynamic intensity of nineteenth-century romanticism. Free of princely patronage, Beethoven was sustained by publishers and by music lovers in the rising middle class, who applauded his astonishing pianism and supported the composition of sonatas, chamber music, concertos, and symphonies. Deafness began to afflict him at age 28, but he continued his creative work, which culminated in some of the most profound and brilliant instrumental compositions ever written. The unusual choral finale of the Ninth Symphony (his last) gloriously proclaims the composer's faith and his desire for universal brotherhood through transcendent joy.

Oh, Lord, I Want Two Wings

African American Spiritual

1. Oh, Lord, I want two wings to cov-er my face, __ Oh, Lord, I want two wings to cov-er my face, __ Oh, Lord, I want two wings to cov-er my face, __
2. Oh, Lord, I want two gold-en shoes for my feet, __ Oh, Lord, I want two gold-en shoes for my feet, __ Oh, Lord, I want two gold-en shoes for my feet, __
3. Oh, Lord, I want a gold-en harp __ to play, __ Oh, Lord, I want a gold-en harp __ to play, __ Oh, Lord, I want a gold-en harp __ to play, __

And the world can do me no harm. __

Auotharp, harp strum
Piano, accompaniment pattern XVII

OH, MY LITTLE BOY

American Folk Song

Playfully (♩ = 136)

C
Oh, my lit - tle boy, Who made your breech - es?

G7
Oh, my lit - tle boy, Who made your breech - es?

C
Oh, my lit - tle boy, Who made your breech - es?

F   C   G7   C
"Mom - my cut 'em out, and Dad - dy sewed the stitch - es."

Autoharp, strum D
Piano, accompaniment pattern II

213

OH! SUSANNA

Stephen C. Foster
(United States, 1826–1864)

Verse

1. I ____ came from Al - a - ba - ma with my ban - jo on my knee, I'm ____
2. I ____ had a dream the oth - er night when ev' - ry thing was still, I ____

going to Loui - si - an - a, my _____ true love for to see; It ____
thought I saw Su - san - na a' - com - in' down the hill. The ____

rained all night the day I left, the weath - er it was dry; The ____
buck - wheat cake was in her mouth, a tear was in her eye; Says ____

sun so hot I froze to death; Su - san - na, don't you cry.
I, I'm com - in' from the south; Su - san - na, don't you cry.

Refrain

Oh! Su - san - na, oh, don't you cry for me, I've ____

come from Al - a - ba - ma with my ban - jo on my knee.

Autoharp, strum C (verse) and banjo strum (refrain)
Piano, accompaniment pattern IV

"Oh! Susanna" was introduced by the famous Christy Minstrels in 1848. It was an imme-diate hit and soon became the "theme song" of the forty-niners who headed west for the gold-fields of California. In the "Oh! California" version that follows, the washbowl is the miner's gold pan.

214

Oh! California

    F   *C7*
1. I come from Salem City with my washbowl on my knee,

       F   *C7* *F*
I'm going to Californi-ay the gold dust for to see.

                                          C7
It rained all night the day I left, the weather it was dry,

       F   *C7*   *F*
The sun so hot I froze to death, oh, brothers, don't you cry.

Refrain

B♭   *F*   *C7*
Oh! California, that's the place for me,

       F   *C7* *F*
I'm bound for San Francisco with my washbowl on my knee.

  F   *C7*
2. I jumped aboard the 'Liza ship and traveled on the sea,

       F   *C7* *F*
And every time I thought of home, I wished it wasn't me!

                                    C7
The vessel reared like any horse that had of oats a wealth:

       F   *C7*   *F*
I found it wouldn't throw me so I thought I'd throw myself! *(Refrain)*

  F   *C7*
3. I thought of all the pleasant times, we've had together here,

       F   *C7* *F*
I thought I ought to cry a bit but couldn't find a tear.

                                    C7
The pilot's bread was in my mouth, the gold dust in my eye,

       F   *C7*   *F*
And though I'm going far away, dear brothers, don't you cry. *(Refrain)*

  F   *C7*
4. I soon shall be in Fri-is-co and there I'll look around,

       F   *C7* *F*
And when I see the gold lumps there, I'll pick them off the ground,

                                    C7
I'll scrape the mountains clean, my boys, I'll drain the rivers dry.

       F   *C7*   *F*
A pocketful of rocks bring home, so brothers, don't you cry! *(Refrain)*

Formation

Form a single circle of partners, girls on boys' right; face inward.

Dance

Phrase 1: Girls move four steps into the circle while boys clap the beat.

Phrase 2: Girls move four steps backward to their place; boys clap.

Phrases 3 and 4: Boys do the same movements that the girls have just done; the girls clap.

Phrases 5 and 6: All do grand left and right. Boys face clockwise, girls face counterclockwise; they join right hands and move around the circle, alternating left and right hands. On the word "me," all take new partners.

Last phrase: New partners promenade eight steps counterclockwise. On the final beat, all face inward ready to repeat the dance.

OLD BRASS WAGON

American Dance Song

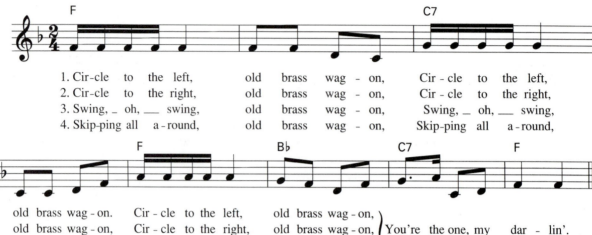

Dance tempo

1. Cir-cle to the left, old brass wag - on, Cir - cle to the left, old brass wag - on. Cir - cle to the left, old brass wag - on,
2. Cir-cle to the right, old brass wag - on, Cir - cle to the right, old brass wag - on, Cir - cle to the right, old brass wag - on,
3. Swing, _ oh, __ swing, old brass wag - on, Swing, _ oh, __ swing, old brass wag - on, Swing,_ oh,_ swing, old brass wag - on,
4. Skip-ping all a-round, old brass wag - on, Skip-ping all a-round, old brass wag - on, Skip-ping all a-round, old brass wag - on,

You're the one, my dar - lin'.

Autoharp, banjo strum

Formation

Form a single circle of partners, girls on boys' right.

Dance

Verse 1: All circle left.

Verse 2: All circle right.

Verse 3: Partners face each other, join hands, and swing once around.

Verse 4: Girls stand on boys' right, forming an inner circle; partners link arms and skip clock-wise around the circle.

216

OLD HUNDREDTH
(Psalm 100, altered)

William Kethe

Composer Unknown

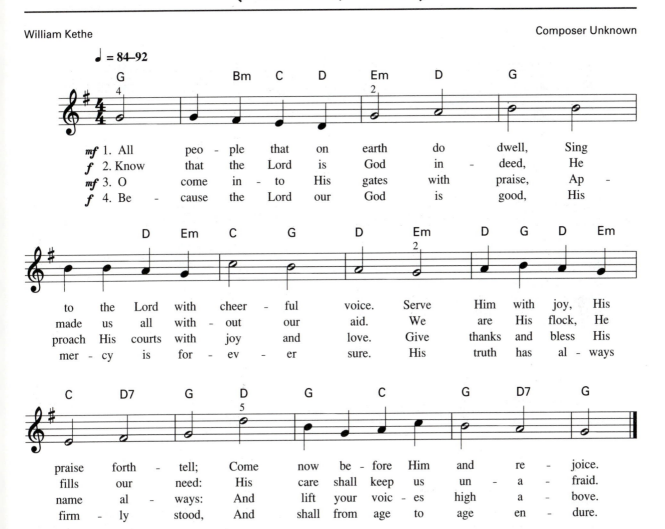

Piano, accompany using chord roots
Soprano recorder

This old psalm tune is of unknown origin. The "Old Hundredth" version first appeared in 1560–61. For the 1953 coronation of Elizabeth II, English composer Ralph Vaughan Williams made a ceremonial arrangement of the tune (with trumpets, organ, orchestra, and chorus). This same arrangement was performed in 1958 for Vaughan Williams's funeral in Westminster Abbey.

OLD JOE CLARK

American Folk Song

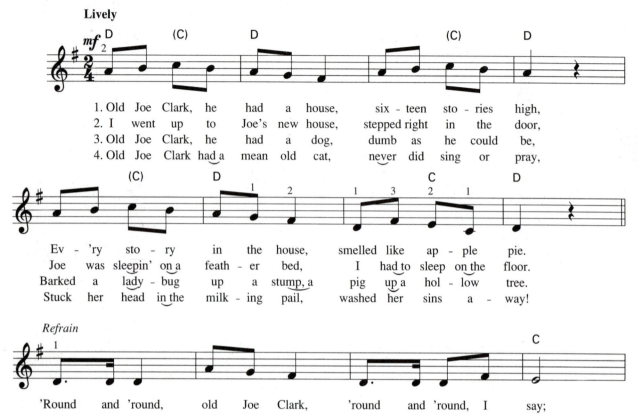

Lively

1. Old Joe Clark, he had a house, six - teen sto - ries high,
2. I went up to Joe's new house, stepped right in the door,
3. Old Joe Clark, he had a dog, dumb as he could be,
4. Old Joe Clark had a mean old cat, never did sing or pray,

Ev - 'ry sto - ry in the house, smelled like ap - ple pie.
Joe was sleepin' on a feath - er bed, I had to sleep on the floor.
Barked a lady - bug up a stump, a pig up a hol - low tree.
Stuck her head in the milk - ing pail, washed her sins a - way!

Refrain

'Round and 'round, old Joe Clark, 'round and 'round, I say;

'Round and 'round, old Joe Clark, dance your cares a - way.

Autoharp (15-bar), drone (Dmaj + Dmin; don't play C chord);
**   strum each downbeat**
Piano, accompaniment pattern II

D
5. Old Joe Clark, he had a wife, name of Mary Lou;

       C   *D*
She had two great big brown eyes, the other two were blue. (*Refrain*)

D
6. Old Joe Clark, he built a house, told his friends "It's neat!"

       C   *D*
He built the floors above his head, the ceilings under his feet. (*Refrain*)

D
7. Old Joe Clark had a violin, played it all the day,

       C   *D*
Never did he fiddle around, all he'd do was play. (*Refrain*)

Play the following pattern on a xylophone throughout "Old Joe Clark."

Play the following rhythm on a xylophone during the song's refrain.

OLD MacDONALD

American Folk Song

1. Old Mac-Don-ald had a farm. E - I - E - I - O. And on that farm he had some {chicks, ducks, pigs,} E - I - E - I - O. With a {chick - chick quack - quack oink - oink} here, and a {chick - chick quack - quack oink - oink} there. Here a {chick, quack, oink,} there a {chick, quack, oink,} ev-'ry where a {chick-chick. quack-quack. oink - oink.} Old Mac-Don-ald had a farm. E - I - E - I - O.

Create an ostinato to play on a xylophone. Find a pattern from the song to use, such as "had a farm."

4. Old MacDonald had a farm, E-I-E-I-O,
   And on that farm he had some turkeys, E-I-E-I-O,
   With a gobble-gobble here, and a gobble-gobble there,
   Here a gobble, there a gobble, ev'rywhere a gobble-gobble,
   Old MacDonald had a farm, E-I-E-I-O.

OLD PAINT

American Cowboy Song

Not too fast

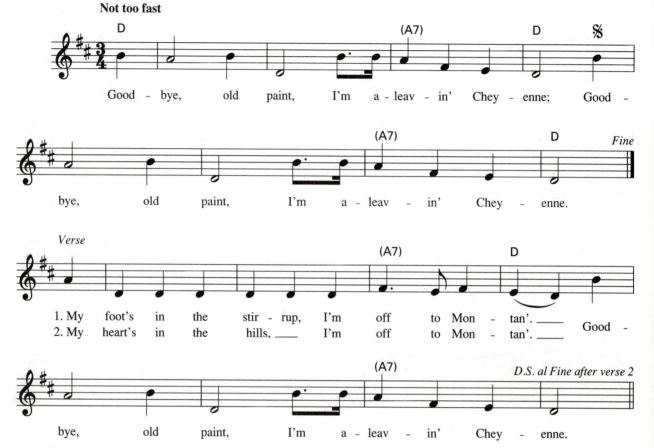

Good - bye, old paint, I'm a - leav - in' Chey - enne; Good -

bye, old paint, I'm a - leav - in' Chey - enne.

Verse

1. My foot's in the stir - rup, I'm off to Mon - tan'. ____ Good -
2. My heart's in the hills, ____ I'm off to Mon - tan'. ____

D.S. al Fine after verse 2

bye, old paint, I'm a - leav - in' Chey - enne.

Autoharp (15-bar), strum H
Guitar, strum 14
Soprano recorder

Play these patterns with "Old Paint."

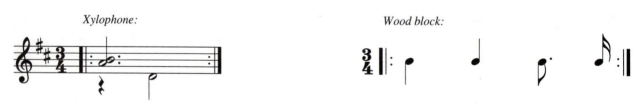

Xylophone:

Wood block:

Read about cowboy songs following "Old Texas."

OLD SMOKY

American Ballad

With feeling

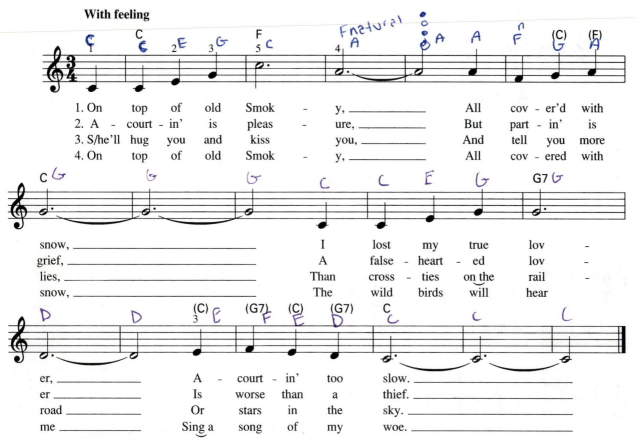

1. On top of old Smok - y, _____ All cov - er'd with
2. A - court - in' is pleas - ure, _____ But part - in' is
3. S/he'll hug you and kiss you, _____ And tell you more
4. On top of old Smok - y, _____ All cov - ered with

snow, _____ I lost my true lov -
grief, _____ A false - heart - ed lov -
lies, _____ Than cross - ties on the rail -
snow, _____ The wild birds will hear

er, _____ A - court - in' too slow. _____
er _____ Is worse than a thief. _____
road _____ Or stars in the sky. _____
me _____ Sing a song of my woe. _____

Autoharp, strum H
Piano accompaniment pattern VII

158

OLD TEXAS

American Cowboy Song

Quietly and not too fast

1. I'm goin' to leave _____ old ___ Tex - as now, _____
2. They've plowed and fenced _____ my ___ cat - tle range, _____
3. I'll take my horse, _____ I'll ___ take my rope, _____
4. Say *a - di - os* _____ to the Al - a - mo, _____

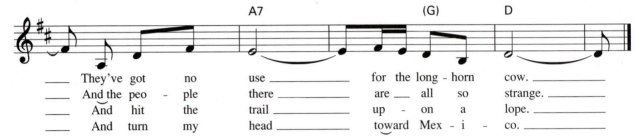

_____ They've got no use _____ for the long - horn cow. _____
_____ And the peo - ple there _____ are ___ all so strange. _____
_____ And hit the trail _____ up - on a lope. _____
_____ And turn my head _____ toward Mex - i - co. _____

Autoharp (15-bar), strum E
Guitar, strum 8 or play melody notes

D
5. I'll make my home on the wide, wide range,

    A7   *D*
For the people there are not so strange.

D
6. The hard, hard ground shall be my bed,

     A7   *D*
And my saddle seat shall hold my head.

Divide into two groups and sing "Old Texas" as an echo song. After group 1 sings "I'm goin' to leave," group 2 begins.

The vernacular of the range was unprintable. It is said that when a cowboy sang in polite company, he would need to whistle nine out of ten verses! No one is certain just how cowboy songs originated or whether the tunes were composed by the men themselves. Most likely they were based on existing melodies, borrowed from popular ballads, railroad songs, or mountain songs of the late nineteenth century. After the cowboy's evening meal, the most musical of the group might strike up a solo as the men sat around the fire or the chuck wagon. Hardly any one singer remembered all the verses, so other men might add stanzas to keep things going. Fortunately, a few collectors relished these songs that eased the loneliness of life on the trail, and preserved them—although in expurgated versions—for later generations.

O Music, Sweet Music

Traditional Round

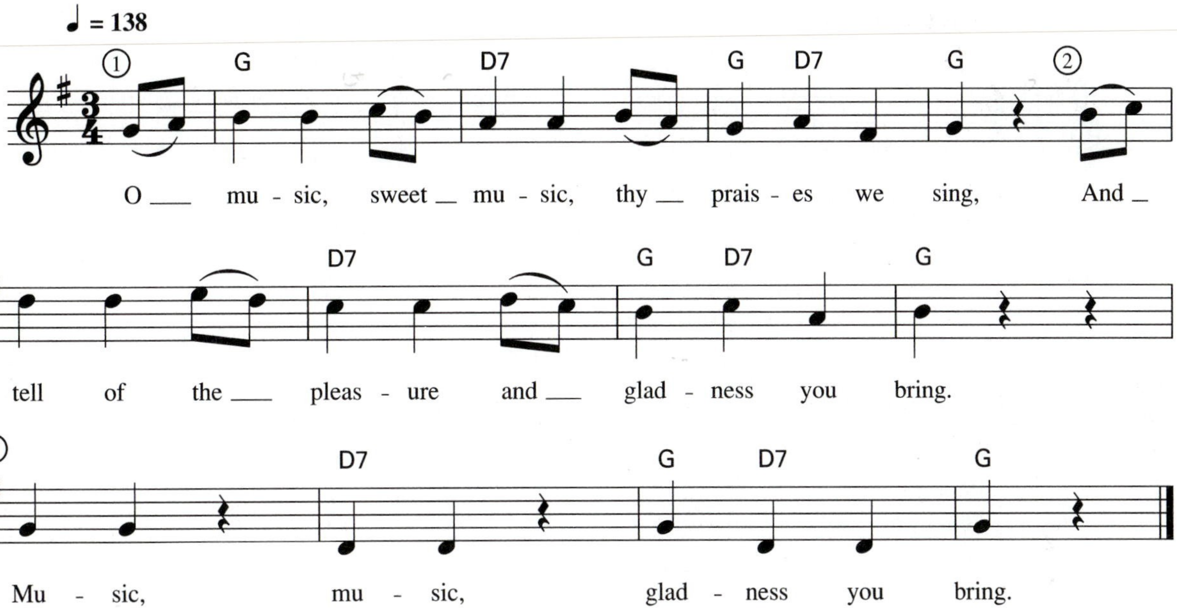
♩ = 138
G D7 G D7 G
O ___ mu - sic, sweet ___ mu - sic, thy ___ prais - es we sing, And ___
D7 G D7 G
tell of the ___ pleas - ure and ___ glad - ness you bring.
D7 G D7 G
Mu - sic, mu - sic, glad - ness you bring.

Autoharp, strum I
Soprano recorder

ONE LIGHT, ONE SUN

Words and music by Raffi

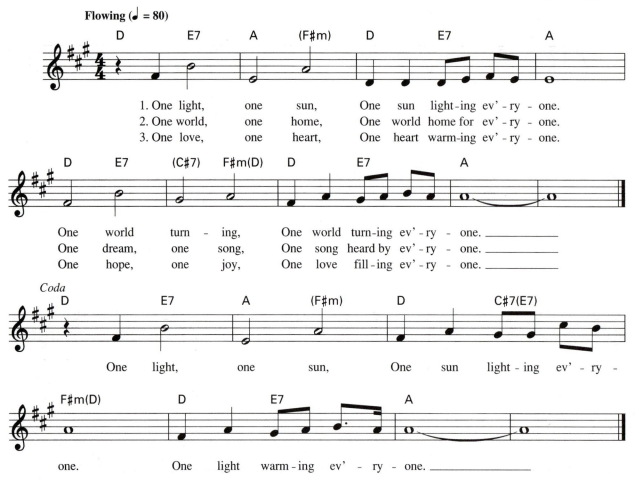

1. One light, one sun, One sun light-ing ev'-ry - one.
2. One world, one home, One world home for ev'-ry - one.
3. One love, one heart, One heart warm-ing ev'-ry - one.

One world turn - ing, One world turn-ing ev'-ry - one. _____
One dream, one song, One song heard by ev'-ry - one. _____
One hope, one joy, One love fill-ing ev'-ry - one. _____

One light, one sun, One sun light - ing ev'-ry -

one. One light warm-ing ev' - ry - one. _____

**Piano, accompaniment pattern XVII (use rolled chords and
solid chords with different verses.)**

One of Those Songs

Will Holt

Gerald Calvin

Begin slowly and get faster to the end

Well, this is one of those songs ___ that you hear now and then, ___ you
one of those songs ___ that can make you re - call ___ a
one of those songs ___ that's so eas - y to hear, ___ you

don't know just where, ___ you don't know just when. ___ It's
ride in the spring - time, a walk in the fall, ___ A
lis - ten just once, ___ then you play it by ear. ___ It's

one of those songs ___ that are o - ver and then, ___ it's
day in the coun - try, a night on the town, ___ the
hummed on ve - ran - - das and strummed on gui - tars, ___ and

one of those songs ___ that start play - ing a - gain. ___
sun com - ing up, ___ or the rain com - ing down. __
all you re - mem - - ber is "lah - dee - dah - dah."

___ Yes, it's just one of those songs ___ that you hear for a while, __ that
___ Or else the eve - ning you part - ed, the morn - ing you met, ___ the
___ But lat - er on you'll re - call ___ it in some oth - er year, ___ you

come in - to fash - ion and go out of style. ___ It's
love of your life ___ you can nev - er for - get. ___ The
may start to smile ___ or you may shed a tear. ___ You'll

225

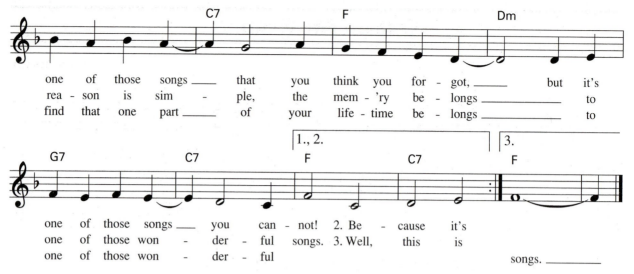

one of those songs ____ that you think you for - got, ____ but it's
rea - son is sim - ple, the mem - 'ry be - longs ____ to
find that one part ____ of your life - time be - longs ____ to

1., 2.

3.

one of those songs ____ you can - not! 2. Be - cause it's
one of those won - der - ful songs. 3. Well, this is
one of those won - der - ful songs. ____

"One of Those Songs." English Lyric by Will Holt. Music by Gerald Calvin.
© Copyright 1958, 1965 by Editions Musicales du Carrousel. Copyright Renewed.
All Rights for the USA and Canada Controlled and Administered by MCA Music
Publishing, A Division of Universal Studios, Inc. International Copyright
Secured. All Rights Reserved.

Autoharp, strum A
Piano, accompaniment pattern XVI

OVER MY HEAD

African American Spiritual

1. O - ver my head   I hear mu - sic in the air,

Yes,   o - ver my   head   I hear mu - sic in the air,

O - ver my   head   I hear mu - sic in the air,

There   must   be   a   God   some - where. _____

Autoharp (15-bar), strum O
Guitar, strum 19

2. In my feet there is dancing in the street, (*Sing three times*)
   There must be joy somewhere.

3. In my heart there's a play about to start, (*Sing three times*)
   There must be joy somewhere.

4. In my eyes there's a rainbow of surprise, (*Sing three times*)
   There must be joy somewhere.

Have a group echo back each phrase, sing in harmony, or improvise upon the three-note melody.

Each verse of "Over My Head" is about a different art and is sometimes called "the National Arts Standards" song. Words for verses 2–4 were written by music educator Will Schmidt.

OVER THE RAINBOW

Edgar Yip Harburg
(United States, 1896–1981)

Harold Arlen
(United States, 1905–1986)

Piano, accompaniment pattern XIV, measures 17–25, XI

OVER THE RIVER AND THROUGH THE WOOD

Lydia M.F.Child
(United States, 1802–1880)

Traditional Melody

Autoharp (15-bar), strum S

Create a dramatization or pantomime to fit the song's words.

"Over the River and through the Wood" is part of a poem by Lydia Child called "A Boy's Thanksgiving Day." Child was one of the most prominent women of her day. Born Lydia Maria Francis at Medford, Massachusetts, she spent most of her life in Boston, where she worked to promote women's right to vote, temperance, and the abolition of slavery. She was author of many popular stories and edited the Juvenile Miscellany, *the first children's monthly periodical in America. Child had strong moral convictions, and with her husband, she opened her home as a link in the Underground Railroad that aided enslaved African Americans.*

PAT-A-PAN

Bernard de la Monnoye   Burgundian Carol (France)

♩ = 138

mf Dm ... A(7) Dm

1. Wil - lie, take your lit - tle drum, Rob - in, bring your flute and
2. Men of old in an - cient days Gave the King of Kings their
3. God and man are now as one, They com-bine as flute and

A(7) ... Dm

come! ⎫
praise! ⎬ Play - ing on the flute and drum, Tu - re - lu - re - lu, pat - a - pat - a -
drum. ⎭

A7 ... Dm A7 Dm A7 *f* Dm

pan, Play - ing on the flute and drum, ⎧ We will cel - e - brate this day!
                                        ⎨ Let us cel - e - brate as they!
                                        ⎩ Sing and dance for joy this day!

Autoharp, strum N
Guitar, strum 22
Piano, accompaniment pattern XI

French words

1. Guillaume prends ton tambourin,
   Toi, prends ta flûte, Robin;
   Au son de ces instruments,
   Tu-re-lu-re-lu, pat-a-pat-a-pan,
   Au son de ces instruments,
   Je dirai Noël gaîment.

2. C'était la mode autrefois
   De louer le Roi des rois,
   Au son de ces instruments,
   Tu-re-lu-re-lu, pat-a-pat-a-pan,
   Au son de ces instruments,
   Il nous en faut faire autant.

3. L'homme et Dieu sont plus d'accord
   Que la flûte et le tambour.
   Au son de ces instruments,
   Tu-re-lu-re-lu, pat-a-pat-a-pan,
   Au son de ces instruments,
   Chantons, dansons, sautons en.

PEACE LIKE A RIVER

Traditional American Song

Autoharp (15-bar), harp strum
Piano, accompaniment pattern XVII

Descant

Verse 2: Joy, fountain . . .
Verse 3: Love, ocean . . .

PIZZA, PIZZA, DADDY-O!

African American Game Song

With spirit (♩ = 84)

Call *Response* *Call*

___ ___ has a boy - friend. *Piz - za, piz - za, dad - dy - O!*
(girl's name)   1   2   3   4   5

1. How'd yah know it?
2. 'Cause she told me.
3. What she call him?
(boy's name) 4. Calls him ___ ___ .
5. Let' - sa sew it.
6. Let' - sa jerk it.
7. Let' - sa swim it.
8. Let' - sa dive it.
9. Let' - sa twist it.
10. Let' - sa spin it.
11. Let' - sa rope it.
12. Let' - sa stoop it.
13. Let' - sa end it.

Response for verses 1–12   *Response for verse 13*

Piz - za, piz - za, dad - dy - O!   *End it, end ___ it, dad - dy O!*

Formation

Players stand in a circle facing the center. One player stands in the center.

Game

Players begin by singing the name of the player in the center. The center player then leads the thirteen calls and motions.

On "Pizza, pizza, daddy-o!" all players sing and perform a five-beat foot pattern:

Beat 1 ("piz"):   Jump, landing with feet apart.

Beat 2 ("za"):   Jump, landing with right foot crossed in front of left.

Beat 3 ("pizza"):   Jump, landing with feet apart.

Beat 4 ("dad"):   Jump, landing with left foot crossed in front of right.

Beat 5 ("O"):   Jump, landing with feet together.

The song stops whenever the center player sings "let's end it." The center player then spins in a circle with eyes closed, arm and pointer finger extended. She stops, her finger identifying the next center player.

PLANTING RICE

Philippine Folk Song

With movement (♩ = 76)

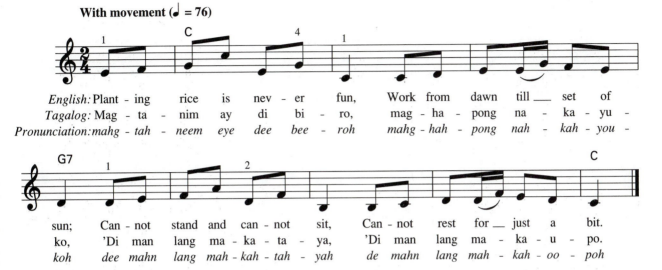

English: Plant - ing rice is nev - er fun, Work from dawn till __ set of
Tagalog: Mag - ta - nim ay di bi - ro, mag - ha - pong na - ka - yu -
Pronunciation: mahg - tah - neem eye dee bee - roh mahg - hah - pong nah - kah - you -

sun; Can - not stand and can - not sit, Can - not rest for __ just a bit.
ko, 'Di man lang ma - ka - ta - ya, 'Di man lang ma - ka - u - po.
koh dee mahn lang mah - kah - tah - yah de mahn lang mah - kah - oo - poh

Autoharp, strum E
Piano, accompaniment pattern III

Formation

Dancers form a circle, facing clockwise. The left arm is extended outward from the body in a half circle, as if cradling a basket of rice seedlings.

Dance steps

The dancer begins with weight on the left foot, ready to move clockwise. Four quick steps RLRL (♩♩♩♩) begin on the upbeat of the song. The quick steps alternate with one slow step R (♩) on the downbeat of each measure.

Arm movements

The dance pantomimes taking rice seedlings from a basket and planting them in the ground. During the quick steps, the right hand gathers seedlings from the basket. The dancer bends at the waist on the long step, extending the right arm downward toward the center of the circle (as if planting the seedlings).

POP, GOES THE WEASEL

English Singing Game

Autoharp (15-bar), strum B

Perform the dance on page 206 along with "Pop, Goes the Weasel."

This dance tune from seventeenth-century England refers to a tool used by London tailors called a "weasel." In hard times, a tailor might pawn ("pop") his weasel to obtain money.

PRECIOUS FRIENDS

Pete Seeger
(United States, b.1919)

Just when I thought _____ all was lost _____ you changed my mind. _____ You gave me hope, not just the old soft soap, You showed that we could learn to share in time. You and I and ev – 'ry-bod – y, I'll keep plug – gin' __ on, _____ Your face will shine _____ so sweet and fair, _____ And when we sing an – oth – er lit – tle sing – a – long _ song. __ We hope that, pre – cious

friends, you will be ___ there, ___ Sing - in' in har - mo-ny,

Pre - cious friends, you will be ___ there. ___

Piano, accompaniment pattern XV

RAINBOW SISTER
(Hong Tsai Me Me)

English words adapted
by Patricia Hackett

Chinese Folk Song

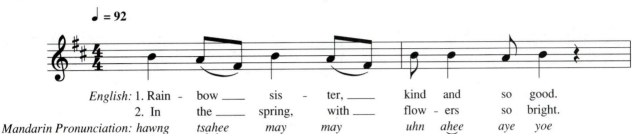

English: 1. Rain - bow ____ sis - ter, ____ kind and so good.
         2. In the ____ spring, with ____ flow - ers so bright.
Mandarin Pronunciation: hawng tsahee may may uhn ahee aye yoe

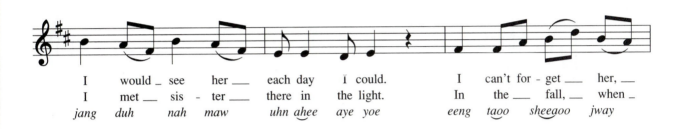

I would _ see her ____ each day I could. I can't for - get ____ her, ____
I met _ sis - ter ____ there in the light. In the ____ fall, ____ when _
jang duh nah maw uhn ahee aye yoe eeng taoo sheeaoo jway

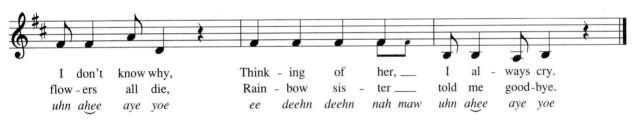

I don't know why, Think - ing of her, ____ I al - ways cry.
flow - ers all die, Rain - bow sis - ter ____ told me good-bye.
uhn ahee aye yoe ee deehn deehn nah maw uhn ahee aye yoe

English lyrics used by permission of The McGraw–Hill Companies,
from *Share the Music,* Grade 5. Copyright © 1995.

Play these patterns on a xylophone with "Rainbow Sister." Create another pattern for wood block.

"Rainbow Sister" is a well-known Chinese folk song about a girl named Hong Tsai. The English words express the familiar tale of a boy longing for his girlfriend ("sister"), who has said goodbye to him.

Perform a Chinese ribbon dance with "Rainbow Sister." Tack a three-foot-long strip of fabric onto the end of a twelve-inch stick. Use movement ideas from the illustrations that follow. Have changes of movement correspond to the phrases in "Rainbow Sister." Or replace sticks with scarves and create a scarf dance. (Scarf dancers are said to portray heavenly beings scattering flowers.)

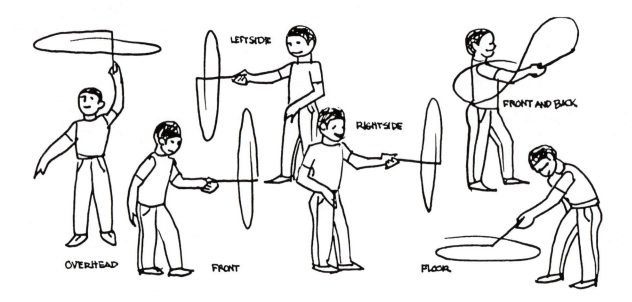

OVERHEAD FRONT LEFT SIDE RIGHT SIDE FRONT AND BACK FLOOR

Rajasthan Folk Melody

Quickly (♩ = 116–120)

"Rajasthan Folk Melody" is from Rajasthan, a state in northwest India, where it is played on the shahnai. The shahnai is a double-reed instrument about two feet long, made of wood, and has a flaring metal bell at the end. It may be descended from a Persian instrument and is possibly a thousand years old. In the Mogul period (sixteenth–eighteenth centuries), the shahnai was used along with kettledrums and other instruments and was played several times daily at palaces and at the tombs of holy men. Today the shahnai is still played along with small kettledrums (also of Persian origin) and is a popular instrument in folk dance and theater, for wedding music, at mosques, temples, tombs, and at folklore shows and concerts.

India is a huge country with one of the oldest civilizations in the world. From the beginning, music has been a part of that culture. All kinds of music (and dance) are found: classical, religious, folk, and popular. The music of north India (Hindustani) is different from that of south India (Carnatic), but their origins are similar. The two styles share the same main elements of Indian music: drone, melody, rhythm, and improvisation. Music and religion are linked, because music has long been associated with devotion and the temple. Beginning in the fourteenth century, classical Hindustani music was supported by Muslim courts and the upper class. A tremendous variety of instruments are found, including many plucked strings (sitar, sarod, vīnā, tambura), drums (tabla, mridangam, tavil), and winds (bansuri, shahnai, nagaswaram). The European violin is used in south India.

RECREATION OF THE BALARI WOMEN

West African Folk Song
(Republic of the Congo)

Hay yah wil lee, yah koo lahm bee lahm bway, Way

kihn zoo pway kwan jee, Yah koo lahm bee lahm bway.

     The ancient musical traditions of Africa endure. South of the Sahara, music remains an important social and personal expression. In traditional African life, music marked the important rites of passage of an individual: birth, puberty, marriage, and death. For these occasions, the professional musician was paid for services. At other times, cohesive, blended voices of a group accompanied communal work efforts such as cultivating, harvesting, and canoeing. In these songs, everyone conformed to an established, orderly plan of work and singing. Music was important in religious celebrations and in work, but also for sheer entertainment.

     This song is from the Republic of the Congo, an equatorial state that borders western Zaire along the Congo and Ubangi rivers. The Balari people live in the southwestern region above Brazzaville, the capital city. A young wife complains in this low-pitched, good-natured song that she does not have enough utensils to cook properly. Singing without musical instruments, she provides her own accompaniment of body sounds: hand clapping or patting, slapping of thighs or upper arms, or finger snapping. Using body percussion while you sing, keep a steady beat ♩ until you become agile enough to try ♪♪ or ♬♬.

RIDING IN THE BUGGY

American Folk Song

♩ = 80–84

C **G7**

1. Rid-ing in the bug-gy, Miss Ma - ry Ann, Miss Ma - ry Ann, Miss
2. I ___ got a house _ in Bal - ti - more, ___ Bal - ti - more, ___

C **G7** **C**

Ma - ry Ann, Rid-ing in the bug-gy, Miss Ma - ry Ann, She's a long ways from home.
Bal - ti - more, I ___ got a house _ in Bal - ti - more, And it's six sto - ries tall.

Refrain

F **C**

Who waits for me? Who waits for me?

G7 **C**

Who waits for me, my la - dy, Who waits for me?

Autoharp, strum A
Piano, accompaniment pattern XI

RITSCH, RATSCH

Swedish Folk Song

Quickly (♩ = 84)

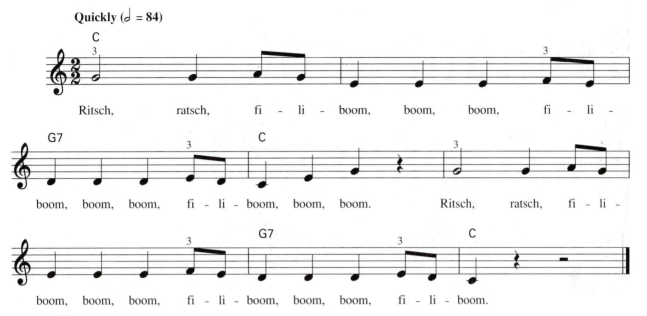

Ritsch, ratsch, fi – li – boom, boom, boom, fi – li –

boom, boom, boom, fi – li – boom, boom, boom. Ritsch, ratsch, fi – li –

boom, boom, boom, fi – li – boom, boom, boom, fi – li – boom.

Auotharp, banjo strum
Piano, accompaniment pattern XI

ROCK-PASSING SONG

West African Play Song
(Ghana)

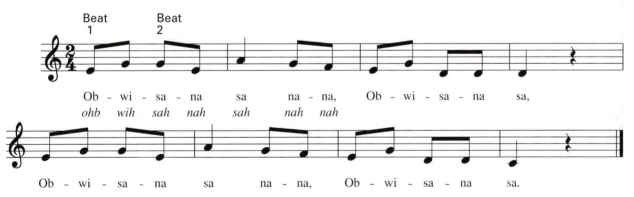

Beat 1 Beat 2

Ob – wi – sa – na sa na – na, Ob – wi – sa – na sa,
ohb wih sah nah sah nah nah

Ob – wi – sa – na sa na – na, Ob – wi – sa – na sa.

Meaning

Oh, Gramma, I just hurt my finger on a rock.

Formation

Players sit in a circle, each holding a pebble.

Game

Players sing during the game. Use the right hand to pass the pebble counterclockwise and to pick it up. On beat 1, place the pebble in front of the player on the right. On beat 2, pick up the pebble that is now in front of each player. Alternate these two movements throughout the song.

On the last note of the song there should be a pebble in front of each player. Any player who has no pebble, or has several, must leave the game circle.

ROCKY MOUNTAIN

American Folk Song

♩ = 80

E

1., 2. Rock - y moun - tain, rock - y moun - tain, Rock - y moun - tain {high, sky,

(B7)   **E**

When you reach that rock - y moun - tain, {Hang your head and cry. Spread your wings and fly.

Refrain   **B7**

Do, do, do, do, Do re - mem - ber me,

E   **(B7)**   **E**

Do, do, do, do, Do, re - mem - ber me.

Guitar, strum 7

ROLL OVER

American Singing Game

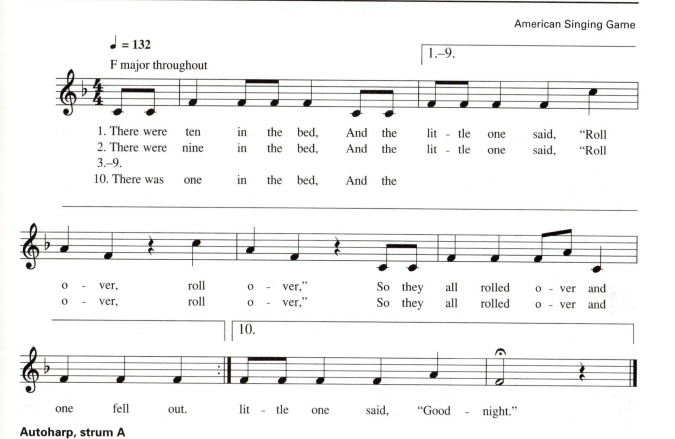

♩ = 132

F major throughout

1.–9.

1. There were ten in the bed, And the lit – tle one said, "Roll
2. There were nine in the bed, And the lit – tle one said, "Roll
3.–9.
10. There was one in the bed, And the

o – ver, roll o – ver," So they all rolled o – ver and
o – ver, roll o – ver," So they all rolled o – ver and

10.

one fell out. lit – tle one said, "Good – night."

Autoharp, strum A
Guitar, strum 2

Formation

Ten players stand side by side in a line.

Game

Players sing during the game. On the words "roll over," players rotate their forearms one over the other. On "they all rolled over," each player turns around in place, and the child on the right end of the line falls down (or kneels). The same actions are repeated nine times until only one player remains standing during verse 10. This player sings a solo "Good night" and the game ends.

RONDE
(from *The Third Little Music Book,* 1551)

Anonymous
Compiled by Tylman Susato
(born Cologne? ca. 1500;
died Antwerp? ca. 1561)

Soprano recorder

The Renaissance extended from about 1420 to about 1600 and brought a new emphasis on the human being. This new humanism was a part of a general move toward the secular, as opposed to the sacred. It was the age of scientists (Copernicus, Galileo) and of explorers (Cortez, Balboa, Magellan, Marco Polo). It produced a unique group of artistic giants, including painters and sculptors such as Michelangelo, Leonardo da Vinci, and Raphael. These artists applied the newly invented system known as perspective, which gave their works a sense of depth. Similarly, Renaissance composers such as Palestrina and Gabrieli gave their music a kind of audible depth by creating several harmony parts (voices) that were equal and in careful relation to each other. This was the beginning of harmony as we now know it in Western European art music. Music printing began in 1473 and greatly aided the growth of music. Sacred music (the Mass and the motet) was coming to the end of a long period of development. A large number of different wind instruments (including the recorder) were built and played in sets (consorts). Music for specifically designated instruments was performed everywhere. Social dancing was extremely popular, and music such as "Ronde" used the steady, predictable rhythms that were common by the end of the Renaissance.

'ROUND AND 'ROUND

West Indian Singing Game

English: 'Round and 'round we must go, Bom, ma - ka - le - li,* chee, cheem, bom.
Pronunciation: *bom mah-kah-lay - lee chee cheem bom*

(fill in child's name)

Down | Miss
Mis–ter | — — you must go, Bom, ma - ka - le - li, chee, cheem, bom.
bom mah-kah lay - lee chee cheem bom

* Makaleli *is an African game of self-defense performed with sticks and stylized moves.*

Autoharp, strum C

Formation

Boys and girls stand in a circle, holding hands, with one player in the middle.

Game

Players sing and circle clockwise. On "Down, Miss _____," the center player touches a child in the circle on the head while singing the child's name. The player who was touched then crouches down while continuing to move with the rest. The game continues until all players are "down."

ROW, ROW, ROW YOUR BOAT

Traditional Round

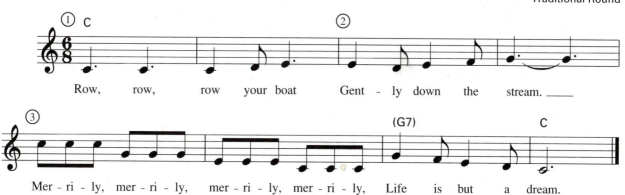

Row, row, row your boat Gent - ly down the stream. ____

Mer - ri - ly, mer - ri - ly, mer - ri - ly, mer - ri - ly, Life is but a dream.

Autoharp, strum B

ROYAL GARDEN BLUES

Clarence Williams
(United States, 1893–1965)
Spencer Williams
(United States, 1889–1965)

1. Hon, don't you hear that trom-bone moan?__ Just lis-ten to that
2. That weep-in' mel-an-cho-ly strain, __ Say, but it's sooth-in'

sax-o-phone, _ Gee, hear that clar-i-net and flute, _
to the brain. _ Just wan-na get right up and dance, _

Cor - net a-jazz-in' with a mute, __ Makes . me just throw my-
Don't care, I'll take most an-y chance, _ No o-ther blues I'd

self a-way, __ When I hear 'em play.
care to choose, _ But Roy-al Gar-den blues.

Autoharp, improvise a strum
Piano, accompaniment pattern XV

In 1924 the legendary Leon "Bix" Beiderbecke (United States, 1903–1931) recorded "Royal Garden Blues" with the Wolverines. Bix was on cornet, backed by five other musicians on trombone, clarinet, banjo, drums, and piano. This was Chicago-style jazz: music that had moved upriver from New Orleans after Storyville, the infamous red-light district, was shut down in 1917. Bix grew up listening to early recordings by the Original Dixieland Jass Band, little dreaming that he would one day sit in with the greats: King Oliver, Louis Armstrong, and Jimmie Noone. Theirs was "hot" jazz: music full of short phrases and changing harmonies as in "Royal Garden Blues" (but with the rhythms never played as straight as they are written above). Beiderbecke's distinctive cornet tone was the result of self-taught fingerings that helped create a lyrical style of improvisation. Bix died a young man of 28, admired and imitated by jazzmen, but appreciated by only a handful of listeners. Fortunately, his genius has endured through the magic of recordings that delight today's jazz fans.

SAIL AWAY, LADIES

American Play-Party Song

1. Ain't no use to sit and cry,
2. I've got a home in Ten - nes - see,
3. Ever I get my new house done,
4. Come a-long boys and go with me,

Sail a - way, la - dies, sail a - way.

You'll be an an - gel bye and bye,
That's the _ place I wan - na be,
I'll give the old one to my son,
We'll go _ down to Ten - nes - see,

Sail a - way, la - dies, sail a - way.

Refrain

Don't you rock 'im, die - dy - o,
Don't you rock 'im, die - dy - o,
Don't you rock _ 'im, die - dy - o,
Don't you rock 'im, die - dy - o.

Autoharp (15-bar), banjo strum
Guitar, strum 5

SAKURA
(Cherry Blossoms)

English words by
Patricia Hackett

Japanese Folk Song

♩ = 72

English: Sa - ku - ra,   sa - ku - ra,   Cher - ry blos - soms   fill   the __ sky,
Japanese: Sa - ku - ra,   sa - ku - ra,   Ya - yo - i - no   so - ra - wa
Pronunciation: sah - koo - rah   sah - koo - rah   yah - yoh - ee noh   soh - rah - wah

Pet - als drift - ing   ev - 'ry - where.   Are they mist or   are they _ cloud? Love - ly blos - soms
Mi - wa - ta - su   ka - gi - ri.   Ka - su - mi - ka   ku - mo - ka,   Ni - o - i - zo
mee - wah - tah - soo   kah - gee - ree   kah - soo - mee - kah   koo - moh - kah   nee - oh - ee - zoh

scent the _ breeze.   Sa - ku - ra,   sa - ku - ra,   Let's all   go __ to see.
i - zu - ru   i - za - ya,   i - za - ya   mi ni   yu - ka - n.
ee - zoo - roo   ee - zah - yah   ee - zah - yah   mee nee   yoo - kah - n

Play one of the following accompaniments throughout "Sakura."

250

Formation

The following movements can be performed while seated or standing.

Starting position

Palms together in a prayerlike position in front of the chest.

Movements

All movements should be large, flowing, and graceful.

Measure 1: Raise the right arm overhead in a circular movement up and to the right, stopping just above the shoulder level, palm up. The left hand remains at chest level.

Measure 2: Raise the left arm overhead in a circular movement up and to the left, stopping just above the shoulder level, palm up. The right hand remains just above shoulder level, palm up.

Measure 3: Bring palms quickly together in front of the chest. Then repeat the measure 1 movement.

Measure 4: Repeat the measure 2 movement.

Measure 5: Bring arms together overhead, forming a large circle.

Measure 6: Hold the measure 5 position.

Measure 7: Hold both arms to the right side, with the right arm slightly higher. Hold arms vertically, away from the body. Turn head to the *left*.

Measure 8: Hold the measure 7 position.

Measure 9: Hold both arms to the left side, with the left arm slightly higher. Hold palms vertically, away from the body. Turn head to the *right*.

Measure 10: Hold the measure 9 position.

Measure 11: Repeat the measure 1 movement,

Measure 12: Repeat the measure 2 movement.

Measure 13: Repeat the measure 1 movement.

Measure 14. Repeat the measure 2 movement.

A refined, highly cultivated art music flowered in Japan, with its roots in ancient court and Buddhist ritual music. At the same time, a lively stream of folk music served the people, accompanying their work, dance, and local ceremonies. Although indigenous music flourished during the isolation of the Edo period (1615–1868), the twentieth-century push toward modernization brought with it the influence of Western music. In the wake of World War II, the practice of traditional music and arts was retained mostly by the elderly or more conservative elements of society. Resurgent nationalism is reversing this trend, but even now, traditional music is heard less often on the media than at the business dinner. There, an elderly executive may sing a song such as "Sakura" for the pleasure of his guests.

SALLY, GO 'ROUND THE SUN

Version 1

rightAmerican Folk Song

Autoharp, strum each downbeat

Version 2

Collected by John Lomax
in Atmore, Alabama (1934)

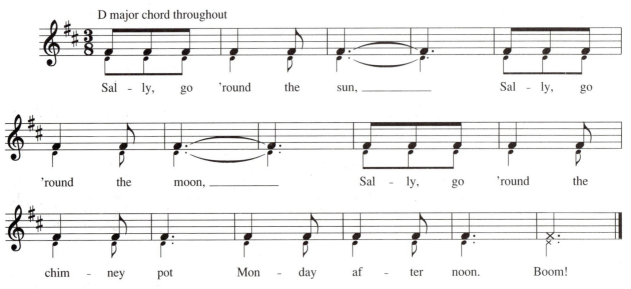

Autoharp (15-bar), strum each downbeat
Guitar, strum each downbeat

Formation: Players form a circle and join hands.

Game: Players walk to the right while singing the song. On "boom," they do a little jump and change direction. Hands remain joined. On the next repetition of the song, players circle left.

When version 1 is sung as a round, form two concentric circles. Each circle moves in a different direction. The circle performing part 2 of the round starts moving after four measures.

SANDY LAND

American Play-Party Song

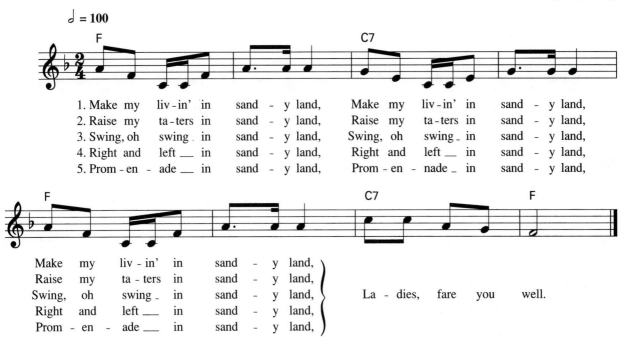

♩ = 100

1. Make my liv-in' in sand - y land, Make my liv-in' in sand - y land,
2. Raise my ta-ters in sand - y land, Raise my ta-ters in sand - y land,
3. Swing, oh swing in sand - y land, Swing, oh swing in sand - y land,
4. Right and left in sand - y land, Right and left in sand - y land,
5. Prom - en - ade in sand - y land, Prom - en - nade in sand - y land,

Make my liv - in' in sand - y land,
Raise my ta - ters in sand - y land,
Swing, oh swing in sand - y land,   La - dies, fare you well.
Right and left in sand - y land,
Prom - en - ade in sand - y land,

Autoharp, banjo strum
Piano accomapaniment pattern IV

Formation

Players choose a partner and form a single circle. Girls are on the right so that players alternate boy, girl, boy, girl, and so forth. All join hands.

Dance

Verse 1: All walk to the left.

Verse 2: All walk to the right.

Verse 3: Partners swing, linking right arms, and skip in a small clockwise circle.

Verse 4: Partners face each other and begin grand right and left. (In grand right and left, players clasp right hands and quickly pass their partner on the right. Then they clasp left hands with the next dancer and pass on the left, alternating right and left hands throughout.) Repeat verse 4 until original partners meet again.

Verse 5: All promenade around the circle with girls on the boys' left.

SARASPONDA

Sa - ra - spon - da, sa - ra - spon - da, sa - ra - spon - da, ret, set, set. Sa - ra -

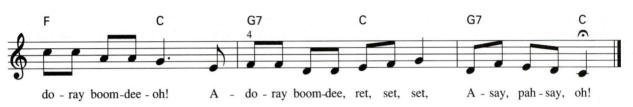

spon - da, sa - ra - spon - da, sa - ra - spon - da, ret, set, set. A - do - ray - oh! A -

do - ray boom-dee - oh! A - do - ray boom-dee, ret, set, set, A - say, pah - say, oh!

Piano, accompaniment pattern XVI

Sing throughout as an ostinato, or as an introduction:

Boom-da, boom-da, boom-da, boom-dah.

The words of "Sarasponda" imitate the sounds of a spinning wheel. The turning wheel, posts, and spools can make rhythmic sounds such as "ret, set, set."

SATURDAY NIGHT

West African Song
(Nigeria)

𝅘𝅥 = 100

Ev - 'ry - bod - y loves Sat - ur - day night. _____
Ga Pronunciation: maw - feeah moe - nee smaw haw beh keh _____

Ev - 'ry - bod - y loves Sat - ur - day night. _____
maw - feeah moe - nee smaw haw beh keh

Ev - 'ry - bod - y,
maw - feeah moe - nee

ev - 'ry - bod - y,
maw - feeah moe - nee

Ev - 'ry - bod - y,
maw - feeah moe - nee

ev - 'ry - bod - y,
maw - feeah moe - nee

Ev - 'ry - bod - y loves Sat - ur - day night. _____
maw - feeah moe - nee smaw haw beh keh

Autoharp, strum each downbeat
Piano, accompaniment pattern V (play solid chords)

Sing "Saturday Night" in other languages.

Spanish

C   G7   C
A todos   les   gusta   la   noche   del   sábado
ah toe-thoes layss goo-stah lah noe-chay dayl sah-bah-doe

French

C   G7   C
Tout le   monde   aime   samedi   soir
too leh   mawnd   ehm   sah-meh-dee   swahr

German

C   G7   C
Alle   haben   Sonnabend   gern
ah-leh   hah-behn   sone-aahn-bend   gairn

Japanese

C   G7   C
Doyobi   no   yoru   minna   suki
doh-yoe-bee noh yoe-ru mee-nah soo-kee

255

SAUK-FOX PIPE DANCE SONG

Native American Song
Transcribed by Patricia Hackett

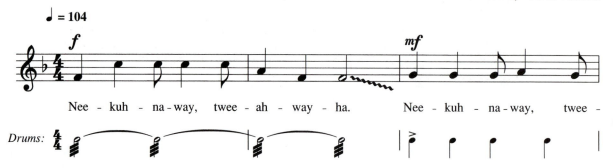

Nee - kuh - na - way, twee - ah - way - ha. Nee - kuh - na - way, twee -

ah - way - ha, Nee - kuh - na - way, twee - ah - way - ha, hay, yea,

Nee - kuh - na - way, twee - ah - way - ha, Nee - kuh - na - way, twee - ah - way - hah.

Perform the first two measures of this song at a moderate tempo (♩ = 104) on each sing-through. At measure 3, gradually increase the tempo during the second sing-through, ending at ♩ = 152. Similarly increase the tempo during the third sing-through, finally reaching ♩ = 200. (Sauk-Fox singers perform the final repetition on a single breath.)

Translation

My friend (twee-ah-way-ha) takes care of horses' feet (nee-kuh-na-way)

Formation

Two or three dancers are encircled by spectators. A group of drummers sits around a drum placed just outside the circle. Drummers sing and play; dancers do not sing.

Dance

During the drum roll, the dancers stand in place and quiver, swaying the torso. On the steady beats (measures 3–11), dancers do the war dance, using the traditional toe-heel step. As they dance, they hold the bowl of the calumet (peace) pipe in one hand, stem outward. They offer it (symbolically) to the various spectators in the circle but do not actually give away the pipe.

"Sauk-Fox Pipe Dance Song" is from the repertoire of a Sauk-Fox/Tonkawa tribal singer. Formerly chair of Native American Studies at San Francisco State University, he has been an active singer at powwows and cultural fairs throughout the western states and Oklahoma, where he sang with the famous Ponca singers. He describes the quivering movements of this pipe dance as mimicking the ruffled grouse of the prairie. The calumet, a long, ceremonial pipe, is symbolically offered to spectators (by dancers) to celebrate peace.

The Sauk ("SAK") and Fox people lived along the Mississippi north of St. Louis, Missouri. Both groups originated elsewhere, but they formed a close alliance after hostile encounters with the French and with competing Native American groups. In 1804 they were forced by the American government to cede their tribal lands. This resulted in a bitter struggle, led—but ultimately lost—by their famous chief, Black Hawk (1767–1838).

SCARBOROUGH FAIR

English Ballad

Moderately

Am · C · G(E) · Am

1. Are you go - ing to Scar - bo-rough Fair? _____
2. Tell her to make me a cam - bric shirt, _____
3. Tell her to wash it in yon - der dry well, _____
4. Tell her to hang it on yon - der thorn, _____
5. Tell her to find me an a - cre of land, _____

C · Am · D · Am

Pars - ley, sage, rose - mar - y, and thyme. _____

Oh,
With -
Where
Which
Be -

C · G

send my love ___ to one who lives there, _____ For
out a nee - dle or stitch - es that show, _____ And
wa - ter ne'er sprang, _ nor rain - drops fell, _____ And
never bore blos - som since Ad - am was born, _____ And
tween the sea ___ foam and the sea sand, _____ Or

Am · Dm · F(Em) · (G) · Am

once she was a true love of mine. _____
2, 3, 4: she shall be a true love of mine. _____
5: nev - er be a true love of mine. _____

Autoharp (15-bar), strum J
Piano, accompany using chord roots

"Scarborough Fair" was popularized by contemporary American minstrels—professional singers and instrumentalists. In its purest form, however, the ballad is a story sung by an unaccompanied amateur. The soloist stretches out syllables in the melody or leaves irregular spaces to think of what comes next. Early American balladeers often sang "out of tune" or in archaic scales; instruments were unavailable or inappropriate. Later, when singers played instruments, they chose unfretted banjos, fiddles, or dulcimers. They were of variable pitch, and the singer was still free to "bend" the melody or rhythm, as in old-style balladry. The use of the fretted guitar—popular in this country only since the late 1920s—usually restricts the freedom of the ballad singer. The minstrel of today, however, is often an accomplished instrumentalist.

THE SEA SERPENT
(La Víbora)

English words by
Patricia Hackett

Central American Singing Game

♩ = 96

English: Oh, the sea __ ser-pent, sea __ ser-pent from the sea, Come and fol - low,
Spanish: A la ví-bo-ra, la ví-bo-ra, la de la mar, por a - quí pue -
Pronunciation: ah lah vee-boh-rah lah vee-boh-rah lah day lah mar pour ah - key pway -

fol - low me. Un - der the arch - way run and run right a - long, as the
den pa - sar, Los de a de - lan - te cor - ren mu - cho y los de a -
dehn pah - sahr lohs dayzyah day - lahn - tay coer - rehn moo - cho ee lohs day ah -

oth - ers come be - hind. Trás, trás, trás, Cam - pa - ni - ta
trás se que - da - rán. Trás, trás, trás. Cam - pa - ni - ta
trahs say kay - dah - rahn trahs trahs trahs cahm - pah-nee - tah

lift the arch, let the oth - ers pass. _____ An - gel, or the
de o - ro, de - ja - me pa - sar. _____ Con to - dos mis
deh oh - roh day - hah-may pah - sahr cohn toh-dohs mees

de - - vil, who will be the last? _____
hi - - jos me - nos el de a - - tras.
ee - - hos meh - nohs ehl day ah - - trahs

Autoharp, strum C
Piano, accompany using chord roots

Literal translation

Sea serpent, pass through here. The ones in front run, the others follow behind.
Little golden bell, let us all go through—except the last one!

259

"The Sea Serpent" game from Nicaragua is similar to the "London Bridge" game. Two players form a bridge (arch) with their arms; one player represents an angel, and the other represents a devil. Other players walk in line under the bridge, singing as they move. On the words "tras, tras, tras," the bridge is lowered over the player underneath; arms around their captive, the players sway gently three times from side to side. On "campanita," the captive is released and the game continues. On "el de atras," the bridge is lowered again, capturing a player. After a whispered conference with the "bridge people," the captive chooses either angel or devil and then goes to stand behind that player. The game continues until all players are behind one of the bridge people. A tug-of-war between the two sides ends the game and determines the winning side.

"The Sea Serpent" is sung everywhere in Central America. In Mexico, the "bridge players" represent a bell, and players sing "pam, pam, pam" (instead of "tras, tras, tras"). The syllable "pam" imitates the sound of the campanita *("little bell").*

SEMINOLE DUCK DANCE

Native American Song
(Florida)
Transcribed by Patricia Hackett

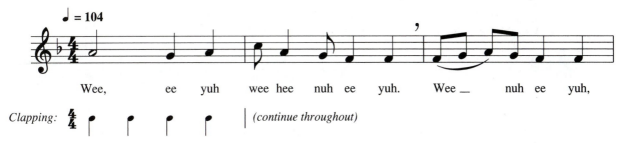

Wee, ee yuh wee hee nuh ee yuh. Wee ___ nuh ee yuh,

Clapping: *(continue throughout)*

wee hee nuh ee yuh. Wee hee nuh ee yuh, wee hee nuh ee yuh.

Formation

Everyone sings the song, clapping a quarter-note beat, while standing or sitting in place. As the song is repeated, the dance leader moves randomly among the spectators and soon joins hands with one individual. The selected person dances (and sings) along with the leader and selects a third person to join hands and join the line. This process continues until everyone is part of a serpentine line of singing dancers.

Dance

Beginning with the right foot, dancers slide feet forward along the floor, alternating right, left, right. This movement continues throughout.

"Duck Dance" is sometimes the first dance or "mixer" at a powwow. A master of ceremonies typically begins the song and acts as dance leader.

SHABAT, SHALOM
(Song for the Sabbath)

Hebrew Song

♩ = 80

Hebrew: Sha-bat, sha - lom, sha-bat, sha - lom, sha-bat, sha - lom, sha-bat, sha -
Pronunciation: shah-baht shah - lohm

lom, sha - lom! Sha-bat, sha - bat, sha-bat, sha - lom. Sha-bat, sha -

lom, sha-bat, sha - lom, Sha-bat, sha - bat, sha-bat, sha - bat, sha - lom.

Autoharp, strum C
Piano, accompaniment pattern II

SHAKE MY SILLIES OUT

Words and music by Raffi and
Bert and Bonnie Simpson

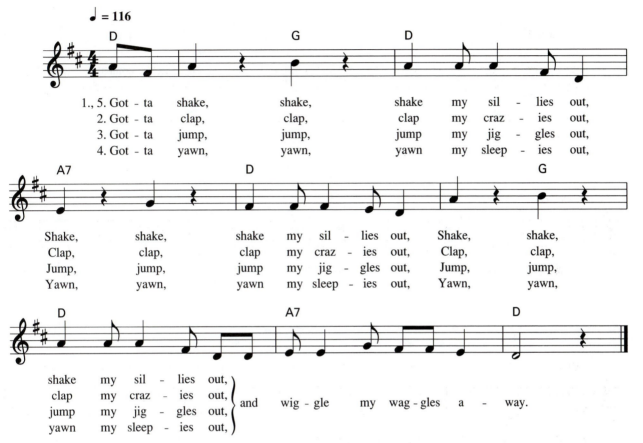

1., 5. Got-ta shake, shake, shake my sil-lies out,
2. Got-ta clap, clap, clap my craz-ies out,
3. Got-ta jump, jump, jump my jig-gles out,
4. Got-ta yawn, yawn, yawn my sleep-ies out,

Shake, shake, shake my sil-lies out, Shake, shake,
Clap, clap, clap my craz-ies out, Clap, clap,
Jump, jump, jump my jig-gles out, Jump, jump,
Yawn, yawn, yawn my sleep-ies out, Yawn, yawn,

shake my sil-lies out,
clap my craz-ies out, } and wig-gle my wag-gles a-way.
jump my jig-gles out,
yawn my sleep-ies out,

Autoharp (15-bar), use a different strum (and pick) for different verses

SHE'LL BE COMIN' 'ROUND THE MOUNTAIN

Southern Mountain Song

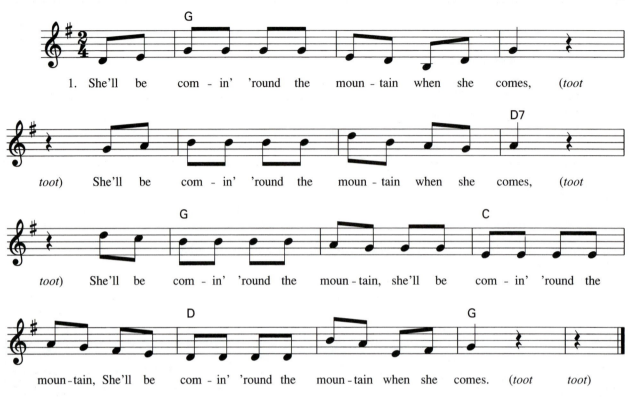

1. She'll be com-in' 'round the moun-tain when she comes, *(toot toot)* She'll be com-in' 'round the moun-tain when she comes, *(toot toot)* She'll be com-in' 'round the moun-tain, she'll be com-in' 'round the moun-tain, She'll be com-in' 'round the moun-tain when she comes. *(toot toot)*

Autoharp, strum C
Piano, accompaniment pattern IV

2. She'll be driving six white horses
   when she comes . . . (whoa back, toot, toot)

3. Oh, we'll all go out to meet her,
   when she comes . . . (hi there, whoa back, toot, toot)

4. Oh, we'll all have chicken and dumplings
   when the she comes . . . (yum, yum, hi there, whoa back, toot, toot)

5. She will have to sleep with Grandma
   when she comes (*snoring sound,* yum, yum, hi there, whoa back, toot, toot)

Perform appropriate sounds (with actions) during the rests in the melody. (See verse 1.)

At the end of each verse, repeat the sounds and actions of previous verses in reverse order.

SHOES FOR BABY JESUS
(Zapatos para el Niño Jesús)

English words by
Patricia Hackett

Hispanic Christmas Song
Transcribed by Patricia Hackett

Smoothly (♩ = 63–66)

English:	God's	ti - ny	child	is	so	poor __	but __	fair,
Spanish:	1. El	Ni - ño	Dios	es	tan	po - - -		bre,
Pronunciation:	ehl	nee - nyoh	deeohs	ess	tahn	poh - - -		bray

See	how	He	lies	in	a	sta - ble __	bare;	Three	lit - tle
Que	no	tie - ne	ni	cu - ni - - ta;				Tres	an - gel -
kay	noh tee–eh - nay	nee coo - nee - - tah						trayss	ahng - hel -

an - gels have	come __	to __	care,		Now	they will	build	Him	a
li - tos del	cie - -	lo,			La	van a ha -	cer	de	pa -
lee - tohs dehl	cee–aye - -	loh			lah	vahn ah -	sair	day	pah -

Faster (♩ = 88–92)

⑰

cra - - dle __	fair.		Man - y	kings	ar - rive	to
ji - - - ta.			El	mo - re - no	po - ne
hee - - - tah			ehl	moh - ray - noh	poh - nay

praise	Him __	bear-ing	shoes	so	rich	and	new,	But the	cho - sen	gift	for
u - na __		y el __	ru - bio	po - ne	tres,			Y el mas	chi - co	se	tro -
oo - nah		ee ehl	rroo - byoh	poh - nay	trayss			ee ehl mahs	chee - coh	say	troh -

Much faster (♩ = 104–108)

Em

Je - sus, _____ is a hum - ble wood - en shoe.
pie - sa pu - es trae lo me - nos diez.
pyaye - sah poo-ehss try loh may - nohs dee ehz

Sleep, ti - ny
Po - nen y
poh - nehn ee

B7

king, rest your head and dream some more,
po - nen y vuel - ben a po - ner.
poh - nehn ee voo—ehl - behn ah poh - nehr

Now the
Y ya
ee yah

Em

moon is in the heav'n, and the sun is at the door.
tie ne su cu - ni - ta El Ni - ño de Be - lén.
tee ehn aye soo coo - nee - tah ehl nee - nyoh day bay - lehn

Am   Em   B7   Em

Mm. _____

Guitar: 2/4 strum pattern

B ↑ ↓ ↑ ↓ ↑ | B ↑ ↓ ↑ ↓ ↑ | B ↑ ↓ ↑ ↓ ↑ | B ↑ ↓ ↑ ↓ ↑

Guitar, strum 6 at beginning of song. At measure 17, change to the strum shown under the last line of humming.

The Spanish version of "Shoes for Baby Jesus" consists of three verses. They are condensed above into a single English verse in which each section of sixteen measures corresponds to one Spanish verse. (All three Spanish verses may be found in earlier editions of this book.)

SHOO, FLY

Billy Reeves

Frank Campbell

With a strong beat

Shoo, fly, don't both - er me, Shoo, fly, don't both - er me.

Shoo, fly, don't both - er me, For I be - long to some - bod - y.

1. I feel, I feel, I feel, I feel like a morn - in' star; I
2. I hear, I hear, I hear, I hear all the an - gels sing; I

feel, I feel, I feel, I feel, I feel like a morn - in' star. Oh,
hear, I hear, I hear, I hear, I hear all the an - gels sing. Oh,

Autoharp (15-bar), strum C (refrain) and E (verse)
Guitar, strum 8
Piano accompaniment pattern IV

"Shoo, Fly" was a favorite nonsense song during the Civil War that later became a popular fiddle tune and singing game.

SIDE BY SIDE

Harry Woods

Oh, we ain't got a bar - rel of mon - ey,

may - be we're rag - ged and fun - ny, But we'll trav - el a - long __

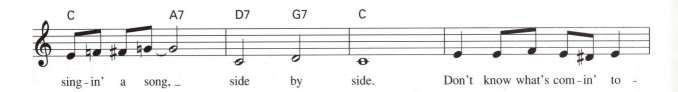

sing - in' a song, __ side by side. Don't know what's com - in' to -

mor - row. May - be it's trou - ble and sor - row, But we'll

trav - el the road __ shar - in' our load, __ side by side.

Through all kinds of weath - er, __ what if the sky should fall, Just as

long as we're to-geth-er, it does-n't mat-ter at all. When they've
all had their quar-rels and part-ed, we'll be the same as we
start-ed, Just trav'-lin' a-long ___ sing-in' a song, ___

1. side by side. Oh, we

2. side by side. ___

Autoharp, strum N
Piano, accompaniment pattern XVI

THE SIDEWALKS OF NEW YORK

Chales B. Lawlor
(United States, 1852–1925)

James W. Blake
(United States, 1862–1935)

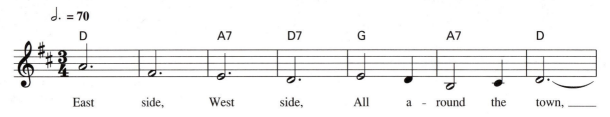

East side, West side, All a - round the town, _____

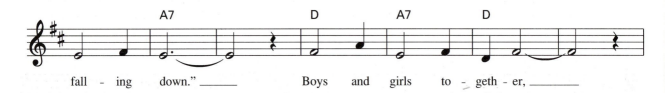

_____ The tots sang "Ring _ A Ros - ie," "Lon - don Bridge is

fall - ing down." _____ Boys and girls to - geth - er, _____

Me and Ma - mie O' Rourke, _____ Tripped the light _ fan -

tas - tic On the side - walks of New York. _____

Autoharp (15-bar), strum H
Guitar, strum 15

Create a medley of Gay Nineties songs by linking "Bye, Bye, Blackbird," "Bicycle Built for Two," "Mister Sun," "Side by Side," and "The Sidewalks of New York."

Lawlor, a vaudeville figure, collaborated with Blake, a hat salesman, to compose this song about their city. It was first performed in New York's Bowery district at the London Theatre.

270

SILENT NIGHT

Josef Mohr
(Austria, 1792–1848)

Franz Gruber
(Germany, 1787–1863)

English: Si - lent night, ho - ly night! All is calm, all is bright
German: Stil - le nacht, Hei - li - ge nacht! Al - les schläft, ein - sam wacht
Pronunciation: *shtih - leh nockkt Hie - lih-geh-nockkt ah - lehs shlayft ine - sahm vahkkt*

'Round yon vir - gin Moth - er and Child. Ho - ly In - fant, so ten - der and mild,
Nur das trau - te hoch - hei - li - ge Paar. Hold - er Kna - be im lock - i - gen Haar,
noor dahs traoo - tuh hoek - hie - lih-guh pahr hohld - ehr knah - beh ihm lockk - ih-gehn hahr

Sleep in heav - en - ly peace, _____ Sleep _____ in heav - en - ly peace.
Schlaf in himm - li - scher Ruh, _____ Schlaf _____ in himm - li - scher Ruh.
schlahf in him - lih-sher roo schlahf in him - lih-sher roo

Guitar, strum 27

    A
2. Silent night, holy night!

    E7   A
Shepherds quake at the sight.

    D   A
Glories stream from heaven afar,

    D   A
Heavenly hosts sing "Alleluia!"

    E7   A
Christ the Savior is born,

        E7   A
Christ the Savior is born.

    A
3. Silent night, holy night!

    E7   A
Son of God, love's pure light!

    D   A
Radiant beams from Thy holy face,

    D   A
With the dawn of redeeming grace,

    E7   A
Jesus, Lord, at Thy birth,

    E7   A
Jesus, Lord at Thy birth.

"Silent Night" was composed on the day before Christmas, 1818, at Oberndorf, Austria. The organ at St. Nicholas Church had broken down, and could not be repaired before the Christmas Eve services. So Franz Gruber, the church organist, composed "Silent Night" and presented it on Christmas Eve, with guitar accompaniment. The poem was provided by Josef Mohr, the church pastor and local schoolmaster. Shortly after it was composed, "Silent Night" was popularized by a touring troupe of singers from the Tyrol.

SIMPLE GIFTS

Joseph Brackett
(United States, 1797–1882)
(American Shaker Song)

♩ = 56

'Tis the gift to be sim - ple, 'tis the gift to be free, 'Tis the

gift to come down where we ought to be, And when we find our - selves _ in the

place just _ right 'Twill _ be in the val - ley of love and de - light. When true sim -

plic - i - ty is gained, To bow and to bend we will not be a - shamed. To

turn, _ to ___ turn, _ will _ be our de - light And by turn - ing, turn - ing we come 'round right.

Autoharp, strum C (high to low, using only eleven bass strings)
Soprano recorder

The legacy of the Shakers is well known today because they are admired for their piety, their ingenuity, and the articles they created for their everyday use. Shaker worship was deeply devotional, but different from other religions because it involved dancing, singing, and shouting. Therefore they were called Shakers, or sometimes Shaking Quakers. They believed that through such agitation, one received the gift of prophecy. (A version of this religious dance has even become part of the modern dance repertory.) Their ingenuity was expressed in many inventions, including the buzz saw, the threshing machine, and the common clothespin. Today, people from around the world visit Shaker villages and admire the purity and simplicity of their designs, particularly the simple, clean lines of their furniture and implements.

Shakers developed from a French Protestant sect, whose persecuted members fled to England and merged with radical Quakers. Englishwoman Ann Lee brought these beliefs from England to America in 1774. After a time, the Shakers settled near Albany, New York, where they gained many members. As a utopian religious group, Shakers sought to realize perfection through their communal living. They believed that a life without sin was possible only through withdrawal from the world, into their own villages. At the movement's peak in 1826, there were eighteen Shaker villages in eight states.

Singin' in the Rain

Arthur Freed

Nacio Herb Brown

I'm sing - - in' in the rain, just sing - - in' in the rain; What a glo - - ri-ous feel - ing, I'm hap - - py a - gain! I'm laugh - ing at clouds so dark up a - bove. The sun's _____ in my heart _____ and I'm read - - y for love. Let the storm - - y clouds chase ev' - ry - one _____ from the place; Come on _____ with the rain, I've a smile _____ on my face! I'll walk down the lane with a hap - - py re - frain, And sing - in' _____ just sing - in' in _____ the rain! _____

Autoharp, strum O
Piano, accompaniment pattern XVI

SING WE NOEL
(Noël Nouvelet)

French Carol

English: Christ - mas comes a - new, O, let us __ sing No - el!
French: No - ël nou - ve - let, No - ël chan - tons i - ci,
Pronunciation: noh - el noo - veh - lay noh - el shahn - tohn ee - cee

Glo - ry to God, now let your __ prais - es swell!
De - vo - tés gens, cri - ons a __ Dieu mer - ci!
day - voh - tay jahn kree - ohns ah dyou mare - cee

Refrain

Sing we No - el for Christ, the new - born King, No - el!
Chan - tons No - ël pour Le Roi nou - ve - let No - ël!
shahn - tohn noh - el poor lay rwah noo - vay - lay noh - el

Sing we no - el for Christ, the new - born King!
Chan - tons no - ël pour Le Roi nou - ve - let!
shahn - tohn noh - el poor lay rwah noo - vay - lay

Christ - mas comes a - new, O, let us __ sing No - el!
No - ël nou - ve - let, no - ël chan - tons i - ci!
noh - el noo - vay - lay noh - el shahn - tohn ee - cee

Autoharp, strum C
Piano, accompany using chord roots

"Sing We Noel" can be performed as a round during phrases 1, 2, and 5. (Sing in unison during phrases 3 and 4.)

Six Little Ducks

Traditional American Song

1. Six lit-tle ducks that I once knew,
2. Down to the riv-er they would go,

Fat ones, skin-ny ones, fair ones, too.
Wibble wobble, wib-ble wobble, to and fro.

But the one lit-tle duck with the

feath-er in his back: He ruled the oth-ers with a "quack, quack, quack,"

"quack, quack, quack." He ruled the oth-ers with a "quack, quack, quack."

Autoharp, strum N
Guitar, strum 20
Piano, accompaniment pattern XVI

Create a pantomime that depicts the song's words.

SIYAHAMBA

Traditional South African
Freedom Song

English: We are march - - ing in the light __ of God. __ We are
Zulu: Si - ya hamb' - - e - ku - kha - nye - ni kwen - khos' - si - ya

march-ing in the light __ of God. __ We are march - - ing in the
hamb' - e - ku - kha - nye - ni kwen - khos' __ Si - ya hamb' - - e - ku - kha -

light __ of God. __ We are march-ing in the light __ of God. __ Si - ya -
nye - ni kwen - khos' __ Si - ya hamb' - e - ku - kha - nye - ni kwen - khos' __

ham - ba _____ Si - ya - ham - ba _____ We are
(Si - ya - ham - ba) (Si - ya - ham - ba) Si - ya -

march - ing in the light _____ of God. _____ Si - ya -
hamb' - e - ku - kha - nye - ni kwen - khos' _____

ham - ba _____ Si - ya ham - ba, _____ We are
(Si - ya - ham - ba) (Si - ya - ham - ba) Si - ya -

march-ing in the light of God, ____ We are ____
hamb' - e - ku - kha - nye - ni kwen - khos' ____ Si - ya ____

Pronunciation guide
see-yah-ham-bah-koo-kah-nyeh-nee kwen-kos
see-yah-hahm-bah

When performing "Siyahamba" in a choir formation, use some ideas from the Zulu *iscathamiya* style: Sway with a subtle, easy body movement, in a slow tempo. The body can first lean gently to the left, and then to the right. Use a rocking motion, or take small steps from side to side.

South Africa has a complicated musical history, with many different styles. Its popular music, which favors the voice, has been strongly influenced by Europe and America. Much South African popular music reflects the overlapping sounds and call-and-response techniques of traditional African music, along with harmonies derived from hymns and African American spirituals.

A distinctive a cappella (unaccompanied) vocal style developed after World War I within South Africa's emerging Zulu working class. Rural migrants worked in mines and factories but had to leave their families behind and live in all-male hostels. In the hostels, they developed a weekend social life based on vocal and dance group competitions. The style became widely popular when played on Radio Zulu in the 1960s.

This Zulu choral style is the specialty of Ladysmith Black Mambazo, a vocal group that performed often on Radio Zulu, becoming famous for their rich harmonies and the subtle lyrics of leader Joseph Shabalala. The group also features restrained dance routines called iscathamiya *(from the Zulu, meaning "to stalk or step softly"). Black Mambazo was introduced to the West in 1986 by Paul Simon. Simon's album* Graceland *sold seven million copies and helped Ladysmith Black Mambazo establish an international career. (Based on information in* World Music: The Rough Guide.*)*

Nelson Mandela

SKIP TO MY LOU

American Play-Party Song

With spirit

Refrain

C   G7

Skip,   skip,   skip   to   my   Lou,   Skip,   skip,   skip   to   my   Lou,

C   G7   C

Skip,   skip,   skip   to   my   Lou,   Skip   to   my   Lou,   my   dar - lin'.

Verse

                                  G7

1. Flies   in   the   but - ter - milk,   shoo, shoo, shoo!   Flies   in   the   but - ter - milk,   shoo, shoo, shoo!
2. Lost   my __ part - ner,   what'll   I   do?   Lost   my __ part - ner,   what'll   I   do?
3. I'll   get an - oth - er one,   better   than   you,   I'll   get an - oth - er one,   better   than   you,
4. Can't   get   a   red bird, a   blue bird'll   do,   Can't   get   a   red bird, a   blue bird'll   do,

Make up your own verses

C   G7   C

Flies   in   the   but - ter - milk,   shoo, shoo, shoo!
Lost   my __ part - ner,   what'll   I   do?   Skip   to   my   Lou,   my   dar - lin'.
I'll   get an - oth - er one,   better   than   you,
Can't   get   a   red bird, a   blue bird'll   do,

Autoharp, banjo strum
Guitar, strum 4
Piano, accompaniment pattern IV

Nineteenth-century Protestant communities in the south, particularly in Texas and Oklahoma, disapproved of social dancing. Even in square dancing, arms could encircle the waist of a partner. And of course, square dancers were accompanied by "the devil's own instrument," the fiddle. Therefore, the play-party, a sung dance, accompanied by the singing and hand clapping of the dancers themselves, was developed. Line, circle, and partner formations were permitted, as long as there was no embracing. The play-party gave teenagers and young marrieds a chance for fun and frolic but still satisfied parents and grandparents—who sometimes joined in. This homemade entertainment was popular on the frontier, and it spread westward wherever people made their own amusements.

SOMETIMES I FEEL LIKE A MOTHERLESS CHILD

African American Spiritual

Moderately, with expression

1. Some-times I feel like a moth-er-less child, ____
2. Some-times I feel like I'm al - most gone, ____

Some-times I feel like a moth-er-less child; ____ Some-times I
Some-times I feel like I'm al - most gone; ____ Some-times I

feel like a moth-er-less child, ____ A long way ____ from
feel like I'm al - most gone, ____ A long way ____ from

home, _____ A long way ____ from home. _____

Autoharp, one strum each downbeat
Piano, accompany using chord roots

THE SONG OF ALI MOUNTAINS
(A Li Shan Jr Ge)

Deng Yu Pying
English words by
Patricia Hackett

Song from Taiwan
Hwang You Di

Lively, but expressively (♩ = 63)

English: Green, green hills will soar, blue, blue seas will
Mandarin: Gau shan chying, jyan shwei
Pronunciation: gow shahn chying tseeyehn sshway

roar; Pret-ty girls of A - li, grace-ful as the wa - ter,
lan. A li shan de gu nyang mei ru shwei ya,
lahn ah lee shahn dee goo neeyahng may jruu sshway yah

Hand-some A - li boys are strong as the hills.
A li shan de shan nyan jwang ru shan.
ah lee shahn dee shahn neeyahng tjwahng jruu shahn

Girls only:
Ah!

Boys only:
Ah!

All:
Pret-ty girls of A - li, grace-ful as the
A li shan de gu nyang mei ru
ah lee shahn dee goo neeyahng may jruu

wa - ter, Hand - some A - li boys are strong _ as the hills. _____
shwei ya, A li shan de shan nyan jwang _ ru _____ shan. _____
sshway yah ah lee shahn dee shahn neeyahng tjwahng jruu shahn

Autoharp, strum E

Play patterns 1 and 2 on xylophones for "The Song of Ali Mountains." Play pattern 3 on a wood block.

Perform a Chinese ribbon dance with this song. For directions, refer to "Rainbow Sister."

This song describes an indigenous tribe who live in the central mountains of Taiwan. The Alishan is a range of eighteen peaks, many of which are famous for their views of clouds and sunrises. The song's words compare the girls (see following illustration) and boys of Ali to the evergreen mountains and blue streams—each inseparable from the other.

Girls of Ali Mountain

SONG OF PEACE
(*Finlandia*)

Lloyd Stone

Jean Sibelius
(Finland, 1865–1957)

1. This is my song, a song for all the na - tions, _____ A song of
2. My coun-try's skies are blu - er than the o - cean, _____ And sun-light

peace for lands a - far and mine. _____ This is my home, the
beams in clo - ver - leaf and pine. _____ But oth - er lands have

coun - try where my heart is, _____ Here are my hopes, my dreams, my ho - ly
sun - light, too, and clo - ver, _____ And skies are ev' - ry - where as blue as

shrine; _____ But oth - er hearts in oth - er lands are beat - ing _____
mine. _____ O hear my song, a song for all the na - tions, _____

____ With hopes and dreams as true and high as mine. _____
____ A song of peace for their land and for mine. _____

Autoharp, strum melody rhythm

Composed by Jean Sibelius in 1899, "Finlandia" was quickly adopted as a symbol of Finnish national aspirations. The words above are used in Christian education by the American Presbyterian Church Board.

THE SONG OF THE WORLD'S LAST WHALE

Pete Seeger
(United States, b. 1919)

1., 6. I heard the song _____ of the world's last whale, _____
2. It was down off Ber - mu - da _____ Ear - ly last spring, _____
(3.) did–n't just hear grunt - ing _____ I did–n't just hear squeaks, _____
4. Down in the Ant - arc - tic _____ The har - poons wait, _____
5. So here's a lit–tle test _____ To see how you feel, _____

_____ As I rocked in the moon - light _____ and reefed the
_____ Near an un–der - wa - ter moun - tain _____ Where the hump - backs
_____ I did–n't just hear bel - lows, _____ I did–n't just hear
_____ But it's up - on the land _____ They de - cide my
_____ Here's a lit - tle test for this age _____ of the au–to - mo -

sail, _____ It - 'll hap-pen to you _____ al - so with - out
sing. _____ I low-ered the mi - cro - phone _____ A quar-ter mile _____
shrieks. _____ It was the mus - i - cal sing–ing _____ And the pas–sion - ate
fate. _____ In Lon - don Town _____ They'll be tell - ing the
bile. _____ If we can save _____ Our sing-ers in the

fail, If it hap-pens to me _____ sang the world's last whale. _____
down, Switched on the re - cor–der _____ And let the tape spin round. _____ 3. I
wail, That came from the heart _____ Of the world's last whale. _____
tale, If it's life or death _____ For the world's last whale. _____
sea, Per - haps there's a chance _____ To save you and me. _____

Autoharp (15-bar), harp strum. Use a different pick (felt, plastic, leather) to fit the mood of different verses. (Measure 14 could be without strumming.)

SORIDA

African Greeting Song
(Zimbabwe)
as sung by Dumišanî Maraire

Shona: So - ri - da! So - ri - da, ri - da ri -
Pronunciation: soe - tree - dah

da, da - da - da - da, da - da - da - da, ri - da ri -

da, da - da - da - da, da - da - da - da, ri - da ri - da!

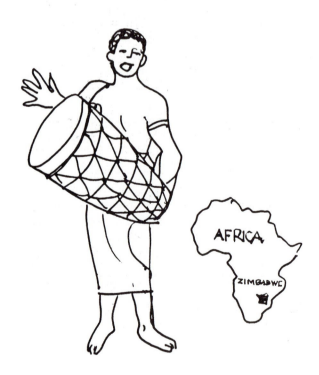

284

THE SOUND OF SILENCE

Paul Simon
(United States, b. 1941)

♩ = 96

1. Hel-lo dark-ness, my old friend, I've come to talk with you a - gain,

Be-cause a vi-sion soft-ly creep - ing, Left its seeds while I was sleep - ing

And the vi - sion _____ that was plant-ed in my brain _____ still re - mains _____

_____ With-in the sound of si - lence. ___

2. In rest-less dreams I walked a -
3. And in the nak-ed light I
4. _ "Fools!" said I "You do not

lone   Nar-row streets of cob-ble-stone   'Neath the ha-lo of a
saw   Ten thou-sand peo-ple may-be more, Peo-ple talk-ing with-out
know   Si-lence like a can-cer grows,   Hear my words that I might

street   lamp, _   I turned my col-lar to the cold and damp _
speak - ing ___   Peo-ple hear-ing with-out lis-ten-ing ___
teach   you, _   Take my arms that I might reach ___ you." _

When my eyes were stabbed _ by the flash of a ne - on light
Peo - ple writ - ing songs _____ that voic - es ____ nev - er share
But my words _____ like si - lent ____ rain-drops fell,

2.,3.

that split the night _____ and touched the sound of si - lence. ____
and no - one dares _____ dis - turb the sound of si - lence. ____

4.

And ech - oed _____ in the wells of si - lence. ____

5. And the peo - ple bowed and prayed To the ne - on god they

made. And the sign flashed out its warn - ing. ____

In the words that it was form - ing, ___ And the sign said "The

words of the proph-ets are writ - ten on the sub - way walls _____ and ten-e-ment

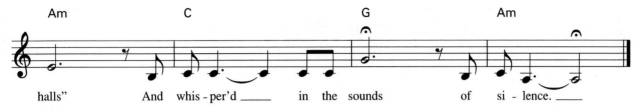

halls" And whis-per'd _____ in the sounds of si-lence. _____

Autoharp, strum N (use a different pick for each verse)
Guitar, strums 23 and 18 on different verses (To sing *The Sound of Silence* in
    C minor with guitar, place the capo in fret 3 and play the chords shown above.)

SPIN, MY TOP
(*S'evivon*)

Hebrew Song

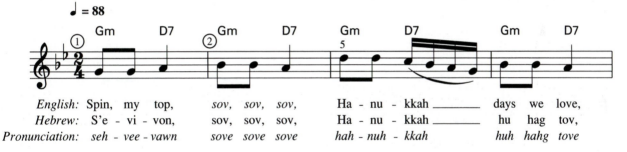

English:	Spin, my top,	*sov, sov, sov,*	Ha - nu - kkah _____	days we love,
Hebrew:	S'e - vi - von,	sov, sov, sov,	Ha - nu - kkah _____	hu hag tov,
Pronunciation:	seh - vee - vawn	sove sove sove	hah - nuh - kkah	huh hahg tove

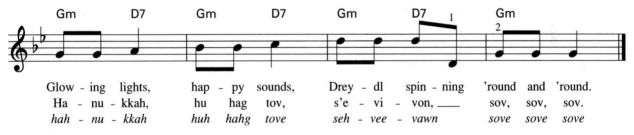

Glow - ing lights, hap - py sounds, Drey - dl spin - ning 'round and 'round.
Ha - nu - kkah, hu hag tov, s'e - vi - von, _____ sov, sov, sov.
hah - nu - kkah huh hahg tove seh - vee - vawn sove sove sove

Autoharp, strum D
Piano, accompany using chord roots

SPRING HOME
(Heng Chwun Folk Song)

English words by
Patricia Hackett

Chinese Folk Song
(Taiwan)

With movement (♩ = 80)

English: See how our land is al- ways spring; Sweet breez-es blow and
Mandarin: Yi nyan rung yi you chwun tyan, Fan tu sya jung
Pronunciation: *yee nyehn roong yee yoh chwuun tyehn fahn too sshah juung*

birds al- ways sing. See how our land is fair each
mang tyan byan. Tyan li yang myau you lyu
mahng tyehn byehn thehn lee yahng myahoo yoh luu

day, Our fields are home, For work and for play.
lyu, Jya jya hu hu pu feng nyan.
luu jyah jyah huu huu puu fuhng nyehn

Play these patterns on a xylophone with "Spring Home."

① Play 7 times   Last 2 measures   ② Play 7 times   Last 2 measures

The high cultures of the Far East were already ancient when Marco Polo first glimpsed their wonders in the thirteenth century. A flourishing trade with distant lands had long conveyed new goods and ideas to Asia—along with music, instruments, and dance. China, Korea, and Japan synthesized these foreign introductions, absorbing them into their prevailing arts and culture. Each nation created a distinctive musical style, but they all shared similar traits. All possessed a refined art music to accompany court and ritual functions and a rich and varied folk music for other festivals and ceremonies. Vocal music was most often for solo performers, but string, woodwind, and percussion instruments might play in groups of several hundred at lavish court spectacles in China.

STANDIN' IN THE NEED OF PRAYER

African American Spiritual

It's me, it's me, oh Lord, Stand-in' in the need of
prayer; It's me, it's me, Oh Lord, Stand-in' in the need of
prayer.

1. Not my fa – ther nor my moth – er, but it's me, oh Lord,
2. Not my broth – er nor my sis – ter, but it's me, oh Lord,

Stand-in' in the need of prayer; Not my fa – ther nor my moth – er, but it's
Stand-in' in the need of prayer; Not my broth – er nor my sis – ter, but it's

me, oh Lord, Stand – in' in the need of prayer.

Guitar, strum 26 (refrain) and 19 (verse)
Piano, accompaniment pattern XII

THE STAR-SPANGLED BANNER

Francis Scott Key
(United States, 1779–1843)

John Stafford Smith
(England, 1750–1836)

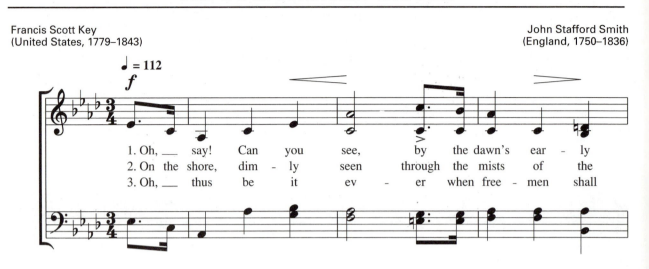

1. Oh, __ say! Can you see, by the dawn's ear - ly
2. On the shore, dim - ly seen through the mists of the
3. Oh, __ thus be it ev - er when free - men shall

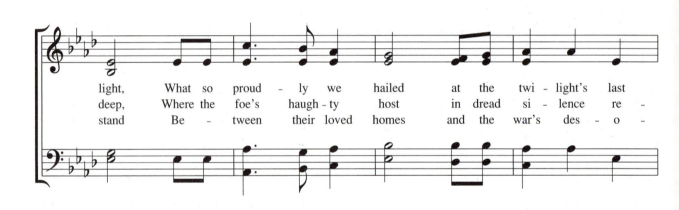

light, What so proud - ly we hailed at the twi - light's last
deep, Where the foe's haugh - ty host in dread si - lence re -
stand Be - tween their loved homes and the war's des - o -

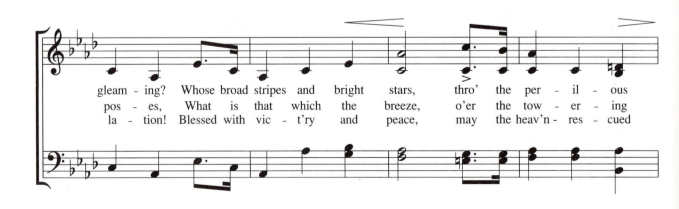

gleam - ing? Whose broad stripes and bright stars, thro' the per - il - ous
pos - es, What is that which the breeze, o'er the tow - er - ing
la - tion! Blessed with vic - t'ry and peace, may the heav'n - res - cued

wave _____ O'er the land _____ of the free and the home of the brave?
wave _____ O'er the land _____ of the free and the home of the brave?
wave _____ O'er the land _____ of the free and the home of the brave?

An American flag waves both day and night over Ft. McHenry in Baltimore and over a grave at Frederick in northwestern Maryland. These commemorate the attorney Francis Scott Key and the incident in 1814 that inspired him to write "The Defense of Ft. McHenry," later entitled "The Star-Spangled Banner." Key and a friend undertook a mission to secure the release of an American physician held prisoner on a British flagship. The venture was successful, but their boat was detained in Chesapeake Bay by the British, who began a bombardment of nearby Ft. McHenry. The shelling stopped during the night, but only after the morning fog lifted could the Americans see their flag still flying over the fort. On that very day—September 14—Key set down his verses. The text was immediately associated with a well-known hymn tune, already familiar to Key. Since 1931, "The Star-Spangled Banner" has been our official national anthem.

THE STORKS
(Gólya, Gólya, Gilice)

English words by
Patricia Hackett

Hungarian Folk Song

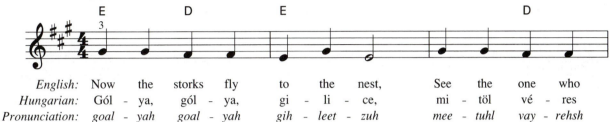

Simply, but not too slowly (♩ = 144)

| | E | D | E | | D |

English: Now the storks fly to the nest, See the one who
Hungarian: Gól - ya, gól - ya, gi - li - ce, mi - töl vé - res
Pronunciation: goal - yah goal - yah gih - leet - zuh mee - tuhl vay - rehsh

| E | | D | E |

stops to rest; Some-thing must have hurt the bird, Let us sing to
a lá - bad. Tö - rök gyer - ek el - vá - gta, Mag - yar gyer - ek
ah lah - bahd toh - roh(k) jeh - reh(k) ehl - vag - tah mahg - jahr jehr - ehk

| D | E | | D | E |

get him cured. Sing songs! Play drums! Mu - sic helps to heal you.
gyó - gyit - ja, Síp - pal, do - bal, Ná - di - he - ge - dü - vel.
joh - jeet - jah shee - pahl doh - bahl nah - dee - heh - geh - doo - val

Piano, use accompaniment pattern XI

In the literal translation of this song, Magyar children try to heal a stork hurt by Turkish children. This reflects a historic animosity between the Magyars (the founders of the Hungarian state) and the Turkish people, who were in frequent conflict from the fifteenth through the eighteenth centuries. "The Storks" may also describe the ancient shamanistic practice of healing the sick through song.

ST. PAUL'S STEEPLE

English Melody

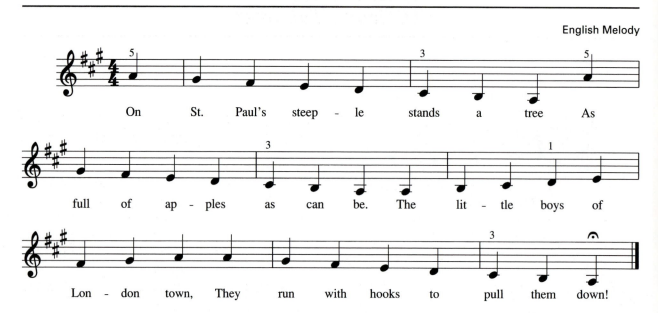

On St. Paul's steep - le stands a tree As

full of ap - ples as can be. The lit - tle boys of

Lon - don town, They run with hooks to pull them down!

THE STREETS OF LAREDO
(The Cowboy's Lament)

American Cowboy Song

Verse 6 may be sung as a refrain throughout.

Autoharp (15–bar), strum H or J (verse 6, strum I, high to low)
Guitar, strum 14 (verse 6, strum 16)
Piano, accompaniment pattern VII

SUMER IS ICUMEN IN
(Summer Is A-Coming In)

English Round (ca. 1240)

Soprano recorder

Translation

Summer is coming, the cuckoo sings loudly. The seeds in the fields and the woods grow. The cuckoo sings merrily. Cuckoo. Ewe bleat after lambs, cow after calf, the bull rises, the buck grazes. The cuckoo sings merrily. Cuckoo. How well sings the cuckoo. Never stop singing!

SYMPHONY NO. 1 IN C MINOR
Opus 68
Theme from fourth movement

Johannes Brahms
(Germany, 1833–1897)

Soprano recorder

Since the early nineteenth century, the symphony has been the large-scale, serious composition it remains today. Haydn, Mozart, Beethoven, and Brahms developed symphonic masterpieces, weaving and reweaving their musical ideas within the orchestral texture. Symphonic form typically includes three or four sections (movements) of varying character, tempo, and length. The first and fourth movements are often dramatic and move in a fast tempo. The second is usually slower and more pensive, and the third movement may be a quick, playful dance. Symphonies are usually designated by number, but in the fervor of nineteenth-century Romanticism, a few have acquired programmatic subtitles.

TAKE ME OUT TO THE BALL GAME

Jack Norworth

Albert von Tilzer

Autoharp, strum J

TAKE THE "A" TRAIN

Billy Strayhorn
(United States, 1915–1967)

Play last measure on piano

Piano, accompaniment pattern XI

"Take the 'A' Train" was the theme song of America's greatest jazz composer and arranger, Edward "Duke" Ellington (1899–1974). His orchestra, renowned for its precision and coordination, was as much Duke's instrument as was his piano. Working with exceptionally gifted individual performers (on trumpet, clarinet, saxophone, trombone, drums, and bass), Duke molded a group sound that was to become his trademark. Instruments were combined to produce tonal effects not possible with individual instruments. It was a well-rehearsed "big band" sound with a driving rhythm—a sound appreciated by jazz enthusiasts around the world. Throughout his long career, Ellington remained an innovator, always searching for new techniques and forms of expression.

TEDDY BEAR

American Play Song

Jump-rope tempo

1. Ted - dy bear, Ted - dy bear, turn a - round, _____
2. Ted - dy bear, Ted - dy bear, say your prayers, _____

Ted - dy bear, Ted - dy bear, touch the ground.
Ted - dy bear, Ted - dy bear, go up - stairs. Ted - dy bear, Ted - dy bear,

show your shoe, _____ Ted - dy bear, Ted - dy bear, that will do!

THANKS FOR THE FOOD

Danish Folk Song

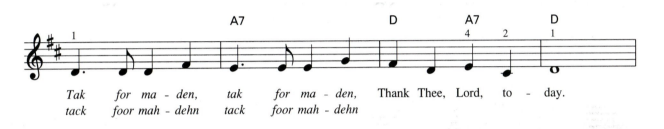

Tak   for ma - den,*   tak   for ma - den,   Bless this food   we   pray;
tack   foor mah - dehn   tack   foor mah - dehn

Tak   for ma - den,   tak   for ma - den,   Thank Thee, Lord,   to - day.
tack   foor mah - dehn   tack   foor mah - dehn

Strength - en, love, and   guide   us,   Stay Thou close be - side   us;

Tak   for ma - den,   tak   for ma - den,   Bless this food   we   pray.
tack   foor mah - dehn   tack   foor mah - dehn

"Tak for maden" means "Thanks (to God) for the food."

Autoharp (15-bar), strum L
Guitar, strum 2 or 22
Piano, accompaniment pattern XI

THANK YOU FOR THE CHRIS'MUS

Jamaican Folk Song

Autoharp, strum L
Piano, accompaniment pattern XI

Many cultures have left their mark on the islands of the Caribbean, including those of Spain, France, Great Britain, North and South America, and the African nations. The music of Cuba, Jamaica, Haiti, and Trinidad reflect both African and Hispanic contacts, with the African traits especially strong. Instruments of African derivation dominate traditional Caribbean music making: drums of all sizes, iron bells, horns, stamping tubes, and even oversized thumb pianos. (As in Africa, voices supplied the desired effects in regions where instruments were banned or were unavailable.) Complicated rhythms are the "norm," with syncopations and cross-rhythms performed in a strict, unvarying tempo.

THERE'S JUST SOMETHING ABOUT A SONG

Janet and Ted Wilson

Piano, accompaniment pattern XVI (play solid chords)

THIS BEAUTIFUL WORLD
(Nani Ke Ao Nei)

Mary K. Puku'i
(Honolulu, Hawaii)

♩ = 44

1. I - lu - nǎ, la i - lu - nǎ, Na mǎ - nu o ka lě - wa.
A - bove, __ up a - bove, __ The birds __ fly so high. __

2. I lǎ - o, la i lǎ - o, Nā pu - a o ka ho - nu - a.
Be - low, __ down be - low, __ The earth's _ flow - ers __ grow. __

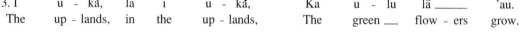

3. I u - kǎ, la i u - kǎ, Ka u - lu lā _____ 'au.
The up - lands, in the up - lands, The green __ flow - ers grow.

4. I kai, la i kai, Nā i - a o ka - mo a - na.
The sea, in the sea, The fish __ swim so __ free. __

5. Ha - 'i - na mai Ka - pu - ǎ - na, A he hǎ - ni - ke ao nei.
Now this __ ends my _ song, __ Of a beau - ti - ful world.

Pronunciation Guide

Unstressed vowels	*Stressed vowels*
ā as in father	ǎ as in above
ē as in they	ě as in set
ī as in see	i as in sit
ō as in hoe	ǒ as in obey
ū as in too	ǔ as in book

Consonants	*Other*
k as in kodiak	' indicates a glottal stop
w sounds w after *o* and *u*	
w sounds soft "v" after a, e, and i	

When no stress is indicated, use a pronunciation between the stressed and unstressed vowel.

"Nani Ke Ao Nei" is a *mele hula* (literally "chant dance") composed by Mary K. Puku'i in the style of the ancient chants heard by Captain James Cook and his men in 1778. A *mele hula* documents and comments on the religious, historical, social, and psychological elements of Hawaii's culture. Hawaiian music is still orally transmitted and performed by experienced musicians, many of whom express the same cosmic energy (*mana*) that inspired traditional creativity.

"Nani Ke Ao Nei" consists of a series of couplets: two (short) phrases using two pitches a minor third apart (*sol–mi*). (Chants can use up to six pitches.) Like all mele hulas, "Nani Ke Ao Nei" has a regular meter and is accompanied by gestures and by an instrument. Although sticks are used here, a mele hula can be accompanied by one of several instruments made of gourd, bamboo, coconut, pebbles, skin, or wood.

In a mele hula, singers use husky, deep-chested voices; the goal of a singer is to have a pleasant and continuous sound throughout the chant. In some meles, there is room for individual interpretation. A dance using only hand and arm movements accompanies "Nani Ke Ao Nei," to interpret the words. (There is also a type of chant without dance.)

A mele hula is usually sung in groups, sometimes sitting, sometimes standing. "Nani Ke Ao Nei" is a seated hula. During a standing hula, hands, hips, and sometimes feet keep the rhythm, so that three different rhythms go on simultaneously: that of the chant, that of the dance, and that of the accompanying instrument.

"Nani Ke Ao Nei" describes the natural beauties of Hawaii, making it especially appropriate for an Earth Day celebration. Or students might compose their own mele hula, describing the beauty of their particular region.

Perform "This Beautiful World" with the choreography that follows. Choreography is by Mary K. Puku'i.

Dancers sit in a row. One dancer gives the calls.

KAHEA (Call): "Ho'omakaukau!" (Get ready! Dancers pick up sticks, which they have
"Pa!" (Begin. Literally, "strike.") placed on the floor in front of themselves.)

(The drawings show the dancer's position from either the front or side, depending on which angle is clearer. The dancer's legs do not move from side to side during the dance. The letter R or L next to the drawings indicates which stick should be on top during striking.)

KI'I PA: These gestures are the introduction, the interludes between verses and the closing movements. On the last four beats if the Ki'i pa, the caller calls the first two or three words of each couplet.

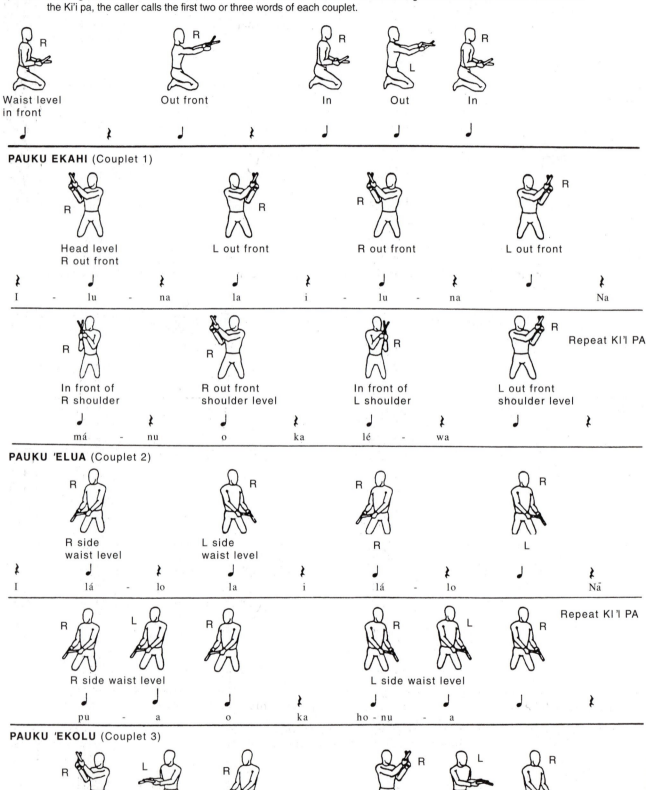

PAUKU EKAHI (Couplet 1)

PAUKU 'ELUA (Couplet 2)

PAUKU 'EKOLU (Couplet 3)

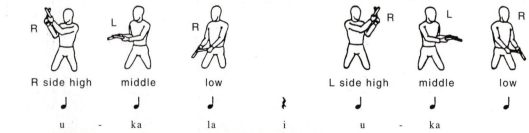

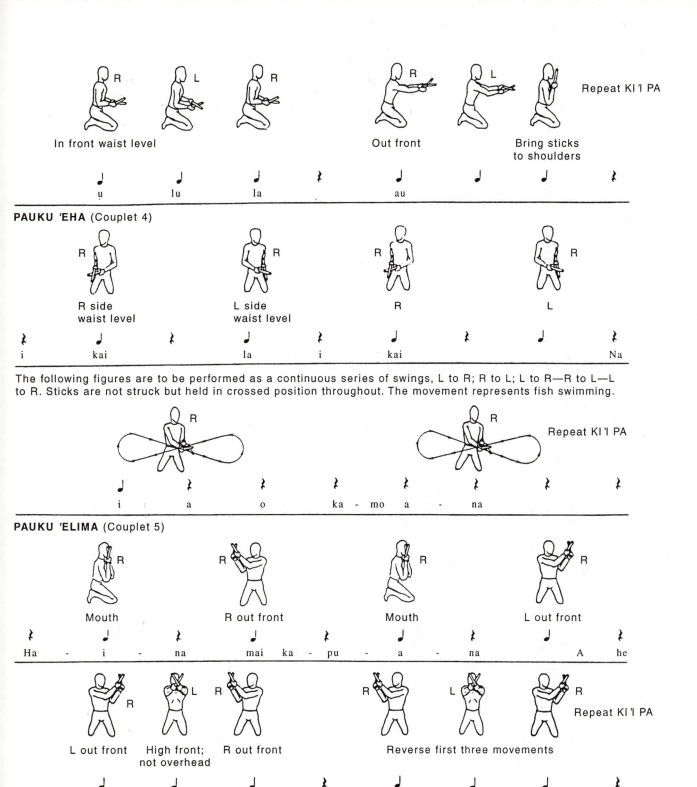

In front waist level

Out front

Bring sticks to shoulders

Repeat KI'I PA

u lu la au

PAUKU 'EHA (Couplet 4)

R side waist level

L side waist level

R

L

i kai la i kai Na

The following figures are to be performed as a continuous series of swings, L to R; R to L; L to R—R to L—L to R. Sticks are not struck but held in crossed position throughout. The movement represents fish swimming.

Repeat KI'I PA

i a o ka - mo a - na

PAUKU 'ELIMA (Couplet 5)

Mouth

R out front

Mouth

L out front

Ha - i - na mai ka - pu - a - na A he

L out front

High front; not overhead

R out front

Reverse first three movements

Repeat KI'I PA

na - ni - ke an nei

The closing KI"I PA requires one extra tap forward. The dancers drop their heads slightly on the last tap and all recite the closing dedication:
"HE INOA NO NA KAMALI'I
Translation: This is a name song for children

THIS LAND IS YOUR LAND

Words and music by Woody Guthrie
(United States, 1912–1967)

Verse

1. As I was walk - ing _____ that rib - bon of high - way, _____
2. I've roamed and rambl - ed _____ and I fol-lowed my foot - steps _____
3. When the sun came shin - ing, _____ and I _____ was strol - ling, _____

_____ I saw a - bove me _____ that end - less sky - way, _____
To the spark - ling sands of _____ her dia - mond des - erts, _____
And the wheat fields wav - ing, _____ and the dust clouds rol - ling, _____

_____ I saw be - low me _____ that gold - en val - ley, _____
And all a - round me _____ a voice came sound - ing, _____
As the fog was lift - ing _____ a voice was chant - ing, _____

_____ This land was made for you and me. _____

Refrain

This land is your land, _____ this land is my land, _____

_____ From Cal - i - for - nia _____ to the New York is - land, _____

_____ From the red - wood for - est _____ to the Gulf Stream wa - ters; _____

308

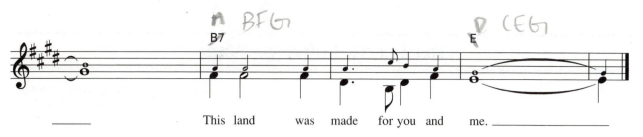

This land was made for you and me. _____

Guitar, strum 20

   E   *A*   *E*
4. In the square of the city in the shadow of the steeple,

     B7   *E*
By the Relief Office I seen my people;

       A   *E*
As they stood there hungry, I stood there wondering if,

B7   *E*
This land was made for you and me. (*Refrain*)

   E   *A*   *E*
5. As I went walking, that dirty old highway,

     B7   *E*
I saw a sign that read private property,

     A   *E*
But on the other side it didn't say nothing,

B7   *E*
That side was made for you and me. (*Refrain*)

   E   *A*   *E*
6. Nobody living can ever stop me,

     B7   *E*
As I go walking that freedom highway;

     A   *E*
Nobody living can make me turn back,

B7   *E*
This land was made for you and me.
(*Refrain*)

Woodrow Wilson Guthrie, American folk singer, guitarist, and composer of ballads, was born in Okemah, Oklahoma, on July 14, 1912. By the age of 13, he was earning his living as a wandering singer, performing in saloons, migrant labor camps, and "hobo jungles" (where the homeless men of the 1930s camped). Later he composed ballads, performed on radio, and wrote a newspaper column. His songs are filled with stories of how ordinary people became victims of the 1930s depression. He also celebrates the great beauty of the American landscape in songs such as "This Land Is Your Land," one of his nearly one thousand songs. Woody's son Arlo Guthrie (born 1947) is also a songwriter, composing "Alice's Restaurant" and starring in the 1969 film of the same name. Woody influenced many singers and songwriters, including Bob Dylan. After a long battle with Huntington's disease, Woody died in 1967 in New York City.

Woody Guthrie

THIS LITTLE LIGHT OF MINE

African American Spiritual

With a swing

1. This lit - tle light of mine,   I'm gon-na let it shine,
2. Ev' - ry - where I go,

This lit - tle light of mine,   I'm gon-na let it shine.
Ev' - ry - where I go,

This lit - tle light of mine,   I'm gon-na let it shine,   Let it
Ev' - ry - where I go,

shine,   let it   shine,   let it   shine. _____

Autoharp, strum N
Piano, accompaniment pattern XVI

THIS OLD HAMMER

African American Work Song

Heavily (♩ = 44)

1. This old ham-mer _____ killed John Hen - ry, _____
2. This old ham-mer _____ shines like sil - ver, _____

_____ This old ham-mer _____ killed John Hen - ry; _____
This old ham-mer _____ shines like sil - ver; _____

_____ This old ham-mer _____ killed John Hen - ry; ___
_____ This old ham-mer _____ shines like sil - ver; ___

But it won't kill me, _____ But it won't kill me. _____
But it rings like gold, _____ Yes, it rings like gold. _____

Guitar, strum 21
Piano, accompaniment pattern XI

311

THIS OLD MAN

English Folk Song

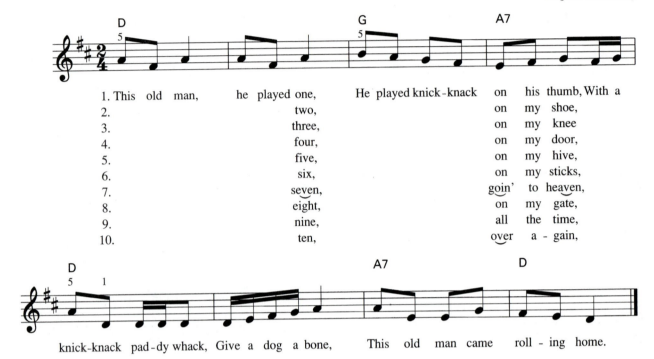

1. This old man,   he played one,   He played knick-knack   on   his thumb, With a
2.   two,   on   my   shoe,
3.   three,   on   my   knee
4.   four,   on   my   door,
5.   five,   on   my   hive,
6.   six,   on   my   sticks,
7.   seven,   goin' to heaven,
8.   eight,   on   my   gate,
9.   nine,   all   the time,
10.   ten,   over   a - gain,

knick-knack pad-dy whack, Give a dog a bone, This old   man came   roll - ing home.

Autoharp (15-bar), use strums C, D, and E on different verses
Guitar, strum 4
Piano, accompaniment pattern III

THIS TRAIN

African American Spiritual

♩ = 160

D   **(A7)**   **D**

1., 4. This train   is   bound for glo - ry,   this   train, _____   This train   is
2.   This train   don't carry no gam-blers,   this   train, _____   This train   don't
3.   This train   don't carry no li - ars,   this   train, _____   This train   don't

Am   **A7**   **D**

bound   for   glo - ry,   this   train; _____   This   train   is
carry   no   gam - blers,   this   train; _____   This   train   don't
carry   no   li - ars,   this   train; _____   This   train   don't

D7   **G**

bound   for   glo - ry,   Don't   car - ry none   but   the   right-eous and   ho - ly,
carry   no   gam - blers,   No   hyp - o - crites,   no ___   mid - night   ram - blers,
carry   no   li - ars,   No   hyp - o - crites   and ___   no ___ high   fli - ers,

D   **A7**   **D**

This   train   is   bound   for   glo - ry,   this   train. _____

Guitar, strum 2
Piano, accompaniment pattern XVI

African Americans created spirituals as music for worship during the era of slavery. They were collective expressions of a cohesive group, communicating with their God through music. Vividly pictorial, spirituals often told a story in which concepts were depicted in earthly terms. Heaven became a place where the poor might enjoy material abundance and where the streets might be paved with gold. Spirituals described a straightforward ethical code, with salvation the reward for those who spurned drinking, lying, and the like. Trains appear frequently in texts, along with rocks and rivers. Double meanings were common in spirituals: The train was probably a symbol of redemption as well as a means of escape from slavery.

THREE BLIND MICE

Thomas Ravenscroft
(England, ca. 1582–ca. 1633)

Three blind mice, ___ Three blind mice, ___ See how they run! ___

See how they run! _____ They all ran af - ter the farm - er's wife, She

cut off their tails with a carv - ing knife, Did you

ev - er see such a sight in your life as three blind mice?

Autoharp, strum B

"Three Blind Mice" first appeared in Deuteromelia (1609), a collection of rounds published and apparently composed by Ravenscroft, who is also known for his anthems and psalm
settings. The foregoing melody of "Three Blind Mice" is remarkably similar to the 1609 version,
except that the original words were somewhat different.

THREE ROGUES

Traditional American Song

3. The mil-ler he stole corn, The wea-ver he stole yarn, And the
4. The miller got drown'd in his dam, The weaver got hung in his yarn, And the

3. He stole some corn, he stole some yarn, Oh ___
4. Got drown'd in his dam, got hung in his yarn,

lit-tle tai-lor boy stole broad-cloth e-nough to keep the three rogues warm, To
de - vil __ caught the little tai-lor boy with the broad-cloth under his arm, With the

(oh) ___ rogues warm, Oh ___
his arm,

keep the three rogues warm, To keep the three rogues warm, And the
broad-cloth under his arm, With the broad-cloth under his arm, And the

___ to keep three rogues, Oh ___ to keep three rogues, Oh ___
with the broad-cloth under, with the broad-cloth under,

lit-tle tai-lor boy stole broad-cloth e-nough to keep the three rogues warm.
de - vil __ caught the little tai-lor boy with the broad-cloth under his arm.

THROW IT OUT THE WINDOW

American Nonsense Song

Quickly

1. Make up a rhyme and sing it in time, And throw it out the
2. Lit - tle Jack Horn - er sat in a cor - ner Eat-ing his Christ - mas
3. Hump - ty Dump - ty sat on a wall, _____ Hump - ty Dump - ty
4. Lit - tle Miss Muf - fet sat on a tuf - fet, Eat-ing her curds and
5. Jack _____ and Jill went up _____ the hill, To fetch a pail of
6. Lit - tle Tom Tinker got burned with a clink-er, And he be - gan to
7. See, _____ saw, _____ Mar - ger - y Daw, _____ Jack shall have a new
8. O - li - ver Twist _____ can't _____ do this: _____ Touch his knees and

(1) win - dow! _____ Make up a rhyme _____ and sing it in time, And
(2) pie, _____ Stuck in his thumb _____ and pulled out a plum, And
(3) had a great fall, _____ All the king's hors - es and all the king's men, _____
(4) whey, _____ A - long came a spid - er and sat down be - side her, And
(5) wat - er, _____ Jack _____ fell down _____ and broke _____ his crown, And
(6) cry: _____ "Ma! _____ Ma! _____ And
(7) mas - ter, _____ He _____ shall have but a pen - ny a day, And
(8) touch _____ his toes, _____ Clap _____ his hands _____ and o - ver he goes, And

Refrain

(1) throw it out the win - dow! _____
(2) threw it out the win - dow! _____
(3) Threw him out the win - dow! _____
(4) threw her out the win - dow! _____
(5) threw it out the win - dow! _____
(6, 7, 8) throw him out the win - dow! _____

The win - dow, _____ the win - dow, _____ the

sec - ond sto - ry win - dow. _____ Make up a rhyme and

sing it in time and throw it out the win - dow! _____

Autoharp, strum B

317

TIDEO

American Game Song

Pass one win-dow, ti - de - o, Pass two win-dows, ti - de - o,

Pass three win-dows, ti - de - o, Jin-gle at the win-dow, ti - de - o.

Ti - de - o, ti - de - o, Jin-gle at the win-dow, ti - de - o.

Autoharp, strum D
Piano, accompaniment pattern III

Formation

Players stand in a circle with hands joined and arms raised to form arches (windows). One player (it) stands outside the circle.

Game

Measures 1–8: It walks into the circle under one window and out under another, continuing until the word "Tideo." It then stops in front of a player in the circle.

Measures 9–12: The two players link elbows and swing. On the song's repeat, the player from the circle becomes it.

TIE A YELLOW RIBBON 'ROUND THE OLE OAK TREE

Irwin Levine
L. Russell Brown

Piano, accompaniment pattern XVI

TODAY CHRIST IS BORN
(Hodie Christus Natus Est)

Gregorian Chant

Latin: Ho - di - e Chri - stus na - tus ___ est: hó - di -
Pronunciation: hoh - dee - aye kree - stoos nah - toos ehst hoh - dee -

e Sal - vá - tor ap - pá - ru - it; hó - di - e
aye sahl - vah - tohr ah - pah - roo - eet hoh - dee - aye

in ter - ra ___ ca - nunt An - ge - li, lae - tán - tur Arch - án -
in tehr - rah cah - noont ahn - jeh - lee lay - tahn - toor ahr kahn -

ge - li: hó - di - e ___ ex súl - tant
jeh - lee hoh - dee - aye ehk - sool - tahnt

ju - sti ___ di - cén - tes: ___ Gló - ri - a
joo - stee dee - chehn - tahs gloh - ree - ah

in ex - cél - sis De - o, ___ al - le - lú - ia.
in ehk - chehl - sees day - oh ah - lay - loo - yah

Soprano recorder

Translation

Today Christ is born. Today the Savior hath appeared. Today Angels sing on earth, and Archangels rejoice. Today the just exult, saying Glory to God in the highest, alleluia.

Gregorian chant is Western civilization's most ancient music still in use. For centuries the liturgical chant of the Roman Catholic Church, these subtle and free-flowing melodies probably originated in the synagogues of Jerusalem. The chant is named in honor of Pope Gregory I, who systematically reorganized the music of the church during his papacy from 590 to 604. Conveying a transcendent peace, the pure melody of Gregorian chant endures as a magnificent expression of humankind's religious faith.

TOEMBAI

Israeli Round

♩ = 100

Am **Em** **B7** **Em**

① Toem – bai, toem – bai, toem – bai, toem – bai, toem – bai, toem – bai, toem – bai.
toom – buy toom – buy toom – buy toom – buy toom – buy toom – buy toom – buy

Am **Em** **B7** **Em**

② Tra la la, la la la la la, La la la la la la.

Am **Em** **B7** **Em**

③ Tra la la la la, La la la la la, La la la la la, la.

Guitar, strum 2

TOP OF THE WORLD

John Bettis

Richard Carpenter

With movement

1. Such a feel - in's com - in' o - ver me, _____
2. Ev - 'ry - thing ___ I want the world to be, _____

There is won - der in ___ most ev - 'ry - thing ___ I
Is now com - ing true ___ es - pe - cial - ly ___ for

see; _____ Not a cloud in the sky, ___ got the sun in my
me; _____ And the rea - son is clear, ___ it's be - cause you are

eyes, and I won't ___ be sur - prised ___ if it's a dream.
here, you're the near - est thing to heav - en that I've seen. ___

Refrain

I'm on the top of the world _____ look-in' down on cre-a-

- tion and the on - ly ex - pla - na - tion I ___ can ___ find,

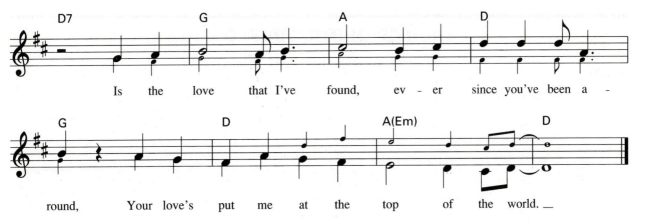

Is the love that I've found, ev - er since you've been a -

round, Your love's put me at the top of the world. __

Guitar, strum 2 (verse), strum 23 (refrain)

"TROUT" QUINTET IN A MAJOR
(Fourth movement theme)

Franz Schubert
(Austria, 1797–1828)

Andantino (♩ = 104)

(Original key: D major)

(violin)

Soprano recorder

Schubert's famous "Trout" Quintet was composed for violin, viola, cello, double bass, and piano. The fourth movement is an example of theme and variations form.[6]

The ideals of nineteenth-century Romanticism infused music with a subjective, emotional lyricism. Some of the Romantic composers who sought greater freedom of form and expression were Beethoven, Schubert, Mendelssohn, Chopin, Wagner, Brahms, and Tchaikovsky. No longer subsidized by royal patrons, music began to serve a rising middle-class audience. For the typical nineteenth-century artist, music transcended both time and place; it was the perfect expression of the soul.

[6] Found in *Bowmar Orchestral Library*, Series 3, "Ensembles Large and Small."

Turn! Turn! Turn!
(To Everything There Is a Season)

Words from Ecclesiastes
Adaptation and words by Pete Seeger
(United States, b. 1919)

Guitar, strum 23; at measure 9, one strum for each measure
Piano, accompaniment pattern XVII

A member of a well-known musical family, Pete Seeger has been active on the folk-music scene since his student days at Harvard University. Seeger is a composer, a performer, a political activist, and a leader in the environmental effort to save New York's Hudson River from pollution. He presently assists the Music Educators National Conference as honorary chairperson of the "SingAmerica!" campaign.

TURN ME 'ROUND

African American Spiritual

Ain't gon - na let no - bod - y turn me 'round, _____

turn me 'round, ___ turn me 'round. ___ Ain't gon - na

let no - bod - y turn me 'round, ___ Keep on a - walk - in',

Keep on a - talk - in', Walk - in' all o - ver this ___ land.

Guitar, scratch or brush the melody rhythm
Piano, accompaniment pattern XI

TURN THE GLASSES OVER

American Singing Game

Walking tempo

I've been to Haar - lem, I've been to Do - ver, I've trav -eles all this

wide world o - ver, O - ver, o - ver, three times o - ver,

Find me an - oth - er ship when this trip is o - ver.

Refrain

Sail - ing east, sail - ing west, Sail - ing o - ver the o - cean,

Bet -ter watch out when the boat be-gins to rock, Or you'll lose your girl in the o - cean.

Autoharp, strum A
Guitar, strum 2 or 22
Piano, accompaniment pattern XVI
Soprano recorder

THE TWELVE DAYS OF CHRISTMAS

English Carol

1. On the first day of Christ-mas my true love sent to me A par-tridge in a pear tree.

2. On the sec-ond day of Christ-mas my true love sent to me
3. On the third ___ day of Christ-mas my true love sent to me
4. On the fourth ___ day of Christ-mas my true love sent to me

Two tur-tle doves, And a par-tridge ___ in a pear tree.
Three French ___ hens,
Four call-ing birds,

5. On the fifth day of Christ-mas my true love sent to me

Five gold-en rings; Four ___ call-ing birds; Three French hens;

Two ___ tur-tle doves and a par-tridge ___ in a pear tree.

6. On the sixth day of Christ-mas my true love sent to me
7. On the seventh day of Christ-mas my true love sent to me
8.–12.

Six geese a lay-ing; Five gold-en rings; Four — call-ing birds;
Seven swans a swim-ming;

rit.

Three French hens; Two — tur-tle doves and a par - tridge — in a pear tree.

Autoharp, strum N; for triple-meter measures, strum only on the downbeat.

Piano, accompaniment pattern XVII (play solid chords); for triple-meter measures, play only on the downbeat.

8. On the eighth day . . .
   Eight maids a-milking . . .

9. On the ninth day . . .
   Nine ladies dancing . . .

10. On the tenth day . . .
    Ten lords a-leaping . . .

11. On the eleventh day . . .
    Eleven pipers piping . . .

12. On the twelfth day of Christmas

F

C7   F
My true love sent to me

C7
Twelve drummers drumming;
Eleven pipers piping;
Ten lords a-leaping;
Nine ladies dancing;
Eight maids a-milking;
Seven swans a-swimming;

     F G7 C
Six geese a-laying; Five golden rings;

F   *B♭*
Four calling birds; Three French hens;

G7 *C* *F B♭* *F*
Two turtle doves and a partridge in a

C7 F
pear tree.

TWINKLE, TWINKLE, LITTLE STAR
(Alphabet Song)
(Baa, Baa, Black Sheep)

French Melody

Twin - kle, twin - kle, lit - tle star, How I won - der what you are,
A, B, C, D, E, F, G, H, I, J, K, L,M, N,O, P,
Baa, baa, black sheep, have you an–y wool? "Yes, sir, yes, sir, three bags full.

Up a - bove the world so high. ____ Like a dia - mond in the sky.
Q, R, S, T, U, and V, ____ Dou - ble U and X, Y, Z.
One for my mast - er and one for my dame, And one for the lit–tle boy who lives in the lane."

Twin - kle, twin - kle, lit - tle star, How I won - der what you are.
Now I nev - er will for - get, How to say my al - pha - bet!
Baa, baa, black sheep, have you an–y wool? "Yes, sir, yes, sir, three bags full."

Autoharp (15-bar), strum A
Guitar, play melody notes
Piano, accompaniment pattern XIV
Soprano recorder

330

Tzena, Tzena

English words by
Phyllis Resnick

Israeli Folk Song

① D / G
Tze - na, tze - na, tze - na, tze - na, come in - to the fields and we'll be -
zay - nuh

A7 / D
gin _____ to work the land. Hoe - ing, sow - ing, new things grow - ing,

G / A7 / D
pi - o - neer - ing all to - geth - er, come _____ and lend a hand.

② D / G
Tze - na, tze - na, build - ing a new na - tion,

A7 / D
toil - ing bus - i - ly all day. _____ Soon we'll dance and

G / A7 / D
have a cel - e - bra - tion, But first we'll work and then we'll play.

③ Tze - na, tze - na, (clap) Tze - na, tze - na, tze - na, Tze - na, tze - na,

Tze - na, tze - na, tze - na, tze - na, Tze - na, tze - na,

(clap) Tze - na, tze - na, tze - na, Tze - na, tze - na, Tze - na, tze - na, tze - na.

Autoharp, strum N
Guitar, strum 2
Piano, accompaniment pattern XVI

Form three groups, then perform "Tzena" as a round. Each group can create a pattern of movements for their singing.

UP ON THE HOUSETOP

Benjamin R. Hanby
(United States, 1833–1867)

1. Up on the house - top the rein - deer pause, Out jumps good old
2. First comes the stock - ing of lit - tle Nell, Oh, dear San - ta,
3. Next comes the stock - ing of lit - tle Will, Oh, just see what a

San - ta Claus; Down through the chim - ney with lots of toys,
fill it well; Give her a dol - ly that laughs and cries,
glori - ous fill; Here is a ham - mer and lots of tacks,

Refrain

All for the lit - tle ones' Christ - mas joys.
One that can o - pen and shut its eyes. } Ho, ho, ho! Who would - n't go!
Al - so a ball and a whip that cracks.

Ho, ho, ho! Who would - n't go, _____ Up on the house - top,

click, click, click, Down through the chim - ney with good Saint Nick!

Autoharp (15-bar), strum N
Guitar, strum 19

Create a pantomime or a dramatization for this song.

333

Up the Hickory

American Folk Song

Lively

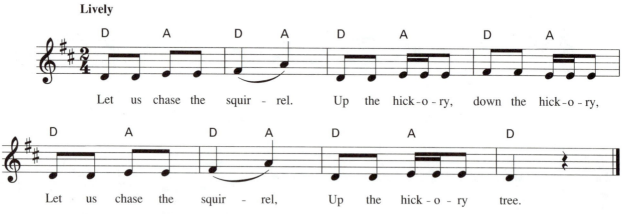

Let us chase the squir - rel. Up the hick-o-ry, down the hick-o-ry,

Let us chase the squir - rel, Up the hick-o-ry tree.

Autoharp (15-bar), strum C (play A7 throughout)
Piano accompaniment pattern II

Üsküdar

Turkish Popular Song

♩ = 96

English: Üs - kü-dar' a Üs - kü - dar' a. See how it rains out here!
Turkish: Üs - kü-dar' a gi - der — i ken al - li-da bir yağ mur,
Pronunciation: uhs - kuh-dahr ah gih - dehr ih kehn ah - lih-dah bihr yahj muhr

Come, my friend and do — not — wor - ry, Friend - ship — keeps — us —
Ka - ti-bi - min se - tre-si u - zun e - te - ği - ça
kah - tih-bih - mihn seh - treh-sih uh - zuhn eh - teh - jih - sah

warm. Friend - ship — keeps — us — warm.
mur. e - te - gi - ça - mur.
muhr eh - teh - jih - sah - muhr

Guitar, strum 3
Piano accompany using chord roots

Üsküdar is a suburb of Istanbul, a Turkish city.

VIVA LA MUSICA

Round

With movement

Italian: Vi - va, vi - va la mu - si - ca, Vi - va, vi - va la
Pronunciation: vee - vah vee - vah lah moo - zee - kah vee - vah vee - vah lah

mu - si - ca, Vi - va la mu - si - ca.
moo - zee - kah vee - vah lah moo - zee - kah

Autoharp (15-bar) strum A
Guitar, strum 2

WADDALY ATCHA

Words and music by Kassel and Stitzel
(United States)

♩ = 112

Wad - da -ly a - tcha, wad - da -ly a - tcha,

Doo - dle -ee - doo, _ doo - dle -ee - doo; _ Wad - da -ly a - tcha,

wad - da - ly a - tcha, Doo - dle -ee - doo, ___

doo - dle -ee - doo. _ It's the sim - pl -est thing, _

noth - in' much to _____ it, _____ All you got to do is

doo - dle - ee - doo it; ___ I like the rest, _ But the

part I love best, _ It goes doo -dle-ee, doo -dle-ee - doo. *Whoo!*

Autoharp (15-bar), banjo strum
Piano accompaniment pattern XV

WAR DANCE

Native American Dance Song
Transcribed by Patricia Hackett

Dance

Dancers move in a large circle, each dancing independently. (For description of steps and costumes, see below.) Music is provided by a group of about six drummer/singers seated around a large drum in the center of the dance area. Only the drummers sing, not the dancers.

Before the intrusion of Europeans, an occasion for "war" on the Great Plains was often to settle a personal feud or to steal ponies from a neighboring group. The instigator of a raid needed to persuade several of his band to join him. He would succeed only if his plan seemed sensible and just. Such skirmishes usually didn't result in fatalities before the days of firearms. Instead, it was important to "count coup." This included taking booty (especially horses) and tagging an enemy or, occasionally, killing him. The groups performed a war dance before a battle to generate courage, or afterward to celebrate and to display their booty.

Today, however, the modern war dance is mainly a display of male dance virtuosity. There are two main styles of dancing. The "straight dance" style is typical of older men, and the dignified steps suit them: The torso is straight, arms are close to the body, and the head and shoulders tilt subtly while they dance a toe-heel step. The "fancy dance" style is favored by younger dancers, who also use a toe-heel step as they twist, cross legs, shake heads, and swirl in place. (But they should not get too wild.) Outfits of fancy dancers include trailing streamers, large leg bells (like sleigh bells), and either a long, feather headdress or a circle of feathers on the lower back. By contrast, the straight dancers wear simple shirts, pants, and headdresses. Women weave in and out among the men and dance with a step-bend.

WASSAIL SONG

English Carol

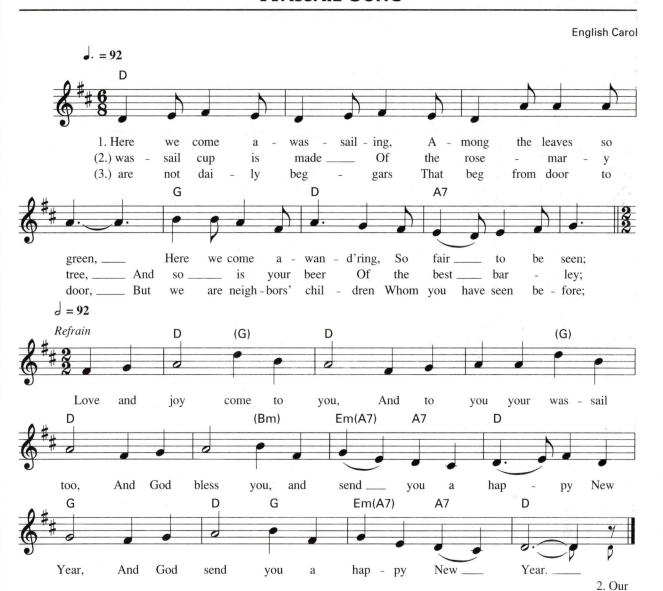

♩. = 92

D

1. Here we come a - was - sail - ing, A - mong the leaves so
(2.) was - sail cup is made ____ Of the rose - mar - y
(3.) are not dai - ly beg - gars That beg from door to

G   **D**   **A7**

green, ____ Here we come a - wan - d'ring, So fair ____ to be seen;
tree, ____ And so ____ is your beer Of the best ____ bar - ley;
door, ____ But we are neigh - bors' chil - dren Whom you have seen be - fore;

♩ = 92

Refrain   **D**   **(G)**   **D**   **(G)**

Love and joy come to you, And to you your was - sail

D   **(Bm)**   **Em(A7)**   **A7**   **D**

too, And God bless you, and send ____ you a hap - py New

G   **D**   **G**   **Em(A7)**   **A7**   **D**

Year, And God send you a hap - py New ____ Year. ____

2. Our
3. We

Autoharp (15-bar), strum B (verse) and strum A (refrain)

4. Call up the butler of this house
   Put on his gold ring;
   Let him bring us up a glass of beer,
   And better we shall sing: (*Refrain*)

5. We have got a little purse
   Of stretching leather skin;
   We want a little money
   To line it well within: (*Refrain*)

6. Bring us out a table
   And spread it with a cloth;
   Bring us out a mouldy cheese,
   And some of your Christmas loaf: (*Refrain*)

7. God bless the master of this house
   And the mistress too,
   And all the little children
   That 'round the table go: (*Refrain*)

8. Good master and good mistress
   While you're sitting by the fire,
   Pray think of us poor children
   Who are wand'ring in the mire: (*Refrain*)

THE WATER IS WIDE
(Waly, Waly)

English Folk Song

$\stackrel{\circ}{=} 63$

F   (C)   Bb   F

1. The wa-ter is wide, _____ I can-not get o'er, And nei-ther
2. I leaned . my back _____ up a-gainst some oak, And thought it
3. Oh, down _ in the mead - ow the oth - er day, All gath-r'ing
4. Oh, love _ is hand - some and love is fine, And love's a

Dm   Bb   C   Bb   F

have _____ I wings to _____ fly, So give me a boat _____ that will car - ry _____
was _____ a trust - y _____ tree, But first it _____ bent _____ and _ then it _____
flow'rs _____ that bloom in _____ May, All gath - r'ing _ flow'rs _____ both _ red and _____
jewel _____ while it is _____ new, But when it is old _____ it _____ wax - eth _____

Dm   Bb   F   Am   C   F

two, And both shall row, my love and _____ I.
broke, And so did love, false love, to _____ me.
blue, I lit - tle thought what love can _____ do.
cold, And fades a - way like morn - ing _____ dew.

Autoharp, free strum
Piano, accompaniment pattern X on each chord change

WEEVILY WHEAT

American Dance Song

1. Char-lie's neat and Char-lie's sweet, Char-lie is a dan-dy,
2. Your weevi-ly wheat's not fit to eat, nei-ther is your bar-ley,
3. Char-lie is a brave young man, Char-lie is a sol-dier,
4. Char-lie is a nice young man, Char-lie is a dan-dy,

Char-lie is a nice young man, he feeds the girls on can-dy.
What I want is the best of rye to bake a cake for Char-lie.
Sword and pis-tol by his side, his mus-ket on his shoul-der.
Char-lie likes to swing the girls, and he can do it han-dy.

Refrain

Rise you up in the morn-ing, all to-geth-er ear-ly; You

need not feel at all a-fraid be-cause I love you dear-ly.

Autoharp, strum A
Piano, accompaniment pattern XVI

Formation

Two lines of five or six couples face each other.

Dance

Verse 1: First couple take both hands, straight across, and "sashay" down the middle (eight counts) and back again (eight counts).

Verse 1, Refrain: Begin the reel; first couple turn clockwise once and a half, hooking right elbows. The first boy turns the second girl, hooking *left* elbows, counterclockwise once around, while the first girl turns the second boy the same way. Then the first couple turn each other once around again with right elbows, and so forth, continuing to the last couple.

Verses 2 and 3: Continue the reel and finish the reeling just before the refrain of verse 3.

Verse 3, Refrain: The last couple join raised hands, forming an arch. Dancers cast off by moving in line to the top and then down the outside. The boys' line casts off to the left, the girls' line casts off to the right; partners meet below the arch and come back up the middle to places. Use a skipping step throughout.

Repeat until each couple has done all figures.

WE GATHER TOGETHER

English version by Theodore Baker

Netherlands Melody

♩ = 76

1. We gath - er to - geth - er to ask the Lord's bless - ing; He
2. Be - side us to guide us, our God with us join - ing; Or -
3. We all do ex - tol Thee, Thou lead - er tri - umph - ant, And

chas - tens and has - tens His will to make known. The
dain - ing, main - tain - ing His king - dom di - vine. So
pray that Thou still our de - fend - er wilt be. Let

wick - ed op - press - ing, now cease _____ from dis - tress - ing. Sing
from the be - gin - ning, the fight _____ we were win - ning. Thou,
Thy con - gre - ga - tion es - cape _____ tri - bu - la - tion. Thy

prais - es to His name; He for - gets not His own.
Lord, wast at our side; _____ all glo - ry be Thine.
name be ev - er praised! _____ Oh, Lord, make us free!

Autoharp, harp strum
Piano, accompaniment pattern VI

We'll Meet Again

Ross Parker
Hughie Charles

Autoharp (15-bar), strum A

English singer Vera Lane made this song a wartime favorite during the dark days of World War II in Great Britain.

WE SHALL OVERCOME

Civil Rights Song

Slowly, with strength and fervor

C	F	C	Am	C	F	C	Am

1., 6. We shall o - ver - come, _____ We shall o - ver - come, _____
2. We'll walk hand in hand, _____ We'll walk hand in hand, _____
(3.) truth will make us free, _____ The truth will make us free, _____ The
4. We are not a - fraid, _____ We are not a - fraid, _____
5. We shall live in peace, _____ We shall live in peace, _____

C F (G7) Am D7 G7 D7 G G7 Am

We shall o - ver come some day; _____
We'll walk hand in hand some day; _____
truth will make us free some day; _____ Oh, ___ deep in my
We are not a - fraid to - day; _____
We shall live in peace some day; _____

C F C F C G7 C

heart, I do be - lieve We shall o - ver - come some day. _____

3. The

Autoharp, strum A
Piano, accompaniment pattern XI
Soprano recorder

Verses sung during the movement for integration include:

We shall brothers be . . .

We shall end Jim Crow . . .

Black and white together . . .

We shall all be free . . .

A Spanish text was sung during the drive to unionize farm workers:

C   F   C Am C   F   C Am
Nostros venceremos, nostros venceremos.

C   F   Am D7 G7 D7 G
Nostros venceremos ahora;

G7 Am   C F   C
En mi corazón yo creo.

F   C G7 C
Nostros venceremos.

What'll I Do with the Baby-O?

American Fiddle Melody

Refrain

What-'ll I do with the ba - by - O? What-'ll I do with the ba - by - O?

What - 'll I do with the ba - by - O? If he don't go to sleep - y - O?

1. Wrap him up in cal - i - co, Wrap him up in cal - i - co,
2. Wrap him up in a ta - ble - cloth, Wrap him up in a ta - ble cloth,
3. Tickle his chin, ___ pull his toes, Tickle his chin, ___ pull his toes,
4. Dance him north, ___ dance him south, Dance him north, ___ dance him south,

Wrap him up in cal - i - co, Send him to his mam - my - O.
Wrap him up in a ta - ble - cloth, Throw him up in the fod - der loft.
Tickle his chin, ___ pull his toes, Dress him up in my cit - y clothes.
Dance him north, ___ dance him south, Pour a little moon - shine in his mouth.

Autoharp, banjo strum
Piano, accompany using chord roots

345

WHAT SHALL WE DO ON A RAINY DAY?

Traditional Song

What shall we do on a rain - y day, Rain - y day, rain - y day?

What shall we do on a rain - y day, When we can't go out to play?

Autoharp (15-bar), banjo strum
Guitar, strum 8

WHEN THE SAINTS GO MARCHIN' IN

African American Spiritual

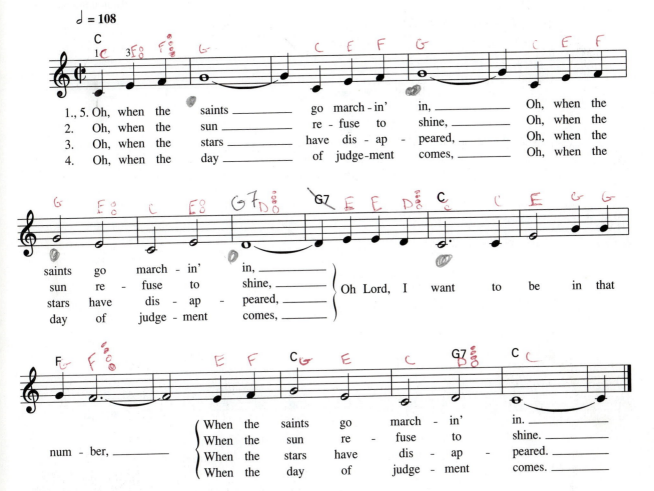

♩ = 108

1., 5. Oh, when the saints _____ go march - in' in, _____ Oh, when the
2.   Oh, when the sun _____ re - fuse to shine, _____ Oh, when the
3.   Oh, when the stars _____ have dis - ap - peared, _____ Oh, when the
4.   Oh, when the day _____ of judge-ment comes, _____ Oh, when the

saints   go   march - in'   in, _____ { Oh Lord, I   want   to   be   in that
sun   re - fuse   to   shine, _____
stars   have   dis - ap - peared, _____
day   of   judge - ment   comes, _____

num - ber, _____ { When the saints go march - in' in. _____
                      { When the sun re - fuse to shine. _____
                      { When the stars have dis - ap - peared. _____
                      { When the day of judge - ment comes. _____

Autoharp, strum A
Guitar, strum 2
Piano, accompaniment pattern XI

WHERE HAVE ALL THE FLOWERS GONE?

Pete Seeger
(United States, b.1919)

Guitar, strum 23 (To sing in C major, place the capo on fret 3 and play the chords shown above.)

WINDS OF MORNING

Tommy Makem
(Ireland)

winds, ___ your mourn-ful sound. Blow, ye from ___ the earth's four

cor - ners, ___ Guide this trav - - 'ler where s/he's bound.

Autoharp (15-bar), harp strum
Guitar, strum 23

WIND THROUGH THE OLIVE TREES

American Christmas Song

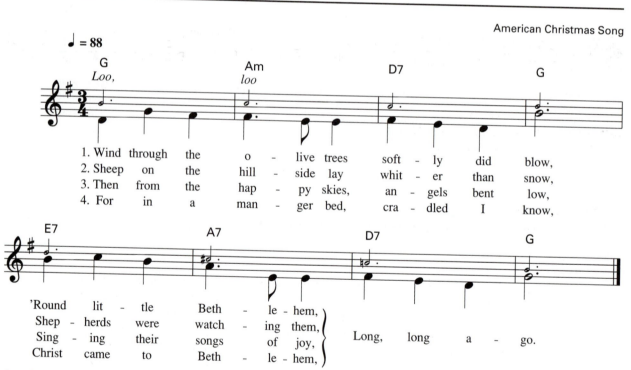

♩ = 88

1. Wind through the o - live trees soft - ly did blow,
2. Sheep on the hill - side lay whit - er than snow,
3. Then from the hap - py skies, an - gels bent low,
4. For in a man - ger bed, cra - dled I know,

'Round lit - tle Beth - le - hem,
Shep - herds were watch - ing them,
Sing - ing their songs of joy,
Christ came to Beth - le - hem,

Long, long a - go.

Autoharp, strum I
Guitar, play melody notes
Soprano recorder

WISHY WASHY WEE

American Folk Song

Verse

Oh, we are two sail - ors come from o'er the sea, If you want to go a - way a - gain, come a - long with me. Oh,

wish - y wash - y, wish - y wash - y, wish - y wash - y wee, If you want to go a - way a - gain, come a - long with me.

Autoharp (15-bar), strum O
Guitar, strum 18 (verse) and strum 26 (refrain)
Piano, accompaniment pattern XI

Formation

Players stand in a large circle with two sailors in the center.

Dance

During the verse, all stand in place while the two sailors link elbows and swing in the center. At the end of the verse on "come along with me," each of the two sailors stops in front of a person standing in the circle. During the refrain, these two join hands. They dance by hopping on the left foot, at the same time sliding the right heel forward, and then hopping on the right foot while sliding the left heel forward. This alternating footwork continues. At the same time, the right hand pushes straight ahead along with the right heel, and then the left hand pushes straight ahead with the left heel, and so forth.

On "come along with me" at the end of the refrain, the four dancers change places. The two players from the circle move to the center and become the new sailors for a repetition of the song. The dance continues until every player in the circle has an opportunity to dance as a sailor.

WORRIED MAN BLUES

American Song

Moderately fast

Refrain: It takes a wor-ried man to sing a wor-ried song. It
1. I went a-cross the river and I lay down to sleep. I
2. I hung ___ down my head and cried just like be-fore. I

takes a wor-ried man to sing a wor-ried song. It
went a-cross the river and I lay down to sleep. I
hung ___ down my head and cried just like be-fore. I

takes a wor-ried man to sing a wor-ried song. I'm wor-ried
went a-cross the river and I lay down to sleep, When I woke
hung ___ down my head and cried just like be-fore. I'm wor-ried

now, but I won't be wor-ried long. _____
up, had ___ shack-les on my feet. _____
now, but I won't be wor-ried long. _____

Autoharp, strum N
Guitar, strum 26
Piano, accompaniment pattern XV

352

YANKEE DOODLE

Words by
Dr. Richard Shuckburgh

Traditional Melody

Brightly

1.　　Fath'r and I went down to camp A - long with Cap - tain Good - win, And
2. And there was Cap - tain Wash - ing - ton Up - on a slap - ping stal - lion, A -
3. And then the feath - ers in his hat, They looked so ver - y fine, ah, I

there we saw the men and boys As thick as hast - y pud - din'.
giv - ing or - ders to his men, I guess there was a mil - lion,
want - ed pes - ki - ly to get To give to my Je - mi - ma.

Verse

Yan - kee Doo - dle keep it up, Yan - kee Doo - dle dan - dy;

Mind the mu - sic and the step, And with the girls be hand - y.

Autoharp, strum C

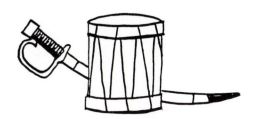

4. And there I see a swamping gun,

 As large as a log of maple,

 Upon a deucéd little cart;

 A load for father's cattle. (*Refrain*)

5. And every time they fired it off

 It took a horn of powder;

 It made a noise like father's gun,

 Only a nation louder. (*Refrain*)

6. And Captain Davis had a gun,

 He kinda clapt his hand on't,

 And stuck a crooked stabbing iron

 Upon the little end on't. (*Refrain*)

7. And there I see a little keg,

 Its heads were made of leather.

 They knocked upon't with little sticks

 To call the folks together. (*Refrain*)

8. And there they'd fife away like fun,

 And play on cornstalk fiddles;

 And some had ribbands, red as blood,

 All wound about their middles. (*Refrain*)

9. The troopers, too, would gallop up

 And fire right in our faces;

 It scared me almost half to death

 To see them run such races. (*Refrain*)

10. I see another snarl of men,

 A-diggin' graves, they told me;

 So tarnal long, so tarnal deep,

 They 'tended they should hold me. (*Refrain*)

11. It scared me so, I hooked it off,

 Nor stopped, as I remember,

 Nor turned about till I got home,

 Locked up in mother's chamber. (*Refrain*)

The amiable mockery of "Yankee Doodle" has been with Americans for more than two hundred years. During the French and Indian War, a British army doctor was the first to create verses poking fun at the ragtag attire of the Colonial fighters. No one knows the origin of the tune or of the epithet "yankee doodle." But the scruffy "Yankees" were as amused by the satire as were the British, and the song was adopted by the Colonials—to become virtually their battle march during the Revolutionary War. "Yankee Doodle" is the state song of Connecticut.

THE YELLOW ROSE OF TEXAS

Traditional American Song

♩ = 126

G

1. There's a yel - low rose in Tex - as, I'm go - in' there to see; No
Refrain: She's the sweet - est lit - tle lad - y that Tex - as ev - er knew, Her
2. Where the Ri - o Grande is flow - ing, and the star - ry skies are bright, We
3. Oh, I'm go - in' back to find her, for my heart is full of woe, And we'll

D7

oth - er sol - dier loves her, no sol - dier, on - ly me. She
(Refrain) eyes were bright as dia - monds, they spark - led like the dew. You may
walked a - long the riv - er, in the qui - et sum - mer night. I
sing the song to - geth - er, we sang so long a - go. I'll

G

cried so when I left her, it al - most broke my heart, And
(Refrain) see a lot of dand - y girls wher - ev - er you may be, But the
think that she re - mem - bers, where we part - ed long a - go; I
play the ban - jo bright - ly, and sing just as be - fore; And the

D7   G   D7   G

if we ev - er meet a - gain, we nev - er - more will part.
(Refrain) yel - low rose of Tex - as, _____ is the on - ly girl for me.
prom - ised to come back a - gain, and nev - er let her go. *(Refrain)*
yel - low rose of Tex - as will be mine for ev - er more. *(Refrain)*

Autoharp, banjo strum
Piano, accompaniment pattern XVI

141

Yesterday

Paul McCartney
(England, b. 1942)

Expressively

Yes - ter - day, all my trou - bles seemed so far a way
Sud - den - ly, I'm not half the man I used to be

Now it looks as tho' they're here to stay _ Oh I be - lieve _ in yes - ter - day. _
There's a shad - ow hang - ing o - ver me _ Oh yes - ter - day _ came sud - den - ly. _

Why she had to go I don't know, she would - n't say. I said

some - thing wrong now I long for yes - ter - day. _____ Yes - ter - day,

love was such an eas - y game to play. Now I need a place to hide a - way, _ Oh

I be - lieve _ in yes - ter - day. _ Mm _____

Autoharp (15-bar), strum each chord change
Piano, accompany using chord roots

YOKUTS GRINDING SONG

Adapted by Patricia Hackett from
tapes 115 and 116 of the Lowie
Museum (Berkeley, Calif.)

Native American Song
(California)

The Tachi Yokuts people lived in California's San Joaquin Valley near Tulare. (Tulare is midway between Bakersfield and Fresno.) More than one hundred Native American groups lived amicably in the central two-thirds of California. No groups practiced agriculture, perhaps because food was usually plentiful. Acorns were a staple and were varied by game, shellfish, berries, seeds, and roots.

Many California Indian songs are similar to the "Yokuts Grinding Song" because they include only a few different pitches and are expressed in one to three short musical phrases. The "song" above is a short version of the original, which was much longer, with the three phrases alternating and repeating in no regular order. Yokuts use slurred enunciation in this acorn grinding song about the magical properties of acorns. (There is no precise translation for the song's words.) The grinding song is accompanied by the striking of a stick of soft elderberry wood about twelve inches long and five-eighths of an inch in diameter. The stick is split through about half its length; the split ends make a "clicking" sound when struck in the palm of the hand.

Zum Gali Gali

Israeli Round

Zum   ga - li   ga - li   ga - li,   Zum   ga - li   ga - li,
zoom   gah - lee   gah - lee   gah - lee   zoom   gah - lee   gah - lee

Zum   ga - li   ga - li   ga - li,   Zum   ga - li   ga - li.
zoom   gah - lee   gah - lee   gah - lee   zoom   gah - lee   gah - lee

1. Pi - on - eers work   hard   on the land,   Men and wom - en   work hand in hand.
2. As they la - bor   all   day _ long,   They_ lift their   voic - es in song.

Autoharp, play drone (Dmaj + Dmin), strum A
Guitar, strum 2
Piano accompaniment pattern XI

The present-day state of Israel was created in 1948 as a homeland for Jews from around the world. Jewish pioneers cultivated the desert beginning in the late 1800s, continuing to the present.

Musical Instruments

THE PIANO

THE GUITAR AND THE UKULELE

THE AUTOHARP

THE SOPRANO RECORDER

_____ *The Piano*

Piano study and performance is rewarding to individuals of all ages because keyboard skills can be applied to several styles of music and to many different musical situations.

Body and Hand Position

Sit directly in front of the middle of the keyboard. You can lean slightly forward, but keep your torso straight. Sit far enough back from the keys that your arms and elbows can move freely.

Your hands, wrists, and forearms should be level with the keyboard. Fingers should remain close to the keys at all times, and the fingers should strike the keys, not press them, with the pad of each finger.

Fingering

The fingers of each hand are numbered 1 through 5, from the thumbs outward: The thumbs are 1; the index fingers, 2; the middle fingers, 3; the ring fingers, 4; and the little fingers, 5. Small arabic numbers appear above, below, or beside the notes in piano music to show the recommended fingering.

The Staff and the Keyboard

Notes on the *treble* (upper) staff are usually played by the right hand, and notes on the *bass* (lower) staff with the left hand. Each note on the staff has an exact location on the piano keyboard.

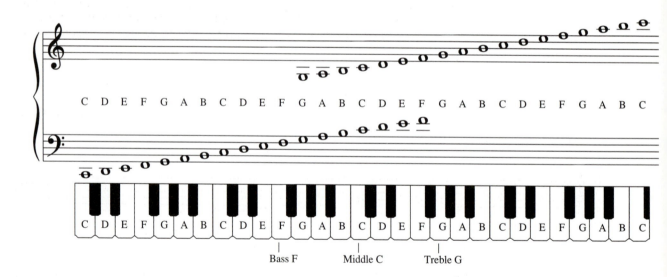

The names of the black keys are as follows:

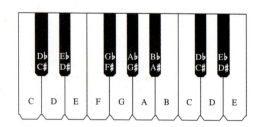

SONGS TO PLAY AND SING

The following songs have right-hand piano fingering. For additional simple melodies to play, see the Classified Index under Piano, Five-Finger Patterns.

Ring around the Rosy

American Play Song

Ring a - round the ros - y, Pock - et full of pos - y,

Ash - es, ash - es, All fall down.

Soprano recorder

"Ring around the Rosy" may describe characteristics of the plague that struck Europe in the fourteenth century: A rose-colored "ring" was an early sign that a blotch was about to appear on the skin; "a pocket full of posies" was a device to ward off stench and infection; "ashes, ashes" is a reference to "ashes to ashes, dust to dust," or perhaps to the sneezing "a-choo, a-choo" that afflicted the lungs of some victims—ending, inevitably, in "all fall down."

Hey, Tswana

African Round

With a steady beat (♩ = 152)

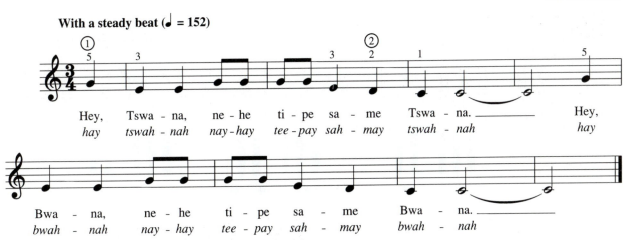

Hey, Tswa - na, ne - he ti - pe sa - me Tswa - na. _____ Hey,
hay tswah - nah nay - hay tee - pay sah - may tswah - nah hay

Bwa - na, ne - he ti - pe sa - me Bwa - na. _____
bwah - nah nay - hay tee - pay sah - may bwah - nah

The simplicity of this song belies the multilayered, percussive sound common to much African music. Typically, a profusion of drums, xylophones, rattles, and metal bells play in solo, in ensemble, and as accompaniment for singing and dancing. Nearly everywhere south of the Sahara, the timbre most admired is a buzzing, rattling, percussive sound.

Hanukkah Candles

Hebrew Folk Song

1. Burn lit-tle can-dles, burn, burn, burn,
2. Eight lit-tle can-dles in a row, } Ha-nu-kkah is here.
3. Dance, lit-tle can-dles, dance, dance, dance,

Burn lit-tle can-dles, burn, burn, burn, Burn so bright and clear.
Eight lit-tle can-dles in a row, Burn so bright and clear.
Dance, lit-tle can-dles, dance, dance, dance, Ha-nu-kkah is here.

Autoharp, strum L

PRIMARY CHORDS IN SELECTED MAJOR AND MINOR KEYS

Three primary (or principal) chords may be used to accompany many melodies. The following diagrams and staff notation show a relatively easy way to move between the three chords. Fingering shown is for the left hand.

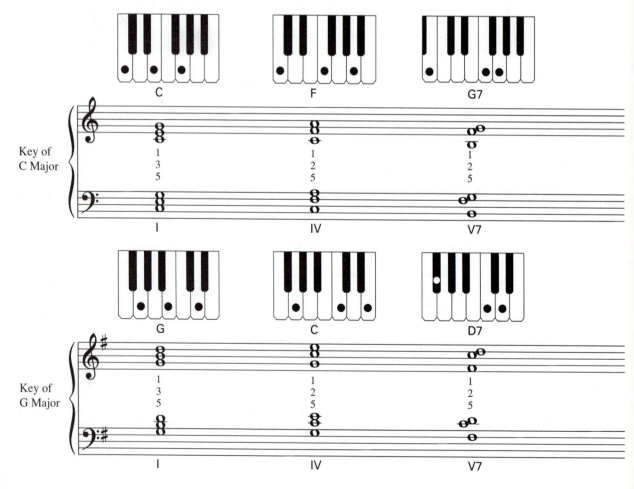

Triple-meter patterns for $\frac{3}{4}$

VI Block chords in 3s

```
1        1        1        1
3        2        2        3
5        5        5        5
```

VII Broken chords in 3s

```
5   1   1    5   1   1    5   1   1    5   1   1
    3   3        2   2        2   2        3   3
```

VIII Arpeggios in 3s

```
5   3   1    5   2   1    5   2   1    5   3   1
```

IX Jump bass in 3s

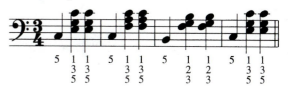

```
5   1   1    5   1   1    5   1   1    5   1   1
    3   3        3   3        2   2        3   3
    5   5        5   5        3   3        5   5
```

X Two-hand rolled chords in 3s

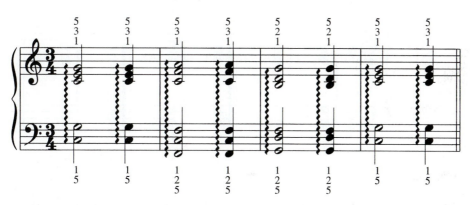

```
5   5   5   5   5   5   5   5
3   3   3   3   2   2   3   3
1   1   1   1   1   1   1   1
```

```
1   1   1   1   1   1   1   1
5   5   2   2   2   2   5   5
        5   5   5   5
```

Quadruple-meter patterns for $\frac{4}{4}$ C $\frac{2}{2}$ ¢

XI Block chords in 4s

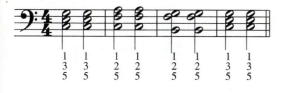

```
1   1   1   1   1   1   1   1
3   3   2   2   2   2   3   3
5   5   5   5   5   5   5   5
```

XII Broken chords in 4s

```
5   1 5   1    5   1 5   1    5   1 5   1    5   1 5   1
    3     3        2     2        2     2        3     3
```

XIII Arpeggios in 4s

```
5 3 1 3   5 2 1 2   5 2 1 2   5 3 1 3
```

XIV Alberti bass style in 4s

```
5 1 3 1 5 1 3 1   5 1 2 1 5 1 2 1   5 1 2 1 5 1 2 1   5 1 3 1 5 1 3 1
```

XV Jump style in 4s

XVI Two-hand alternating style in 4s

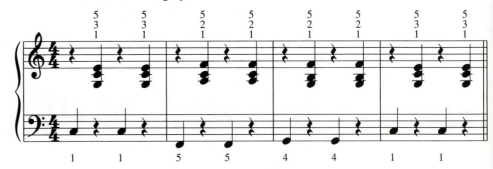

XVII Two-hand rolled chords in 4s

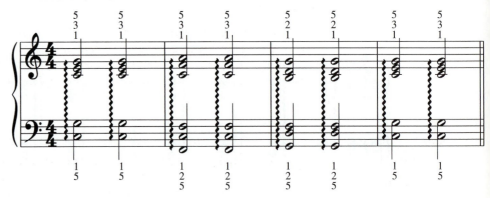

ADDITIONAL CHORDS FOR SONGS IN THIS BOOK

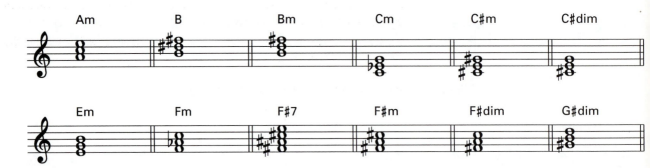

THE GUITAR

The modern guitar is the most widely used musical instrument in the world. Both acoustic and electronically amplified models are available. The acoustic guitar is discussed here.

Body and Hand Positions for Guitar

Hold the guitar with its neck at an upward angle, keeping the face of the instrument almost vertical. When sitting, rest the guitar's waist on the right leg. A neck strap on the guitar makes playing while standing easier.

  The left-hand fingers press down individual strings on the neck of the guitar while the right hand strums the strings near the sound hole. The right forearm rests on the top edge of the guitar, above the bridge. The fingers of the left hand should approach the strings from an arched, nearly vertical position. (Left-handers can finger chords in this same way, or they can restring their guitars, reversing the order of the strings, then use the right hand to finger the chords and the left hand to strum.)

Tuning the Guitar

Although electronic tuners are available, the relative tuning method is the one most commonly used by guitarists. Twist the tuning key while continuously plucking the string to check its pitch. If a string is difficult to tune, lower it well below the desired pitch, and gradually bring it up. (Never raise a string too high, because excessive tension will damage the neck of the guitar.)

Strings

(low) EADGBE (high)

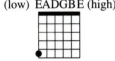

E	Tune the bass E string to a piano or to your pitch pipe.
A	Place your finger just behind the fifth fret of the E string, as shown in the diagram. You will be fingering the correct pitch for the next string, the A string. Pluck the A string and match it to the sound of the note on the E string.
D	Press down the A string at the fifth fret. Pluck the next string, D, and match it to the sound of the note on the A string.
G	Press down the D string at the fifth fret. Pluck the next string, G, and match it to the sound of the note on the D string.
B	Press down the G string at the *fourth* fret. Pluck the next string, B, and match it to the sound of the note on the G string.
E	Press down the B string at the fifth fret. Pluck the top E string and match it to the sound of the note on the B string.

Strum an E minor or E major chord to check your tuning.

GUITAR PITCHES

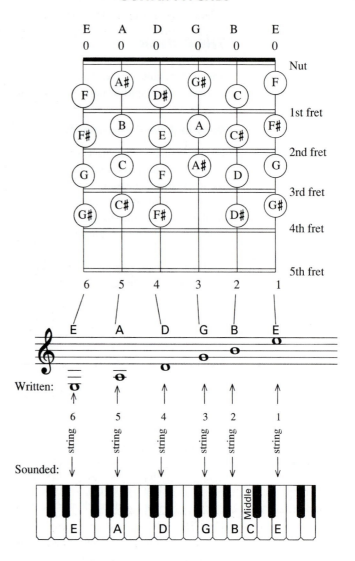

Fingering

Finger designations are shown here. Left-hand fingerings are indicated in chord diagrams; right-hand finger numbers will be used in the chart on various strums for guitar at the end of this section.

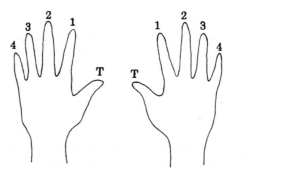

T = thumb
1 = index
2 = middle
3 = ring
4 = little

Guitar Chords

Chord diagrams for guitar look like the fingerboard of the guitar, showing the strings and the frets. Numbers (sometimes circled) show where to place the fingers of the left hand to play chords.

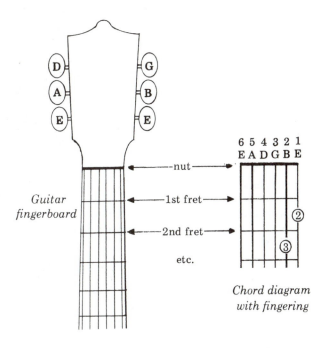

Chord diagram with fingering

A complete chord chart is presented at the end of this section.

For songs to accompany with guitar, see the Classified Index under Guitar Accompaniments (one chord, two chords) and Guitar, Melody Only.

Strums

Six strokes and strums are illustrated and described here. They include the brush stroke, the thumb stroke, the thumb-brush stroke, the arpeggio strum, the thumb-pluck strum, and the syncopated strum, and they are discussed in order of difficulty. (A chart of strums for guitar and ukulele in different meters is presented at the end of this section.) Hold an E major chord to practice the following strums.

Brush stroke

↑

The right-hand thumb sweeps downward across all strings.

Thumb ("rest") stroke

The right-hand thumb plucks and then rests on the next string—for just a moment. The thumb usually plucks the root of each chord (labeled *R* in chord diagrams). The player can also alternate between plucking the root and the fifth of the chord (labeled *5* in chord diagrams.) The low-pitched strings 4, 5, and 6 are usually used for playing a rest stroke. Keep in mind that each chord has a different root and fifth, and these are shown in the chart of chord diagrams that concludes this section.

Thumb-brush stroke

T ↑
thumb brush

This strum is a combination of the brush and the thumb strokes. The thumb of the right hand plucks the string, rests momentarily, then sweeps downward across the remaining strings.

Arpeggio strum

Plucking strings one at a time (arpeggio) adds expression to an accompaniment. While holding a chord with the left hand, place the right-hand fingers as follows:

3

2

1

T

1. Index finger just under the G string
2. Middle finger just under the B string
3. Ring finger just under the high E string

One at a time, snap each finger into the palm of the hand: index (1), middle (2), and ring (3). Do this without moving your arm. Keep each finger on its string until time to play.

The thumb starts the arpeggio strum by plucking the chord root (labeled *R* on the chord diagram).

Thumb-pluck strum

3

2

T   1

thumb pluck

Place fingers as described for the arpeggio strum. The thumb plucks the string and rests, and the remaining fingers (index, middle, ring) *simultaneously* pluck the G, B, and high E strings.

Syncopated strum

♪ ♩ ♪ ♩ ♩

syn - co - pa - ta - ta
↑   ↑   ↓   ↑   ↑

In the syncopated strum, all movements are downward, except for the strum on *-pa*. The index finger should lead each movement.

THE BARITONE UKULELE

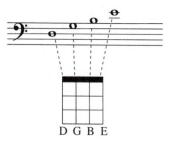

Baritone ukulele tuning

D G B E

The ukulele is a Hawaiian instrument that probably developed from a small Portuguese guitar. The modern ukulele is built in two sizes: the small, higher-pitched soprano and the larger, lower-pitched baritone. Portable, inexpensive, and relatively easy to play, a four-string ukulele can be used for song accompaniments instead of the six-string guitar.

The baritone ukulele is tuned D-G-B-E. This is the same as the four highest guitar strings. Therefore, chord diagrams have four lines. Diagrams for baritone ukulele are presented on a chart at the end of this section ("Chords for Guitar and Baritone Ukulele").

Because the two instruments are similar, almost any song for guitar can be played on baritone ukulele. See the Classified Index under Guitar.

TRANSPOSITION

Transposition changes a melody from one key (scale) to another. Performers often find music that is too high or too low for their voices or instruments. It is helpful to transpose such music, to move it from a higher to a lower key, or vice versa.

Transposition is accomplished in several ways. One way is to label each pitch in the original melody by scale number or by *sol-fa* syllable. Then change each scale number or syllable to the letter name of the new scale. For example, "Twinkle, Twinkle, Little Star" is in the key of C major, whose scale numbers and syllables are as follows:

```
C D E F G A B C
1 2 3 4 5 6 7 1(8)
do re mi fa sol la ti do
```

To transpose "Twinkle, Twinkle, Little Star" to D major, these changes are necessary:

```
D E F♯ G A B C♯ D
1 2 3  4 5 6 7 1(8)
do re mi fa sol la ti do
```

In the transposed version, a new key signature identifies the new tonic. The original and the transposed versions are identical in melodic contour (the upward and downward movement of pitch).

Twinkle, Twinkle, Little Star

(C Major)

Twin - kle, twin - kle, lit - tle star, How I won - der what you are.

Twinkle, Twinkle, Little Star

(D Major)

Twin - kle, twin - kle, lit - tle star, How I won - der what you are.

Transposition by interval distance

Another way to transpose a melody is to use interval distances. First, calculate the interval (up or down) between the original key and the new one. For example, in "Twinkle, Twinkle, Little Star," the interval distance between the key of C major and the key of D major is one whole step (major second) higher. Therefore, the transposed version will be in the key of D major and will have the key signature of D major. When the melody of "Twinkle, Twinkle, Little Star" is transposed up a major second,

C becomes D

D becomes E

E becomes F♯

F becomes G

G becomes A

A becomes B

B becomes C♯

A capo is a small piece of wood or metal that can be fixed across the guitar strings to shorten them. This makes the music sound higher, but the performer plays the same chords as in the original. The capo may be used to transpose music without learning new chord fingerings.

The capo raises all the strings at the same time when clamped around the guitar neck. Each fret on the guitar neck equals one half step. When the capo is placed on the first fret, all strings are one half step higher; on the second fret, one step higher; on the third fret, one and one half steps higher; and so on.

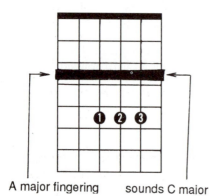

A major fingering   sounds C major

Capo in third fret; use A major fingering

"America, the Beautiful" is notated in the key of A major in this book. To raise the pitch to C major, put the capo on the third fret. The capo now becomes the upper end (nut) of the fingerboard. Retain the fingering for the A major chord. The strings sound three half steps (a minor third) higher, resulting in the C major chord. All the chords in the song will sound three half steps higher. Similarly, the melody is sung three pitches higher (in C major).

STRUMS FOR GUITAR AND UKULELE

Use the following key for abbreviations within the following strum chart.

B	=	brush thumb down across all strings
T	=	thumb ("rest") stroke
T6	=	thumb ("rest") stroke on string 6
T5	=	thumb ("rest") stroke on string 5
↑	=	scratch down with index finger
↓	=	scratch up with index finger
1	=	pluck with the index finger
2	=	pluck with the middle finger
3	=	pluck with the ring finger
3 2 1	=	pluck simultaneously with three fingers

A circled number appears to the left of each strum in the chart. This number can be found below selected songs in the Song Anthology, indicating that a specific guitar strum is suitable for a particular song.

Italic numbers above the notes are a counting system.

Duple meter

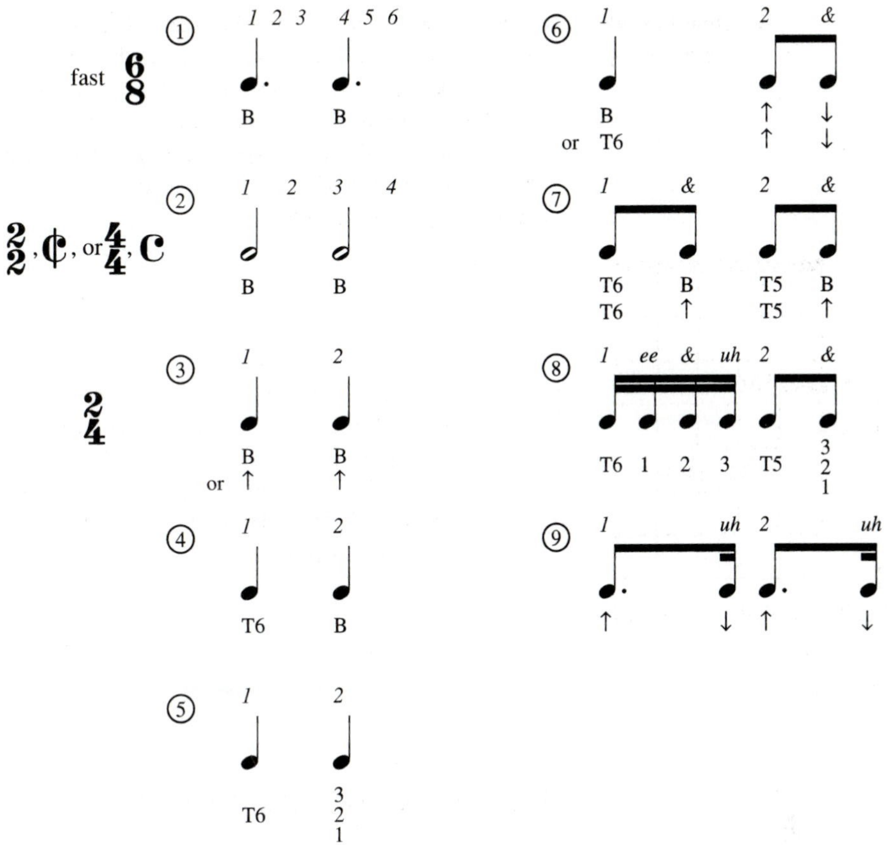

fast $\frac{6}{8}$ ①   *1 2 3*   *4 5 6*   B   B

$\frac{2}{2}$, ¢, or $\frac{4}{4}$, C   ②   *1*   *2*   *3*   *4*   B   B

$\frac{2}{4}$ ③   *1*   *2*   B   B   or ↑   ↑

④   *1*   *2*   T6   B

⑤   *1*   *2*   T6   3 2 1

⑥   *1*   *2*   *&*   B   ↑ ↓   or T6   ↑ ↓

⑦   *1*   *&*   *2*   *&*   T6   B   T5   B   / T6 ↑ T5 ↑

⑧   *1 ee & uh*   *2*   *&*   T6 1 2 3   T5   3 2 1

⑨   *1*   *uh*   *2*   *uh*   ↑ ↓ ↑ ↓

Triple meter

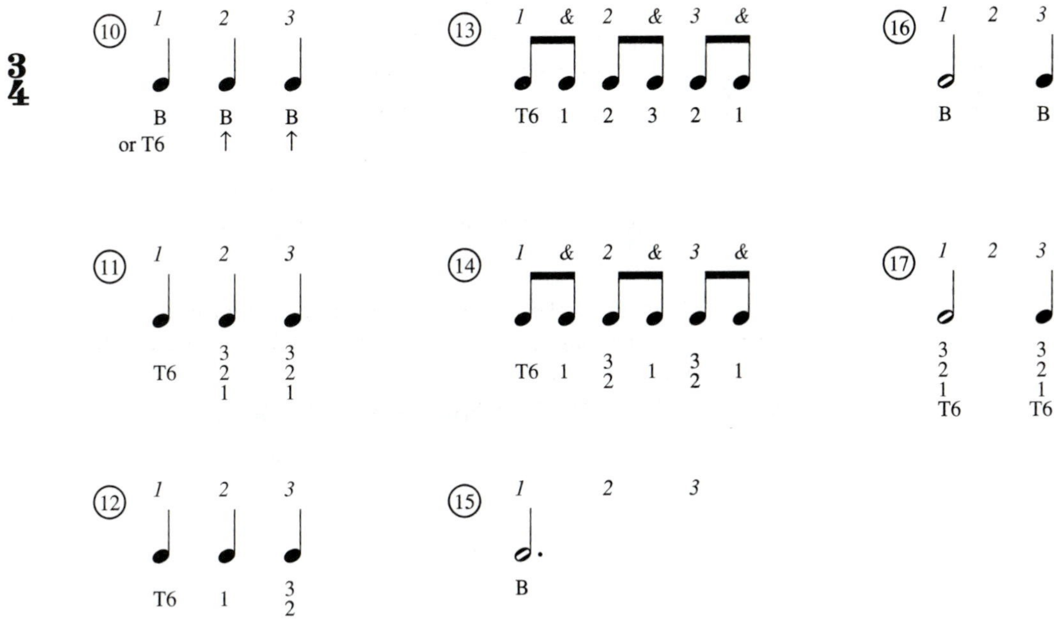

$\frac{3}{4}$

⑩   *1*   *2*   *3*   B B B   or T6 ↑ ↑

⑪   *1*   *2*   *3*   T6   3 2 1   3 2 1

⑫   *1*   *2*   *3*   T6   1   3 2

⑬   *1*   *&*   *2*   *&*   *3*   *&*   T6 1   2 3   2 1

⑭   *1*   *&*   *2*   *&*   *3*   *&*   T6 1   3 2 1   3 2 1

⑮   *1*   *2*   *3*   B

⑯   *1*   *2*   *3*   B   B

⑰   *1*   *2*   *3*   3 2 1 T6   3 2 1 T6

Quadruple meter

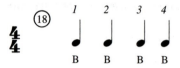

$\mathbf{\frac{4}{4}}$

(18)　1　2　3　4
B　B　B　B

(19)　1　2　3　4
T6　B　T6　B

(20)　1　2　3　4
T6　$\begin{smallmatrix}3\\2\\1\end{smallmatrix}$　T6　$\begin{smallmatrix}3\\2\\1\end{smallmatrix}$

(21)　1　2 & 3　4 &
T6　↑ ↓ T5　↑ ↓

(22)　1　2　3　4
$\begin{smallmatrix}3\\2\\1\end{smallmatrix}$　　$\begin{smallmatrix}3\\2\\1\end{smallmatrix}$
T6　　T6

(23)　1 & 2 & 3 & 4 &
T6　1　2　3　T5　1　2　3

(24)　1 & 2 & 3 & 4 &
T6　1　$\frac{3}{2}$　1　T5　1　$\frac{3}{2}$　1

(25)　1 & 2 & 3 & 4 &
↑　↑　↓　↑　↑

(26)　1　uh 2　uh 3　uh 4　uh
↑　↓ ↑　↓ ↑　↓ ↑　↓

Compound meter

$\mathbf{\frac{6}{8}}$

(27)　1　2　3　4　5　6
T6　1　2　3　2　1

(28)　1　2　3　4　5　6
T6　1　$\frac{3}{2}$　T6　1　$\frac{3}{2}$

(29)　1　2　3　4　5　6
T6　　　$\begin{smallmatrix}3\\2\\1\end{smallmatrix}$

CHORDS FOR GUITAR AND BARITONE UKULELE

The six-string chord diagram is for guitar. The four-string chord diagram is for baritone ukulele.

R means *chord root.*

5 means *chord fifth.*

X means *do not play this string.*

Alternative chord fingerings, in addition to those that follow, do exist for more experienced players.

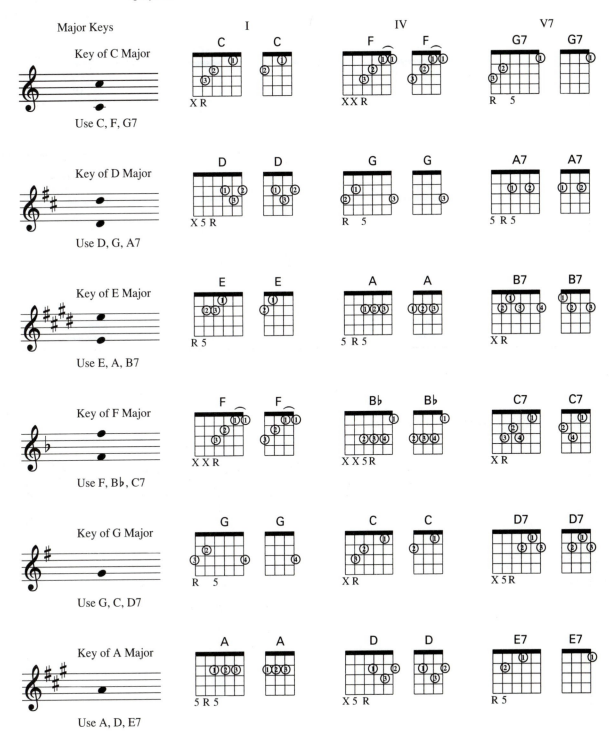

ADDITIONAL GUITAR CHORDS FOR SONGS IN THIS BOOK

For baritone ukulele, use the fingerings on the top four strings of the chord diagrams.

Am	B	3-string B7	Easy Bm	Easy C
5 R 5	X X	X X X	X X X	X X X

Cm	C#m	C#7	C#dim	Dm
X X	X X	X R X	X X	X R 5

Em	Easy F	Fm	Easy F#m	F#7
R 5	X X X	X X R	X X R	X X

F#dim	Easy G	Easy Gm	Easy G7	G#dim
X X X	X X R	X X X	X X X R	X X

The Autoharp is a zitherlike instrument invented about one hundred years ago. It is designed for playing simple harmonies to accompany melodies. Autoharp and Chromaharp are trademark names for similar instruments by different manufacturers. The following information can be applied to either instrument.

Playing Position

Place the Autoharp on your lap or on a tabletop, with its longest side near you. Your left hand will press a chord button, and your right hand will cross over to strum.

Keyboard

The letter name on each chord bar identifies the chord root (the strongest tone of each chord).

Autoharps can have from 5 to 21 chord bars, but the most frequently used are the 12-bar and 15-bar Autoharps. A diagram of the bar arrangements is shown here:

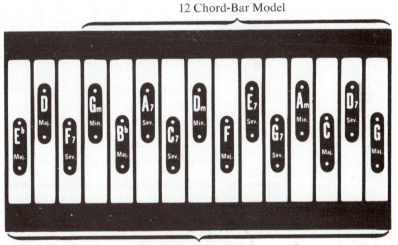

12 Chord-Bar Model

15 Chord-Bar Model

Strums

You can strum with your thumb or the fingernail of your index finger, or you can use a soft or a hard pick. A plastic pick produces a brilliant, "twangy" sound, and a felt pick gives a mellow effect. The pick you select should fit the mood and style of the song.

The basic stroke is an upstroke. It is produced by placing your hand near your body and swinging it outward across the strings (low strings to high strings). An arrow pointing upward indicates an upstroke.

↑ high

| low

The upstroke is often shortened and played in different locations—for example, on the lower or bass strings (close to the body), on the middle strings, or on the higher strings (away from the body).

Accompaniments

Autoharp strokes are used in different ways to create song accompaniments. The accompaniment needs to match the song's rhythm and enhance its character and mood.

An accent is created by playing an upstroke on the lower strings. Common four-beat and three-beat patterns are:

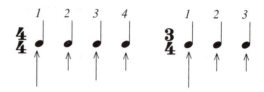

A downstroke toward the body can also be used. An arrow pointing downward indicates a downstroke.

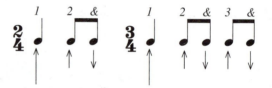

Other accompaniment patterns are possible, many of which are shown at the end of this section, under "Strums for Autoharp." Also described there are special strums such as the harp, banjo, drone (bagpipe), and Middle Eastern strums.

Fingering the Chord Bars

The chord bars are arranged so that the three principal chords are played by the strongest fingers of the left hand. When playing the chord bars, use a pattern of fingering that remains constant throughout the song.

Songs for which Autoharp accompaniment is appropriate are indicated in the Classified Index under the heading Autoharp.

AUTOHARP ACCOMPANIMENTS

Specific Autoharp accompaniments are suggested for many songs in this book. To locate these songs, refer to the Classified Index under Autoharp (12-bar or 15-bar). Songs are listed by key and according to the number of chords needed (one-chord songs, two-chord songs, and so on).

A circled letter appears to the left of each strum in the chart. This letter can be found below selected songs in the Song Anthology, indicating that a specific Autoharp strum is suitable for a particular song.

STRUMS FOR AUTOHARP

↑ = upstroke outward across all strings

↑ = upstroke from middle strings outward

↓ = downstroke on middle strings

Italic numbers above the notes are a counting method.

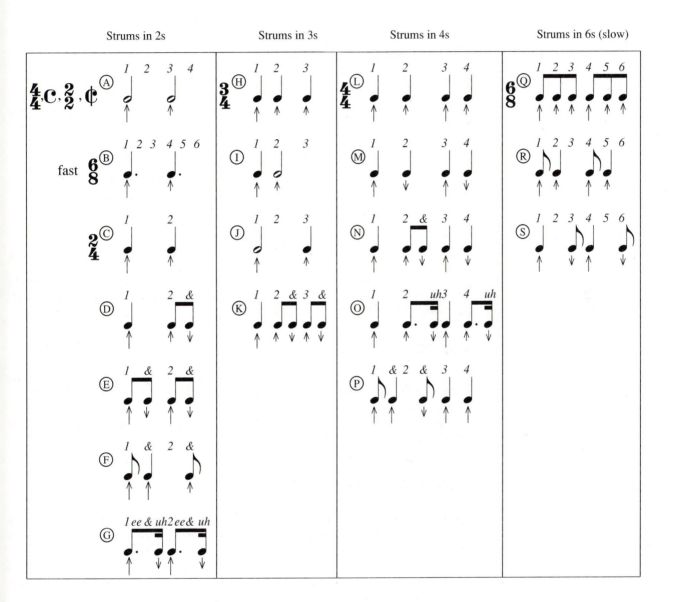

Strums in 2s	Strums in 3s	Strums in 4s	Strums in 6s (slow)

Special Effects

1. *Harp.* Use either a slow upstroke or a slow downstroke, and vary the length of the strum. Use a felt pick.
2. *Banjo.* Strum to the right of the chord bars in a rhythm that is faster than the beat. Use a flat plastic pick.
3. *Drone or Bagpipe.* Press two chord buttons with the same letter names simultaneously, such as G major and G minor. This produces an open fifth.
4. *Middle Eastern.* Press and hold a chord button down while scrubbing or bouncing lightly two or more mallets (rubber or wood) on the strings. This works best with two players.

The soprano recorder is perhaps the most popular of the recorder family and is described here.

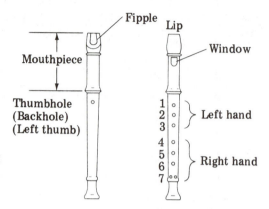

Soprano recorder (back and front views)

Playing Position

Hold the recorder at a 45-degree angle away from the body, with arms in a relaxed position close to the body. Place the mouthpiece between your lips and slightly in front of your teeth (not between the teeth). Close your lips around the mouthpiece and open them slightly to take each breath (the breath is drawn in through the mouth, not the nose).

Breathing

Try to produce a light, steady stream of air, because control of the breath is important for playing in tune. The correct body position for recorder playing is the same as for singing: Keep the shoulders down, the chest elevated, the neck relaxed, and the jaw loose.

Blow more gently on low pitches and increase breath pressure for high pitches. Ration each breath to last through all the notes in a phrase, unless other directions are given.

Use a gentle attack for each note. An explosive attack will produce a penetrating sound and will exhaust your supply of air.

Tonguing

The tongue articulates each note struck by the fingers unless the notes are marked with a slur. The tongue should form the syllable *doo* (or *too*) against the back of the upper front teeth (or the gum just above the teeth). When two or more notes are slurred together, play the notes on a single *doo*.

For short notes (staccato or detached), end the syllable *doo* with the first half of the consonant *t,* as in *doot*.

Fingering

Left-hand fingers cover the top three holes, and the left thumb covers the hole on the back. The left-hand little finger is not used. The four right-hand fingers cover the lower holes. (The little finger covers a pair of holes at the bottom.) The right thumb supports the instrument, as do the lips.

The pads of the fingers (not the tips) cover each hole. Use the fingers as though they were small "hammers" covering each hole. Be sure fingers lift quickly.

Exactly coordinate your fingers with your tonguing.

Fingering Chart for Soprano Recorder
Baroque (English) Fingering

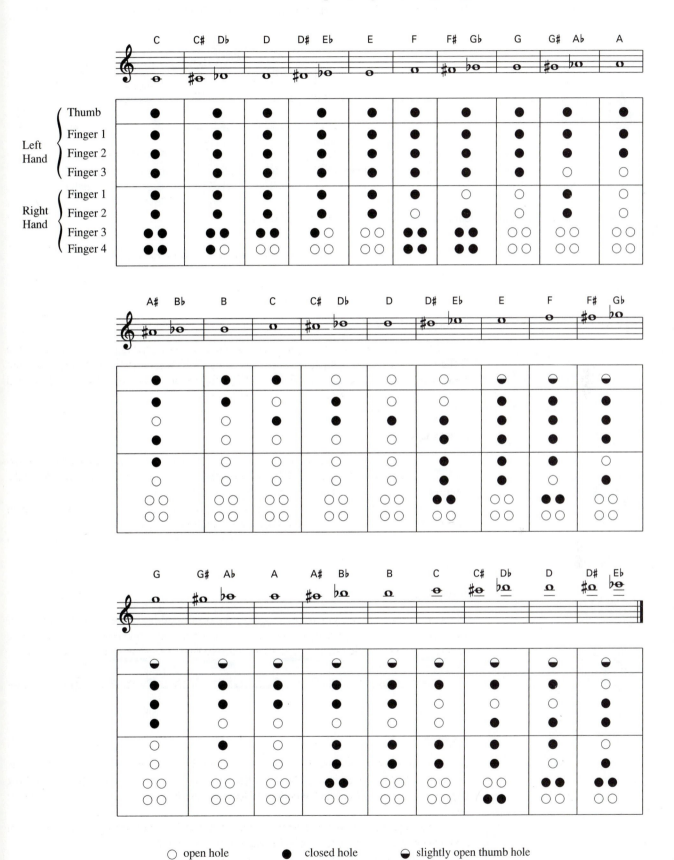

CHANTS TO PLAY AND SING

Counting Chant

Traditional Chant

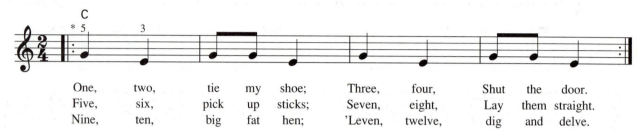

One,   two,   tie   my   shoe;   Three,   four,   Shut   the   door.
Five,   six,   pick   up   sticks;   Seven,   eight,   Lay   them straight.
Nine,   ten,   big   fat   hen;   'Leven,   twelve,   dig   and   delve.

Small numbers in this and the following songs indicate fingerings for keyboard.

Eena, Deena

English Chant

Ee - na,   dee - na,   di - na,   duss.   Kat - la,   wee - na,   wi - na,   wuss,

Spit,   spot,   must   be   done,   Twid - dlum,   twad - dlum,   Twen - ty   one.

Rain, Rain

American Chant

Rain,   rain,   go   a - way!   Come   a - gain   some   oth - er   day.

Bye, Baby Bunting

American Chant

Bye, ba - by bunt - ing, Dad - dy's gone a - hunt - ing;

Catch a lit - tle rab - bit skin To wrap the ba - by bunt - ing in.

Starlight, Starbright

American Chant

Star - light, so bright, First star I see to - night.

Wish I may, wish I might Have the wish I wish to - night.

Lemonade

American Chant

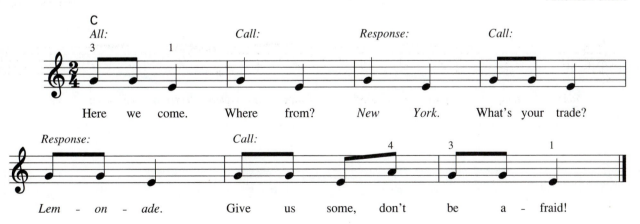

All: Here we come. *Call:* Where from? *Response:* New York. *Call:* What's your trade?

Response: Lem - on - ade. *Call:* Give us some, don't be a - fraid!

A Tisket, A Tasket

American Chant

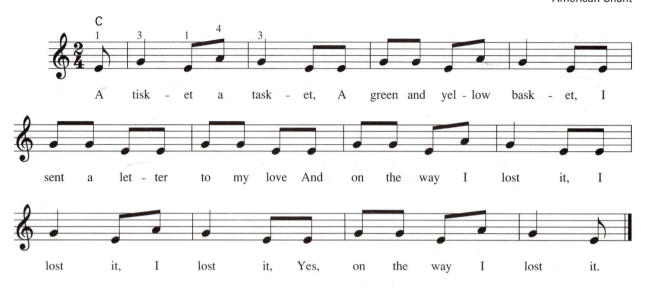

A tisk-et a task-et, A green and yel-low bask-et, I

sent a let-ter to my love And on the way I lost it, I

lost it, I lost it, Yes, on the way I lost it.

Oliver Twist

English Chant

O-li-ver Twist, you can't do this, So what's the use of try-ing;

Touch your knees, touch your toes; Clap your hands and a-round you go!

Tails

American Chant

Rac-coon's got a ring-ed tail, Pos-sum's tail is bare,

Rab-bit's got no tail at all, Just a lit-tle bit-ty bunch of hair. ____

Hot Cross Buns

English Song

Hot cross buns! Hot cross buns! One a pen-ny, two a pen-ny, Hot cross buns!

Mary Had a Little Lamb
(Merrily We Roll Along)

American Song

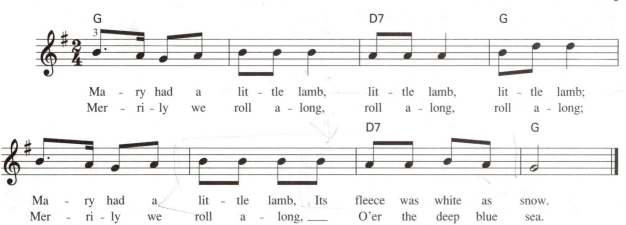

Ma - ry had a lit - tle lamb, lit - tle lamb, lit - tle lamb;
Mer - ri - ly we roll a - long, roll a - long, roll a - long;

Ma - ry had a lit - tle lamb, Its fleece was white as snow.
Mer - ri - ly we roll a - long, O'er the deep blue sea.

Andy Pandy

Traditional

An - dy, Pan - dy, fine and dan - dy, All pop

1. down.
2. up.
3. in.
4. out.

See these chants: "It's Raining," "Ring around the Rosy" (page 361), and "Teddy Bear."

385

APPENDIX A: MUSICAL TERMS, SIGNS, AND SYMBOLS

Dynamic Terms and Signs

pp *Pianissimo*, very soft

p *Piano*, soft

mp *Mezzo piano*, medium soft

mf *Mezzo forte*, medium loud

f *Forte*, loud

ff *Fortissimo*, very loud

sfz *Sforzando*, a sudden strong accent

Crescendo (cresc.). gradually louder

Decrescendo (decresc.). gradually softer

Diminuendo (dim., dimin.). gradually softer

Additional Signs and Symbols

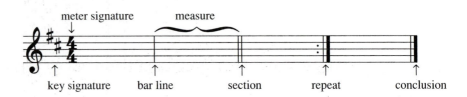

key signature   bar line   section   repeat   conclusion

Da Capo (D.C.), from the start

D. C. al Fine, from the start, ending at *Fine*

Dal segno (D.S.), from the sign

D.S. al Fine, from the sign, ending at *Fine*

Fine, the end

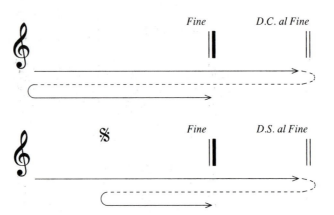

Accents: (＞) slight, (＞) strong, (▲) very strong.

Arpeggio: Play "harp style" from the bottom up.

Breath mark: ᾽

Cantabile: In a singing style.

Dolce: Sweetly.

Fermata (⌒): Hold.

Grace notes (♪♪ ♪): Small notes played quickly; not counted in the rhythm of the measure.

Portamento: Slide the pitch up 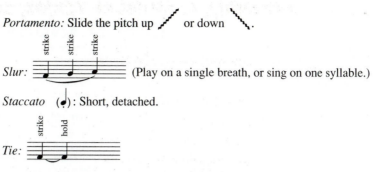 or down ╲.

Slur: (Play on a single breath, or sing on one syllable.)

Staccato (♪): Short, detached.

Tie:

Trill (tr): Rapid alternation with the note above.

= (rapid strokes, as on a drum).

♩ = 76: Tempos are often indicated in *metronome markings.* This example indicates that a metronome (an apparatus that ticks at a desired speed) should be set at 76. The quarter note will be equal to 76 beats or ticks per minute on a metronome.

APPENDIX B: CONDUCTOR'S PATTERNS

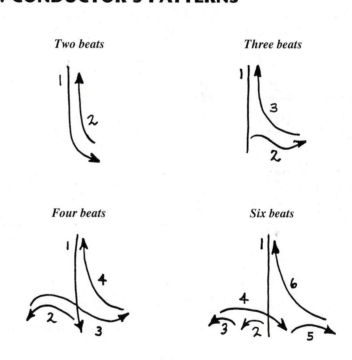

Two beats

Three beats

Four beats

Six beats

CLASSIFIED INDEX

ALPHABETICAL INDEX OF SONGS AND MELODIES

The key is shown in parentheses after the title or source; an upper-case letter designates a major key, and *min* designates a minor key. An asterisk (*) indicates non-English words in addition to the English text.